BEYOND CRISIS

Development Issues In Uganda

BEYOND CRISIS

Development Issues In Uganda

editors:
Paul D. Wiebe
Cole P. Dodge

Co-publishers:
MAKERERE INSTITUTE OF SOCIAL RESEARCH
Makerere University, Kampala
AFRICAN STUDIES ASSOCIATION

Copyright © 1987 by Paul D. Wiebe and Cole P. Dodge

ISBN # 0-918456-60-6

The views expressed by the authors herein do not necessarily represent the views of the organisations with which they are affiliated, nor the views of the editors.

MULTI BUSINESS PRESS
135 NORTH MAIN
Printed in U.S.A. by HILLSBORO, KANSAS 67063

PREFACE

The crises that have affected Uganda in recent years have also affected Makerere University. The work of many academics was cut short, discredited, even destroyed. Many had to flee the country in the interests of their own security or the welfare of their families. Many positions went unfilled. General respect for the importance of free and open discussion, and the role of the university in national deliberations, was undermined. Many university programmes had to be abandoned or were adversely affected due to shortages of personnel, funding and attention.

Makerere University has never once closed its doors, however, and has remained true to the purposes for which it was established. Now as always it remains committed to the promotion of scholarship, understanding, freedom, respect for the individual and human rights, and the promotion of professional and other programmes and services needed in the country.

The Makerere Institute of Social Research was once widely reputed for its superb investigations and analyses of numerous topics of concern to the social sciences. It too has suffered in recent years. But it too has remained true to its mandate and will thrive again, given the opportunity and resources with which to proceed.

This publication by the Institute contains important articles by Makerere and other scholars on issues of concern in contemporary Uganda. My hope is that all of the articles receive the careful attention they deserve. I am delighted that the productive work of the Makerere Institute of Social Research is again so clearly underway.

B. George Kirya
Vice-Chancellor
Makerere University
Kampala, June 1986

FOREWORD

Many developing countries have experienced political and economic problems in the last two decades. These problems have significantly undermined efforts to build viable socio-economic infrastructures that would provide the bases for rational and sustained development. Two decades ago Uganda had a comparatively effective health care delivery system that met the needs of most of her people. Then came the political eruptions and military dictatorships that grew out of the volatile political structures left behind by colonialism and the ineptness and brutality of post-independence leaders. Parochial, conspiratorial and sectarian politics became the order of the day. Gross violations of human rights, mass murder, torture and rape became commonplace. Neglect and mismanagement ran rampant in all sectors. Overall, the cost to Uganda of the political chaos that has occurred during her first two decades of independence has mounted into the hundreds of thousands of lives and the virtual collapse of all of her institutional structures.

Motivated by a commitment to end social and political chaos in Uganda, the National Resistance Movement (NRM) and its armed wing, the National Resistance Army (NRA), waged a successful people's struggle against the oppressive Obote regime, then the succeeding Okello regime, and gained national power in early 1986. The NRM is now engaged in the nationwide mobilisation of the people at the grassroot level into democratic committees in order to assure their participation in the activities and decision-making that affect their own futures and the future of their country. It has also embarked on a programme to revitalise the nation's political, economic, educational, health, family and other institutional structures.

The publication of *Beyond Crisis: Development Issues in Uganda* is a timely contribution to the deeper understanding of the questions and concerns that affect development in Uganda today. The articles included penetratingly examine the forces at work in the country and suggest various proposals that might be considered in effecting agrarian, social and economic reform. One chapter presents a critical analysis of the cooperative movement in Uganda, then makes suggestions concerning how this movement can better serve the people for whom it is intended. Other chapters consider the position of women in the country, challenges to the stability of the family and various political and economic issues. Theoretical issues are raised. Positive and practical recommendations are also raised. All articles deserve careful consideration. Together they are a strong testimony of the intellectual commitment that many members of our academic community share with persons in other spheres of life for the pro-people development efforts that are currently underway.

The NRM Government is irrevocably committed to lifting the scourge of underdevelopment by laying the foundation for a new era of popular and community participation. In this way the people—through their own initiative, participation and struggle will raise the quality of their own social and economic conditions.

The Obote and Okello dictatorships were manifestations of underdevelopment. In the final analysis the struggle by the NRM and the NRA against these dictatorships was a struggle against backwardness and underdevelopment. Thus their removal was not enough. The struggle against injustice and backwardness must not only continue, but indeed be intensified.

The NRM will ensure that the human as well as the material resources of Uganda will be rationally developed and equitably used for the social benefit of all. To this end it is the policy of the NRM Government to consolidate the position of the democratically elected Resistance Committees at both the village and the district levels. The primary objectives of these committees include the democratic mobilisation of the people towards social and economic development.

In the field of health, the embryonic and fragile primary health care programmes currently available will be strengthened by community participation and basic inputs from government. Intersectoral cooperation will be the guiding approach in health care and other development programmes. Democratically established Health Unit Committees will maximise support of the human and material resources available in particular communities and ensure that local health units meet the true needs of the people. The prevention of disease and the promotion of health through community participation, and the strategy of primary health care, will remain the cornerstone of Uganda's health policy.

I wish to congratulate the editors and authors of *Beyond Crisis* for producing such a timely collection of authoritative articles on current development issues in Uganda. I hope the book will be widely read, discussed and used by the people of Uganda in their continuous struggle to consolidate their hard-won democratic gains and to rebuild the country. I hope also that this work helps stimulate further studies and publications on issues concerning development in the country.

Ruhakana Rugunda
Minister of Health
Kampala, June 1986

ACKNOWLEDGEMENTS

Special thanks are due to the people and organisations involved in the formulation and conduct of the seminar out of which this book grew selectively. The seminar was held from 1-6 April 1986 under the auspices of the Makerere Institute of Social Research, the Medical Faculty of Makerere University and UNICEF, Kampala. Dan Mudoola, Director of the Institute, Raphael Owor, Dean of Medicine, A. Wandira, former Vice-Chancellor, and B. George Kirya, Vice-Chancellor of Makerere University, helpfully throughout extended their own services, and the services of their institutions, in formal planning and arrangement. The Carnegie Corporation of New York and the Ford Foundation—through the good offices of Jill Sheffield in New York and Jennifer Sebstad in Nairobi, respectively—provided the funding that enabled the preparation of the papers presented at the seminar, and its organisation. UNICEF funded the research on which the Harmsworth seminar papers were based, served as a base in Kampala from which to coordinate efforts, and provided the various logistical, communications and secretarial services necessary in the conduct of the seminar and the preparation of the seminar papers for publication in the form of a proceedings report. World Relief of Wheaton, Illinois, provided funds towards Paul Wiebe's round-trip travel expenses to Uganda and basic subsistence.

Grace Nakintu-Kyeyune of UNICEF, Kampala, handled the financial and logistical details of the seminar. Mweya Lodge, with its spectacular backdrop of the Ruwenzori Mountains and Lake Edward, and its location within one of Uganda's beautiful game parks, proved to be a delightful and productive seminar setting.

Donna Beth Wiebe worked always with insight and care in preparation of the seminar papers for inclusion in the proceedings report. So did UNICEF secretaries Christine Ssekadde, Grace Kiwanuka and Catherine Aluga-Aleku.

Funding for the publication of this book was made available by the Carnegie Corporation of New York and the Ford Foundation.

CONTRIBUTORS

Firimooni R. Banugire, M.Sc. (Economics) - Associate Professor of Economics, Makerere University; President, Uganda Economics Association, 1976-86; research and writing on income taxation and development planning in Uganda and other African countries.

Cole P. Dodge, M.A. (Social Anthropology), M.Sc. (Public Health) - UNICEF Representative, Uganda; co-editor of *Crisis in Uganda: The Breakdown of Health Services* and of *War, Violence and Children in Uganda.*

Josephine Wanja Harmsworth, M.Sc. (Economics) - private consultant on rural development in Uganda; research on social issues in Uganda; naturalised Ugandan of British origin who has lived continuously in Uganda since 1960.

Elizabeth Hillman, M.D., F.R.C.P. (Child Health) - Professor of Paediatrics, Memorial University of Newfoundland, Canada, and Makerere University; Co-Director of Child Health and Medical Education Programme (CHAMP), a CIDA-funded organisation assisting the Department of Paediatrics, Makerere; past President, Medical Council of Canada.

Vali Jamal, Ph.D. (Economics) - Senior Economist in the Employment Department of the International Labour Office, Geneva.

Tarsis B. Kabwegyere, Ph.D. (Sociology) - Associate Professor and Head, Department of Sociology, Makerere University; Minister of Lands and National Resources, 1979-80; convener of the Moshi Unity Conference in 1979; research and writing on the politics of state formation.

B. George Kirya, M.B.Ch.B., M.Sc. (Microbiology) - Vice-Chancellor, Makerere University.

Dan Mudoola, Ph.D. (Political Science) - Associate Professor in Political

Science, Makerere University, and Director, Makerere Institute of Social Research, Makerere University; writings on institution-building and institutional problems, policies and prospects in various African countries.

Josephine M. Namboze, M.B.Ch.B., M.P.H. (Public Health) - Professor and Head, Institute of Public Health, Makerere University Medical School; first woman medical graduate in eastern, central and southern Africa; extensive writings on immunisation, public health and teaching in a model rural health clinic.

J. M. A. Opio-Odongo, Ph.D. (Rural Sociology) - Associate Professor in Rural Sociology, Department of Agricultural Economics, Makerere University; publications on rural cooperatives and rural development.

Dennis R. Pain, Ph.D. (Urban Sociology), M.Soc.Sci. (Social Work) - Oxfam Field Director for Uganda; brought up in southern Uganda; has taught in various Ugandan schools; research in northern Uganda; trainer of social workers.

Ruhakana Rugunda, M.B.Ch.B., M.P.H. - Minister of Health, Government of Uganda.

W. Senteza-Kajubi, M.A. (Education) - Member and at one time Director of the Institute of Education in Uganda; Vice-Chancellor of Makerere University between 1977 and 1979; presently Head, Department of Adult and Higher Education.

Hilda Mary Kabushenga Tadria, Ph.D. (Social Anthropology) - consultant on women in development, Eastern and Southern Africa Management Institute; previously Associate Professor, Department of Sociology, Makerere University; research on changing economic and gender patterns among peasants.

Paul D. Wiebe, Ph.D. (Sociology) - Professor of Sociology and Anthropology, Bethel College, St. Paul, Minnesota; writings on South and Southeast Asia; co-editor of *Crisis in Uganda: The Breakdown of Health Services.*

Contents

Preface	v
Foreword	vi
Acknowledgement	viii
Contributors	ix
Introduction **Paul D. Wiebe and Cole P. Dodge**	1
The Politics of State Destruction in Uganda Since 1962: Lessons for the Future **T. B. Kabwegyere**	11
The Historical Background to the Uganda Crisis, 1966-86 **W. Senteza-Kajubi**	25
Acholi and Nubians: Economic Forces and Military Employment **Dennis R. Pain**	41
The Problems of Institution Building: The Uganda Case **Dan Mudoola**	55
The Agricultural Cooperative Movement and the Emasculation of Producer Members in Uganda **J. M. A. Opio-Odongo**	65
Changes and Continuities in the Position of Women in Uganda **H. M. K. Tadria**	79

The Ugandan Family in Transition **Josephine Wanja Harmsworth**	91
Rehabilitation or Redefinition of Health Services **Cole P. Dodge**	101
Kasangati Health Centre: Past, Present and Future **J. M. Namboze and E. S. Hillman**	113
Ugandan Economic Crisis: Dimensions and Cure **Vali Jamal**	121
The Impact of the Economic Crisis on Fixed-Income Earners **Firimooni R. Banugire**	137
Appendix A. Seminar Participants	153
Index	155

INTRODUCTION

Paul D. Wiebe and Cole P. Dodge

Political instability, social and physical insecurity, repression and violence have repeatedly surfaced in Uganda over the past several decades. Leader after leader has crossed the political stage, but no national consensus or sense of direction has yet emerged. The underpinnings of democratic rule began to erode soon after independence in 1962 as Apollo Milton Obote made his bid for unchallenged national leadership. They gave way during Idi Amin Dada's chaotic and bloodthirsty rule between 1971 and 1979.[1]

Elections in 1980 brought Obote back to power after the brief post-Amin interim governments of Yusufu Lule, Godfrey Binaisa and a Uganda National Liberation Army-backed military commission. The elections were widely disputed, however, and never brought Obote political legitimacy. As a result, and in combination with the fact that Obote and his supporters had been responsible for numerous manipulations and excesses, both in his earlier period in power and his return to power, guerrilla forces soon organised. Obote resorted to repressive military strategies in response, and the country was soon again plagued regularly by political insecurity and administrative disorder.

Tito and Basilio Okello, the army commanders who organised the July 1985 coup that drove Obote out of the presidency for the second time, were cheered for their action. But their regime brought no respite from the problems and violence that had been mounting. In fact, the second half of 1985 found Uganda divided between the part under the control of the government in Kampala, and the part under the control of the National Resistance Army (NRA), the military wing of the National Resistance Movement (NRM), which had decided to stay out of the Okello Government on the grounds that it really promised no departures from the policies of the regime it had replaced. Its leaders were the leaders of the same army that had served Obote

---

[1] An excellent general account of the Uganda story over recent years is contained in Minority Rights Group (1985). See also Karugire (1979), Mazrui (1975) and Kabwegyere (1974). Avirgan and Honey (1982) report the ending of the Amin years. Much of the recent source material used in this introduction comes from newspaper and magazine articles.

Figure 1.

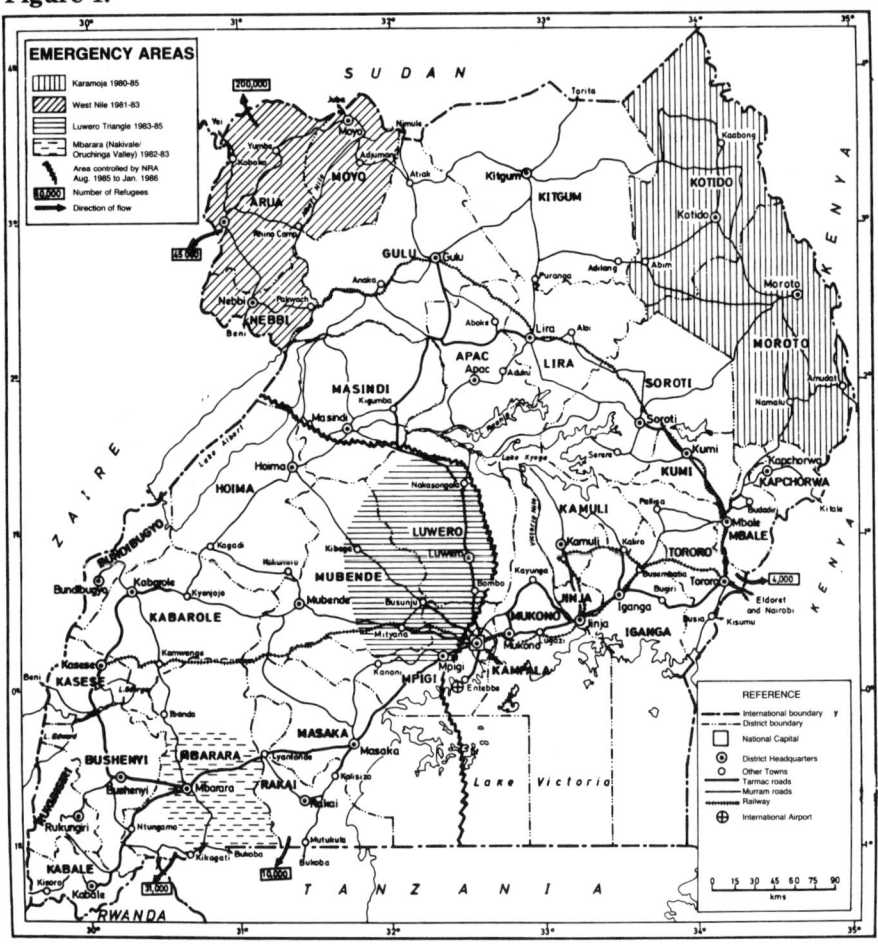

in his heavy-handed rule and represented the same kinds of political and regional interests.

The crises through which Uganda has passed in recent years have taken a terrible toll. Between 100,000 and 500,000 Ugandans lost their lives during Amin's eight-year dictatorship.[2] Perhaps another 200,000 were killed in the "Luwero Triangle" area alone between 1983 and 1985. One estimate for the number of Ugandans living in exile outside the country in 1984 came to 290,000 (see Figure 1). As many as 400,000 other Ugandans in 1984 were displaced from their home territories within the country.

Other dimensions of the toll for Uganda have included the collapse of the country's organised economic sector, attacks on its educational and religi-

---

[2] Estimates of the numbers killed, displaced, forced into exile or otherwise mistreated, vary. The figures reported here can be found in Minority Rights Group (1985), U.S. Committee for Refugees (1985) and Amnesty International (1984).

INTRODUCTION

Figure 2.

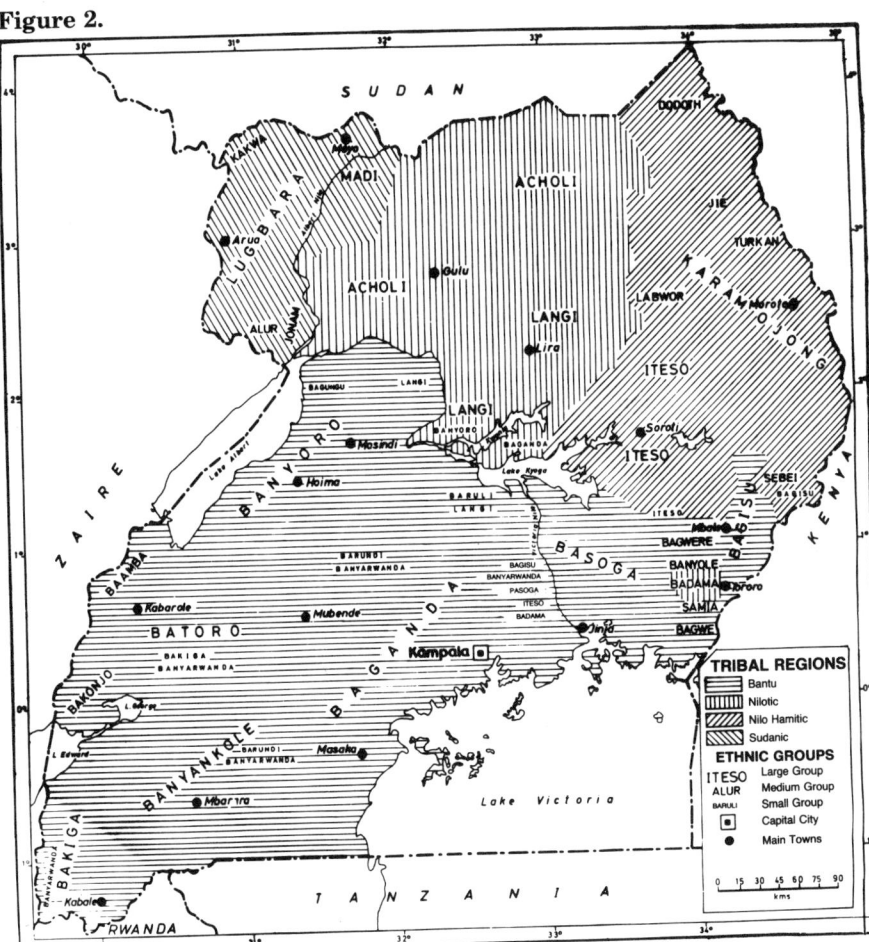

ous institutions, and the undermining of the nation's moral fabric. Whereas Uganda was one of Africa's most developed countries at independence and up to the mid-1970s, by the early 1980s Uganda had to be considered one of the world's "least developed countries".

The reasons for the crises that have beset Uganda are multi-dimensional and deeply rooted. In many ways they stem out of the country's colonial experience, for colonial rule here did little to forge viable central institutions. Indeed it prospered to the extent that it kept the country's principal groupings polarised from each other—in reference to trade, administration, representation and communication—and thus more easily controlled. Prior to independence Ugandans from different parts of the country were never practically encouraged to think of themselves as part of a single national entity.

Other factors that have prevented the emergence of a representative national political system in Uganda have included the continuation of internal struggles for power, external interventions at both international and regional levels, the continuing use of force in the attempt to achieve civil order and the persistence of factions in almost all spheres of public life (see Minority Rights Group, 1985). Uganda's borders contain peoples of four principal language/tribal regions—Bantu, Nilotic, Nilo Hamitic and Sudanic—and some forty different ethnic groups (Figure 2). Leaders have frequently encouraged rivalries for their own advantages and the advantages of their followers, rather than the good of the country. No systematic ideology of national consolidation has been developed. No national language policy has been adopted to enable communication across language barriers. Factions in the ruling elite, army, civil service and opposition groups have generally served parochial interests alone, and religious encouragements have much more commonly followed factional lines than common interests.

BEYOND CRISIS

Uganda is a beautiful country with abundant human and natural resources. Yet it will not be able to move beyond the crises that have so far marked its story without great difficulty. Needed will be strong political resolve informed by meaningful and integrating ideology, and the capacity to get things done. Needed will be a strong government of national reconciliation.

It is still too early to tell whether or not political stability, economic strength, governmental respect for the country's citizenry and personal security will return soon for the people of Uganda. Their chances to move "beyond crisis" are probably better now, however, than they have been for the last twenty years. This is the case because the Okello Government which took over in July 1985 was forced out of power in January 1986 by the National Resistance Army, and the new government of the National Resistance Movement under the leadership of Yoweri Museveni seems thoroughly intent on bringing the country's people back into decision-making processes at local as well as other levels. It seems intent also on rebuilding the country on the basis of its own energies and resources, not on international economic and political dependencies over which it has no control. The International Monetary Fund and World Bank measures introduced during Obote's second term in tackling the country's economic problems did result in the improvement of repayment levels to lending institutions and an improved balance of payments. But they simultaneously necessitated cutbacks in spending for public services and drops in real wages for workers, particularly among the poor (for general comment here, see Cheikh Kane, 1985). The new government's approach will no doubt continue to be a "mixed-economy" approach. It will no doubt also be much more closely linked to the realities and social needs of the Ugandan situation than was the "hard" economic approach under Obote.

Museveni and his people have loudly proclaimed that the people of Uganda are the sovereign force of the country and must be united because of common interests (see NRM, 1985, and Nagenda, 1986). They have argued strongly that tribalism over the years has been encouraged by unscrupulous leaders encouraging artificial interests rather than the real interests of the

INTRODUCTION

people, and that the encouragement of tribal, ethnic, religious and regional differences has stood in the way of national development. They call for the return of democratic rights to the people and the guarantee that the dignity of all Ugandans will be safeguarded. They understand that their acquisition of power was the result of a people's war, not a military coup, and that their chances for success in leadership will rest on the extent to which the people of the country, whatever their local identifications, come to consider the government to be *their* government.

Winston Churchill once referred to Uganda as the "pearl of Africa... an island of gentle manners". Can it become such again? Certainly much more than attractive statements will be necessary. For the sake of the Ugandan people, however, the hope that Uganda will move in the directions so far encouraged by the NRM must be kept alive.

A MWEYA SEMINAR

Earlier or abbreviated versions of all of the papers included in this book were presented at a residential seminar held at Mweya Lodge in southwestern Uganda from 1-6 April 1986. All but two of them—the papers by Vali Jamal (who could not attend the seminar) and Cole Dodge—were prepared specifically for the seminar.

The seminar, which was entitled "Beyond Crisis: Social Development in Uganda", was conceived in 1985 and originally scheduled for July 1986. The name grew out of the hope even in those dark days that the country and its people would be able to move beyond the violence, mismanagement and corruption that continued to characterise public life, and into a period of stability and reconstruction.

The chaos in Uganda that followed the ouster of the Obote regime in July 1985 necessitated a reorganisation of the purposes originally set for "Beyond Crisis". Original research could no longer be developed. Fewer participants could be included. The objectives of the abbreviated project that emerged, however, included the following:

1. To provide Makerere University and other academics with long-term experience in Uganda the opportunity to reflect upon and write about issues concerning social development in Uganda;
2. To provide a forum in which related discussions could be held;
3. To develop recommendations on the basis of the ideas developed and the discussions held for the advantage of the people of Uganda, governmental policy-makers and the representatives of aid agencies;
4. To make available appropriately for wider audiences the materials prepared for the seminar and the results of seminar discussions.

Participation in the seminar by all participants (see Appendix A) was many-sided, frank and vigorous. All of the papers presented at the seminar, plus the recommendations developed during its last two days, are included in the "proceedings" which were reproduced and appropriately distributed in May 1986 under the auspices of the Makerere Institute of Social Research, the Faculty of Medicine of Makerere University and UNICEF, Kampala. Overall, the recommendations made grew out of two basic and common understandings:

1. The awareness that almost all non-traditionally based institutional structures in Uganda over the past decade or more had been distorted to serve narrow or vested interests rather than the interests of the people at large; and
2. The awareness that if the political institutions of the country were again to serve the interests of the people, the people or their representatives would have to be involved at all levels in the initiation, organisation, management, monitoring and evaluation of all programmes affecting their interests.

Considering such bases in understanding, it is not difficult to understand why seminar participants were as hopeful as they were in consideration of the words and the actions of the NRM Government to date.

SOME PERSPECTIVES OF DEVELOPMENT ISSUES IN UGANDA

Development issues abound in Uganda. The displacement and persecution of The Banyarwanda in southwestern Uganda in recent years have caused much distress (Clay, 1984, and Minority Rights Group, 1985). Related issues of settlement and citizenship must be resolved. The rehabilitation of the brutalised "Luwero Triangle" will require much investment, time and effort. Infrastructural and service facilities in West Nile, where the population was repeatedly and terribly abused after the downfall of Amin, and from which thousands upon thousands fled into exile in Zaire and Sudan, will require careful attention. Karamoja in the northeast was treated like a "human zoo" under the British (Cisternino, 1985), and remains cut off from the mainstreams of Ugandan national life to its extreme peril. The 1980 famine in Karamoja, which took the lives of an estimated 50,000 persons (Biellik and Henderson, 1981), was the product of many factors, including drought, the flight from conditions of insecurity by administrative and social service personnel, and the collapse of the region's trade and commercial structures (see Alnwick, 1985; Knutsson, 1985; and Dodge, 1986). It was also the result of the region's isolation and exclusion from consideration during a period of national turmoil. And for just such reasons today Karamoja and its people remain vulnerable to the vicissitudes of nature and the possibility of further unrepresentative consideration. With the routing of the Obote and Okello armies, recruited largely as they were from among the Acholi and the Langi, the confidence of such groups in their position within Uganda has been undermined, and must be restored.

Coffee provides over 95 percent of Uganda's export earnings. But who should profit? The "farm-gate" price of coffee in May 1986 was less than 25 percent of the world price, meaning that the government was banking most of the balance. Many, including certain donor groupings, argue that farmers should receive higher proportional payments, as in fact they do in Kenya and Tanzania. Others argue that a decrease in the government's take at the present time would simply yield a drop in the capacity of the government to provide services to the people, for other forms of revenue collection have either ceased to exist or dried to a trickle. Such persons point out that, for

INTRODUCTION

political reasons, cutbacks in public spending usually mean cutbacks in operational expenditures for social services, and rarely cutbacks in the numbers of civil servants. As a result, little if anything is finally accomplished in solving either the problems of a civil service which is already unhappy, underpaid, inefficient and entrenched, or the need to provide basic human services.

The NRM Government has declared a policy of universal free primary education for the children of the "Luwero Triangle". In general in Uganda, primary schooling is provided on a fee-for-service basis, secondary schooling is partially subsidised and university education is completely subsidised, all of this despite the fact that a good primary educational programme for all children probably benefits a society more than anything else in the long run. What priorities in education are to be established as Uganda moves ahead?

Uganda has forty-eight government and twenty-nine mission hospitals, and 60 percent of Uganda's population lives within ten kilometres of a hospital, health centre or dispensary/maternity unit. Good as such figures are on the surface, problems lurk underneath, particularly in reference to government hospitals. Many facilities here have been destroyed or are in disrepair. Salaries are low and irregularly paid. Personnel and services are heavily concentrated in urban centres (Gish et al., 1982). The overlapping of provisions is common. And emphasis is generally placed on the side of curative rather than preventive or "community" (or "social") approaches in medicine (Cox, 1985, and Mburu, 1985).

Why do mission hospitals tend to manage so much better than government hospitals under conditions such as those through which Uganda has passed in recent years? How will it be possible in the years ahead to guarantee basic health services access to all groups in Uganda? Health and nutrition are not only human imperatives, they are also basic requirements for sustained economic growth (Cheikh Kane, 1985). New courses in the provision of health services will have to be charted.

Various bilateral and other donors provided food assistance to Karamoja, West Nile, "Luwero" and "Mbarara" between 1980 and 1985. The World Food Programme contribution over this period came to 81,911 tons of food commodities, at a value of US$ 37 million. Over the same period Uganda *exported* more than 100,000 tons of maize to Tanzania, while additional food supplies went to waste in certain food surplus areas due to inefficient procedures in the transport and marketing of crops. By 1984 Uganda's government recognised the potentials of maize and beans in cash crop exports and banned the inter-district movement of food crops. This had to do with the control of smuggling. It also had to do with the government's attempt to capitalise on export possibilities. When the rains failed that year in northern Karamoja, Atiak, Nebbi and Kisoro, appeals went out to the World Food Programme and other donors in the attempt to meet shortfalls, even while the prohibition on the internal redistribution of food supplies from food surplus to food deficit areas remained in force.

The introduction of new cropping patterns has in places had unfortunate consequences for nutritional standards as well as for familial and other social relationships. Again, difficulties in access to good farm land, over-concentration in the production of selected crops in particular areas, and procedures in marketing have in places undermined household and community chances for food security.

New approaches are necessary in reference to food and nutrition, health, education, economic and other issues in Uganda. Social infrastructures will have to be rehabilitated. Much will have to be newly constructed. Older patterns in the exercise of power will have to be dismantled. Priorities will have to be established.

The government of the NRM believes that the country's approach in development must be organically integrated and that each household must have access to basic human needs like clean water, adequate food, shelter, health services and education (see Ruhakana Rugunda, 1986). More generally, the government of the NRM is working toward the full implementation of a political programme of development that will revolve around the following themes (NRM, 1985: 44-75):

1. Democracy;
2. The guarantee of security;
3. The consolidation of national unity and the elimination of all forms of sectarianism;
4. The defense and consolidation of national independence;
5. The construction of an independent, integrated and self-sustaining national economy;
6. The restoration and improvement of social services and the rehabilitation of war-ravaged areas;
7. The elimination of corruption and the misuse of power;
8. The redress of errors that have resulted in unequal regional development in the country;
9. Cooperation with other African countries in the defense of human and democratic rights.

The achievement of all such objectives will depend upon the active participation of the Ugandan people at all stages and levels in the determination of their life styles and life chances. But such, of course, is the essence of development.

THIS BOOK

This book is not a manual on development in Uganda, nor an attempt to sketch the possible outlines of development in Uganda. It does not seek to cover even a single broad aspect of development in Uganda in depth.

It is rather a collection of essays about development issues in Uganda by Ugandans and others with long-term Ugandan experience and commitment. Each essay is in a sense self-contained. Together they allow for a general understanding of the complexities, challenges and prospects in the various dimensions of political, social and economic life considered. Hopefully, together they will encourage further reflection, debate, understanding and, above all, participation in the reconstruction of the nation.

Dr. Kabwegyere, in reference to the background of colonial rule in Uganda, examines the anti-people characteristics of the post-independence Ugandan state in the examination of the country's geopolitical reality, civil service, army, judiciary, constitution and economy. Professor Senteza-Kajubi

INTRODUCTION

identifies the historical and socio-cultural factors which, in his position, have contributed to the crisis of political legitimacy and national integration in Uganda. He argues that the single most important task facing Ugandans today is not only some method of enabling a large number of ethnic groups to live together, but also the development of a means of integrating the production and application of new knowledge into the fabric of the country's traditional systems. Dr. Pain reviews what he terms the "economic imperatives" that have been at work in military recruitment in Uganda. In the process he points out that simplistic interpretations of recruitment in terms of prejudicial selection and political machination alone must be avoided. Dr. Mudoola, in his review of the problems of institution building in the country points out how the groups which have so far been most active in attempts to establish political hegemony have themselves generally been economically and culturally marginal to the mainstreams of national life.

Dr. Opio-Odongo's paper is a thorough review of why the cooperative movement in Uganda has failed to ensure that the benefits for which it was established accrue to members, and ends with some thoughts on how the movement might be revitalised. In a review of the position of women in Uganda, Dr. Tadria examines the existing division of labour between males and females within peasant households in reference to the existing gender ideology. She then traces the history of women's organisations in Uganda to show why there is still no effective national forum for women in the country. Ms. Harmsworth explores some of the changes that have been occurring within the institution of the family in Uganda.

The next two papers concern health services. Mr. Dodge examines the possibilities of redefinition in response to the current problems of the Ugandan health services, suggesting alternate strategies including female education, increased budget allocations, a national food and nutrition policy and a developed system of health information. Professors Namboze and Hillman show how the well-known health centre at Kasangati has fared over recent years, and how health delivery systems must be re-oriented if they are to best serve the people in the years ahead.

Dr. Jamal reviews the massive upheavals that have occurred in the formal sector of the Ugandan economy over the past decade and a half, in reference both to its informalisation and to the resilience of Uganda's subsistence sector. In a superb companion paper, Dr. Banugire examines the effects of the economic crisis in recent years on the fixed-income earner.

All of the papers presented draw upon lessons from the past. All offer valuable suggestions. Each identifies the complexities of the challenges that exist in contemporary Uganda. Each also points consistently and forcefully to that which is possible, given institutions representative of the strengths and resilience of the peoples of Uganda, political stability and the return of general security.

REFERENCES

Alnwick, D. J. 1985. "Background to the Karamoja Famine." In Dodge and Wiebe (1985).
Amnesty International. 1984. "Prepared Statement of Amnesty International, USA, on the human

rights situation in Uganda, before the Subcommittee on Human Rights and International Organizations, U. S. House of Representatives on August 9."
Avirgan, Tony and Martha Honey. 1982. *War in Uganda: The Legacy of Idi Amin.* Westport, Connecticut: Lawrence Hill.
Biellik, Robin J. and Peggy L. Henderson. 1981. "Mortality, Nutritional Status and Diet during the Famine in Karamoja, Uganda, 1980." *Lancet,* ii (12 December).
Cheikh Hamidou Kane. 1985. "Africa: Beyond Survival." In UNICEF (1985).
Cisternino, Mario. 1985. "Famine and Food Relief in Karamoja." In Dodge and Wiebe (1985).
Clay, Jason. 1984. "The Eviction of the Banyaruanda: The Story Behind the Refugee Crisis in Southwest Uganda." *Cultural Survival* (Cambridge, Mass.), August.
Cox, P. S. V. 1985. "The Karamoja Health Services: A Proposed Revolution." In Dodge and Wiebe (1985).
Dodge, Cole P. 1986. "Karamoja: Regional Specific Development Needs." Paper presented at the seminar, Beyond Crisis: Social Development in Uganda, Mweya Lodge, Uganda, 1-6 April.
Dodge, Cole P. and Paul D. Wiebe (eds.). 1985. *Crisis in Uganda: The Breakdown of Health Services.* Oxford: Pergamon Press.
Gish, Oscar, C. H. Wood and John Barenzi. 1982. "Health Manpower Development in Uganda." Ministry of Health/UNICEF, Kampala, mimeographed.
Kabwegyere, Tarsis B. 1974. *The Politics of State Formation in Uganda.* Nairobi: East African Literature Bureau.
Karugire, S. R. 1979. *The Political History of Uganda.* Nairobi: East African Literature Bureau.
Knutsson, Karl-Eric. 1985. "Preparedness for Disaster Operations." In Dodge and Wiebe (1985).
Mazrui, A. 1975. *Soldiers and Kinsmen in Uganda: The Making of a Military Ethnocracy.* Berkeley: University of California Press.
Mburu, F. M. 1985. "Evaluation of Government Rural Health Centres and UNICEF Essential Drug Inputs." In Dodge and Wiebe (1985).
Minority Rights Group. 1985. "Uganda and Sudan: The Minority Rights Group Report No. 66." London: The Minority Rights Group.
Naganda, John. 1986. "Yoweri Museveni: My Mission." *New African,* 222 (March).
National Resistance Movement. 1985. *Yoweri Museveni: Selected Articles on the Uganda Resistance War.* Nairobi: NRM.
Ruhakana Rugunda. 1986. "The Effects of Political Mismanagement on Health Services in Uganda." Paper presented at the seminar, Beyond Crisis: Social Development in Uganda, Mweya Lodge, Uganda, 1-6 April.
UNICEF. 1985. *Within Human Reach: A Future for Africa's Children.* New York: UNICEF.
U. S. Committee for Refugees. 1985. "Human Rights in Uganda: The Reasons for Refugees." Washington D. C.: U. S. Committee for Refugees.

THE POLITICS OF STATE DESTRUCTION IN UGANDA SINCE 1962: LESSONS FOR THE FUTURE

T. B. Kabwegyere

The concept of state destruction need not have emotive connotations. If we can talk of state formation we can talk equally of state destruction. In political sociology we have very often talked about nation building, the process of bringing diverse peoples under one political culture.[1] Surely the opposite of nation building is nation destruction. State destruction can be visualised as a process. On the one hand it can be a process whereby the instrument of oppression, the state, is destroyed or transformed for the liberation of the people. On the other, and this is more relevant for our discussion here, oppressive as it is, the state machinery can be perverted for the further intensification of oppression and exploitation. In this latter meaning even the little good one might have been able to discern in the colonial state is dissipated and replaced with the more naked exercise of power and oppression.

The state, according to Lenin, is an "organ of class dominance, an organ of oppression of one class by another; its aim is the creation of order which legalises and perpetrates this oppression by moderating collision between classes" (Lenin, 1933: 71). The dominant class in the colonial era was foreign and imperial. The dominated classes were the diverse African peoples. The colonial class was a relatively homogeneous group in origin, culture and education. The Africans, on the other hand, were separated by linguistic, cultural and geographic barriers, differences in levels of development and, above all, different interests. The Africans did not form a coherent class with articulated interests to counter the dominance of the foreign class. Furthermore, the differences among them were aggravated by the colonial practice of "divide and rule", a practice that was imposed to reduce social interaction and the emergence of a collective consciousness among the oppressed.

The above describes in brief the functioning of the colonial state. The concept of the colonial state, however, differs from the general concept of the state as applicable, for example, in Europe. Much as the state is the instru-

---

1 In earlier work (Kabwegyere, 1974), I have examined the process of state formation in Uganda. In this paper I shall refer only in passing to what has been involved in this process.

ment of a dominant class in imperial Europe, the non-colonial state developed from indigenous and endogenous forces. While the colonial state is imposed by the imperial power, the non-colonial state develops as a result of the interaction of social, historical and economic forces within a given area. The non-colonial state is not imposed from the outside (Lenin, 1933:9).

Unlike the colonial state, the non-colonial state tends to endure because of its distributive function. Surpluses here are reinvested even though they are more to the benefit of the ruling class than the producers of labour, while in the colonial state surpluses are syphoned out to the mother country. As a result, social and economic infrastructures in the colonial state never grow strong but instead continue to deteriorate. This is the basis of the economic dependence and neo-colonialism which characterises colonial and post-colonial states. It also in part explains why colonial and post-colonial peoples engage in the politics of overthrow against their rulers.

The question at this point is what of the Ugandan state was left at the time of independence in 1962 that has been subjected to the politics of destruction? We shall examine each of the following in turn below:
1. Geopolitical identity, or the establishment of legally recognised boundaries, and the establishment of authority within these boundaries;
2. The civil service, or the executive arm of government;
3. The army;
4. The judiciary;
5. The constitution;
6. The economy, satellite though it is in organisation in Uganda;
7. And finally, the sense of hope that characterised the pre-independence political surge against unresponsive colonial rule in Uganda, and has continued to surface from time to time since, however difficult the times.

BOUNDARIES

There are two kinds of boundaries that are important to a state: international boundaries and internal administrative boundaries. The alteration of the former without the consent of neighbours has major political implications. The alteration of internal boundaries is more easily accomplished, but an effective control of territory is a necessary precondition to the existence of the state.

There has been virtually no permanent change in Uganda's legal international boundaries since 1962. In 1978, in a claim that was never vindicated in action, General Idi Amin claimed that Uganda extended to the Kenyan highlands. In 1978 he also claimed the Kagera salient was part of Uganda and tried to implement his definitions in an invasion of Tanzania. This sparked retaliatory action which in turn gave momentum to the liberation war that led to his overthrow in April 1979. Kenya and Tanzania reacted, Kenya in protest rallies throughout the country with threats that not even one inch of Kenya would be ceded to Uganda, the latter with a march of 50,000 troops into Uganda which led to the destruction of both Masaka and Mbarara and a subsequent stay in Uganda until 1981, after a march through the length and breadth of Uganda. During the Amin era, in short, the politics of boundary change surfaced in Uganda with the result that Tanzania became a major factor in Uganda's politics.

Tanzania did not come to Uganda for territorial aggrandisement. Nor did she acquire any territory in her victory over Amin. She was simply reacting to an attack on her territorial integrity.

Nevertheless, Tanzania's presence in Uganda did interfere with Uganda's autonomy. Local territorial integrity was perforated by the presence of Tanzanian troops. A neighbouring power became a major player on Uganda's political stage.

Furthermore, the anti-Amin efforts in Tanzania and elsewhere had all along been searching for an ally in their opposition to Amin, and found in Amin's territorial claim to the Kagera salient, and its consequences, a golden opportunity to develop their strengths. Their meeting in Moshi on 21 March 1979 legitimised Tanzania's entry into Uganda, and with the formation of the Uganda National Liberation Front (UNLF), what they had mounted alongside the Tanzanians as opposition to an attacker turned into a war of liberation.[2]

Amin's desire to alter boundaries weakened the Ugandan state. The Ugandan head of state was defeated in battle. State machinery was brought to a halt. The Ugandan army ran in disarray to the extent that 11 April seemed to mark the beginning of a new era. In fact, it would not be an exaggeration to conclude that the war of liberation overthrew the Ugandan state, though only temporarily, given the reappearance of remnants of the same system on Uganda's political scene later on.

Internally, however, Uganda's boundaries have been changed many times. The first major boundary change followed a referendum which took place in the "Lost Counties" in 1964 and resulted in the return of Buyaga and Bugangazzi to Bunyoro. Amin divided Acholi District into two districts, Gulu and Kitgum. Toro was divided into several districts. When it came to power, the UNLF renamed districts using town names. Over the years the number of districts in Uganda has increased from eighteen to thirty-three. During the brief period he was in office, President Lule established regions as political units under the leadership of regional commissioners.

The reorganisation of districts in general solved the longstanding quarrel between the Batoro, Bamba and Bakonjo, through the establishment of Kasese and Bundibujjo Districts. The end of the Mountains of the Moon guerrilla struggle, with the descent of Ilemangoma from the mountains, was less the result of an ingeneous diplomacy than the end to a struggle for a separate identity.

With the December 1980 election results contested for their authenticity and fairness, guerrilla movements came into being on the Ugandan political scene. What followed from 1981 to the beginning of 1986 was a struggle between Milton Obote's government and the different guerrilla groups fighting to overthrow him. This culminated in the overthrow of Obote on 27 July 1985 and the subsequent near partitioning of Uganda into the part under

---

2 It is not the purpose of this paper to analyse which side was the stronger, the Tanzanian or the Ugandan liberation forces in the war of 1979. Let it suffice to point out that the UNLF was not only a child born in Tanzania but also a child that never grew with the nourishment of the Tanzanian presence in Uganda.

General Tito Okello and the part under Yoweri Museveni, Chairman of the National Resistance Movement (NRM) high command, which ended only with the National Resistance Army (NRA) takeover on 26 January 1986.

By far the biggest internal threat to the state in Uganda has been the guerrilla movements with the NRM being one of the most sophisticated guerrilla movements in post-colonial Africa. Just as Amin was overthrown for his territorial aggrandisement, so was Obote overthrown largely as a result of his failure to control and protect internal boundaries, his inability to control Uganda's geographical territory. The pervasive presence of guerrillas in almost a third of the country and in and around Kampala made it impossible for him to govern. He could go nowhere in the country with the assurance that he was out of the range of guerrilla targeting. Even worse for his regime, his own soldiers turned against him and virtually took over northern Uganda, the part of the country to which he might have fled eventually for sanctuary.

Unlike in 1979, when the Ugandan state was in a sense totally overthrown, the return to exile of Obote in 1985 left trappings of his presence in saddle in the form of Tito Okello and Bazilio Okello, his rebellious lieutenants who were later overthrown by the NRA. But the Okello regime was short lived, for Tito Okello's efforts to come to terms with Yoweri Museveni in the much publicised Nairobi Peace Talks ended in a whimper. His regime could not emerge from the terroristic and anarchic regime of his onetime Commander-in-Chief, Obote: nor could he convince Museveni and the world that he would be a reliable partner in a formulated peace accord. Almost like the 1979 military sweep of the country, early 1986 witnessed an NRA campaign to the very limits of Uganda's borders and the establishment of total territorial control.

There are two main lessons to be learned for the future from the above remarks. First, interference with internationally recognised territorial boundaries has the potential of rocking the state. Secondly, any regime that allows the birth of an effective guerrilla movement within its territory stands the risk of its own overthrow and engenders the subversion of the state. The recent history of Uganda emphasises the importance of these lessons. Because of their relationship with the masses and their subversion of the state, neither Obote nor Okello could withstand a mass supported guerrilla struggle.

THE CIVIL SERVICE

When one talks of a state one is at the same time talking about bureaucratic machinery. The civil service in the Westminister model is the executive wing of government, the government being the policy-making machinery of the state. The reason why bureaucratic machinery is necessary in running a modern state is that decision-making on such a large scale must be guided by impersonal and objective rules to ensure efficiency and effectiveness. It is therefore important, in examing the destruction of the state in Uganda, to look critically at how the civil service operated both in the colonial period and thereafter.

The purpose of colonial administration in Uganda was to establish an efficient system of control. This control took two basic forms. There had to be an efficient control of the people in order to guard against rebellion and opposition, and to harness effectively their energies for surplus production. There also had to be control in order to organise the expatriation of economic surpluses to the mother country. The establishment and practice of divide-and-rule was to guarantee law and order, while the establishment of native administration up to the village level, through the use of chiefs, was to make sure that the masses were kept in place. The contravention of laws, orders-in-council and other edicts that propped up colonial administration was severely punished.

It is very frequently claimed that the colonial civil service was efficient. Indeed it was. For a period of over fifty years, up until independence movements gathered momentum in the late 1950s, to culminate in independence in 1962, rebellions and uprisings in challenge of the status quo were severely curtailed. The colonial government's efficiency in administration did not derive from the effective participation of Ugandans in their own administration, but rather in the operation of suppressive rule and oppression. And therein lay the seeds of colonial destruction, for any system of control that is imposed on the people without their understanding of its purposes and meaning is bound to be rejected, however good it may be, for its operation is in general antagonistic to their interests.

At independence Uganda inherited a system of control that was constructed and operated against the interests of the people and functioned on the basis of rules worked out alone by the imperial establishment. The only difference now was that where you had had Europeans, the Africans set in. No changes in the purposes, functions and inequities of the system were effected. Besides, in that the colonial system did not, and could not, nurture Ugandans to take the places of their colonial masters when they left, the changeover resulted in another of the dynamics that led to the destruction of the civil service. Those who took over did not have the experience necessary to maintain past levels of efficiency in the system, or an interest in upholding authentically its objectives. Permanent secretaries and board chairpersons, as well as ministers at the helm of power, made decisions within the same old framework, while intensifying the operation of the old system. The politics of destruction set in further with a recruitment policy that gained strength during the 1960s, with the recruitment of men and women, not because of their training and capability, but because of their political and social acceptability. Corruption, nepotism and many other evils set in. Effectiveness and efficiency became elusive targets. Amin appointed and fired civil servants on the radio. During Obote's second regime, ministers, members of parliament and party functionaries appointed and fired civil servants on their own, with the cadre worst hit being the chiefs in rural areas. There was such a high turnover in the public service in general during this time that even school teachers, nurses and messengers in offices and parastatals could be fired on the basis of not being party supporters. The arm of politics stretched into industry where management was controlled by party functionaries. A place for a child in school became a highly political issue. The political leanings of a headmaster or other administrator became even more of a political issue.

The lack of adherence to bureaucratic criteria and norms was so pervasive in all sectors that not even the army was spared. Promotions in the army followed no rational criteria other than acceptability to the regime. It took a year to fill the post of Chief of Staff after David Oyite-Ojok died in a plane crash because a politically acceptable army officer could not be found as a replacement. Obote's overthrow in 1971, and his second fall in 1985, can be explained in part in terms of the inefficient operation of the state machine and the ad hoc and irrational manipulation of people and resources.

In the case of the export of economic surpluses, the establishment of marketing boards—namely the Coffee Marketing Board and the Lint Marketing Board—was to organise the collection of exportable produce and control export trade. For his cotton or coffee, the peasant producer was given a fraction of what his produce fetched on the world market. The middleman cadre, composed largely of Asians, benefited from this arrangement to a point where the racially based colonial structure corresponded with the structuring of economic position. Thus, the primary beneficiaries were the colonial elite, and the secondary beneficiaries the Asian middlemen. Only in third position came the African peasant producers.

The bureaucratic characteristics of the marketing boards have increased manyfold over the years, and have found ramification with the introduction of state controlled cooperatives and unions. The country's bureaucratic machinery, in short, has generally served the two functions of controlling the population and syphoning out economic surpluses. That the dawn of independence made no difference, other than in intensifying these functions, is attested to in empirical studies (see Jamal, 1978).

A number of lessons can be learned from the collapse of the civil and public services in Uganda. Uganda inherited a system which was constructed to serve foreign interests. Its efficiency was not in the interests of the people. The retention of the system without modification following independence led to internal problems. Nonadherence to bureaucratic criteria led to inefficiency and collapse. Finally, the manipulative misuse of the resources and people involved in the system was incompatible with the running of a modern state.

Necessary changes must include a redefinition of objectives and targets, a deployment of the right personnel in the right places and a sense of direction. Only if such changes are made can administrative machinery serve the purposes for which it is meant.

THE ARMY

Once again we are thinking about an institution whose beginning and development is to be understood in relation to a colonial background. The white man's burden was shouldered by the use of soldiers. In the early colonial period military activities were termed the "pacification of natives". The Nubians came to Uganda virtually as mercenaries to assist Lugard in his pacification exercises. These exercises were as destructive of human life and property as have been the "exercises" in the Luwero Triangle in recent Ugandan history. The pursuit of Kabarega by Lugard over a period of five years (1894-99) involved large numbers of marauding soldiers. At one stage a figure of 160,000 spearmen moving along with gun support and like army ants was recorded (see Kabwegyere, 1972).

The purposes, organisation and progress of the army in Uganda were all in accordance with the entrenchment and achievement of the objectives of the colonial society. Indian troops were brought in, and some of them later became part of the Asian population to settle in Uganda. The colonial army was the King's army, the King's African Rifles, the king being the King of England. During both the first world war and the second world war, Ugandans participated on the side of the British and their allies.[3]

What kind of army did Uganda inherit at independence? It was a small army of about 1000 men. It was an army constructed along colonial lines. Taller soldiers were considered more qualified than shorter soldiers! Those who were believed to be innately martial were considered best qualified to be fighters. The colonial army was made up of people selected on dubious and superstitious grounds and trained to achieve the dictates of its masters. The most senior officer in 1962 to have passed through the ranks was a sergeant! Natives were believed to be incapable of high rank! After independence the same evils that overwhelmed the public service waxed in the army. The arbitrary behaviour of leaders led to the destruction of the army's authority structure. Promotions were based not on experience and ability but on selfish personal bases. Amin's promotion in the military was not on the basis of his excellence as a soldier but because he was thought to be too stupid to have an interest in taking over the government!

The promotion of Smith Opon-Acak after Oyite-Ojok by Obote was equally bizzare; it assumed that a confidant must come from one's home territory. Bazilio Okello's assumption of the high office of Chief of Defence Forces was more because of his martial chivalry than his foresight and military acumen. Even more destructive for the army was the increasing requirement that the army be the army of the head of state. Loyalty from about 1964 onwards had to be a personal loyalty to the head of state. Officers and men had to sing the praises of the head and wear his portrait, and he personally had to be the source of their satisfaction in service.

One of the ironies in history is that the more the army personifies the head of state, the more likely will he be overthrown by the army (see Janowitz, 1962). This is well illustrated in Obote's two terms of leadership. But the situation in Uganda has illustrated an even worse relationship as well, for a personal relationship between the president and the army, as well as different organs of security, emerged here.

The Ugandan state has suffered more than any other East African state at the hands of its soldiers. Ugandan society has carried the weight of destruction from the army. Human beings have been killed to the point of genocide, and great numbers of those left alive have been abused almost beyond human belief. Society has been terrorised to the point where children's games today are frequently horrible demonstrations of war. The inhumanity of the army has extended to the economy, stretching from the *kon-*

---

3 It is to be pointed out, however, that this involvement opened up new visions and new directions. Robert Kakembo (as reported in Kabwegyere, 1974) writes that the ex-second-world-war soldier brought home a new message and a new outlook in life, one that was to be suppressed under colonial conditions.

doism (armed robberies) in the late 1960s, to military business marauders (*mafuta mingi*) in the 1970s, to rapist looters in the early 1980s. A culture of violence has grown up in Uganda. The army has extended itself into politics by taking over governments. Amin destroyed so much life and hope that his overthrow in 1979 seemed to be the end of a century of misery. Obote's and Okello's overthrows in 1985 and 1986, respectively, were received with sighs of relief.

The Muwanga/Obote military machine that grabbed power in 1980, after extensive involvement by the army in rigged elections, restored a semblance of civilian rule to the country. But Obote's stay in State House between 1981 and 1985 was buttressed by the military and militarism, and the nature of the general confrontation between the army and guerrilla forces between 1981 and 1986 illustrates that from 1962 onwards nothing of the colonial army machinery had changed, other than in relation to the intensification of the negative aspects therein. That the Uganda army since 1962 has been corrupt, inefficient and expensive can be seen with half an eye. Ministers of defence over the years have carried money abroad to buy arms, putting part of the money at their disposal into personal accounts in foreign banks. Internal expenditures on the army have been astronomical.

Uganda has also relied on foreign troops when the local military establishment could not meet the needs of those in power. Thus the Uganda Government kept Tanzanians in the country during 1979-80, Koreans were in Uganda up to the July 1985 coup, and a British Commonwealth team has recently been in Ugandan barracks. In all such cases of foreign presence the questions of state autonomy and security cannot be ignored. Such a presence has also been very costly in financial terms. There is no doubt that one of the most destructive and expensive forces in Uganda since independence has been the army.

On 26 January 1986, in a phenomenon new both in the history of Uganda and the history of Africa, the NRM took over Uganda's government. That people were able to organise themselves in the face of a military dictatorship and work out a force sufficiently strong within the country to overthrow an established government represents a qualitative change in Uganda's and Africa's history. That men, women and children were able to become involved in a movement which grew dramatically over a period of five years and is now in power in Uganda, is an example of what the people can do in the face of oppression and repression if they organise themselves. The assumption of power by the NRM is a promise of hope and portends the beginning of a new reality wherein the gun is a tool to defend, not destroy, human life.

There are a number of lessons to be learned from Uganda's military experience. A colonial and perverted army is an extremely dangerous institution. Uganda, unlike Tanzania in 1964, continued within the colonial tradition, and even the little good that was in the army at independence was destroyed thereafter. To avoid the military destruction and confusion that Uganda has experienced over the past twenty-three years, there must be a people's army. A people's army costs less economically, socially and politically than does a colonial army, for it is integrated into all societal activities in the interest of wider societal causes.

JUDICIARY

In modern states the rule-of-law is a cardinal value. The administration of justice is based on written laws passed by a parliament or an equivalent body. The custodians of law and justice reside in the institution of the judiciary. As an arm of the state the judiciary is supposed to be independent and unencumbered by the whims of policy-makers and implementors.

It is not the purpose of this section to review the history of the judiciary in Uganda, but merely to highlight the inroads of destruction which have stemmed from the mismanagement and perversion of the state. The first obvious inroad into the judiciary was the declaration of the head of state that he was above the law even while he was prone to breaking the law! Given that the president in Uganda since 1967 has been an executive, rather than a ceremonial leader, it has been a tragic blow in the administration of law and justice in the country that he should be above the law. It is true, of course, that the head of state must be protected. Indeed the very institution of the presidency is such that the individual incumbent is kept almost inevitably from the commission of ordinary offences. But the head of state can commit treason, for example, when presidential actions are contrary to the best interests of the society represented. Thus Amin's act of invading Tanzania was a treasonable act, for the cost of his territorial ambitions involved the killing of Tanzanians and hundreds of Ugandans, and the destruction of much property. Similarly, Obote's regime committed genocide in the Luwero Triangle, and for this Obote should be held accountable in a court of law.

The second obvious destructive consequence for the judiciary has been the politicisation of the appointment of the chief justice and judges and other administrators of justice. The manner in which Justice Wambuzi was dismissed by Paulo Muwanga in 1980, then replaced by Justice Masika, was a case of extreme political interference in the affairs of the judiciary, particularly in that it was done on the eve of the elections in order to ensure that an acceptable chief justice would be in place to guarantee Muwanga's choice of leaders after the elections. Furthermore, the fact that the new chief justice was not selected from within the ranks of the senior judges was indicative of an imposition from the outside of a person perhaps less qualified than was necessary, which no doubt interfered with the morale, efficiency and dignity of the legal profession. Finally, the dignity of the legal profession was maligned in the public ridicule of the former chief justice not only by a man like Akena Adoko, but also by Paul Ssemogerere, the leader of the Democratic Party. Both accused the chief justice of direct and personal interference in the administration of justice.

The performance of public prosecutors in the Kyesimira case is another example of the same problem. In fact the Kyesimira case—where the court released Professor Kyesimira, then re-arrested him on the instructions of the Minister of Internal Affairs, then detained him again until after the coup of July 1985—was the grimmest case among so many of its kind of direct interference, and hence destruction, of the judiciary in Uganda. Detention without trial became possible, all as a result of the enactment of the detention act which gave powers to the president to arrest and detain suspects for indefinite periods without trial. The large number of prisoners released after the 1971 coup, and again after the July 1985 coup, were visible manifestations of the weakening of the judiciary institution in Uganda during previous years.

The destruction under consideration here extended to the police who could not bring suspects to justice for fear of victimisation. Cases which involved the army against the people could not be investigated by the police in case evidence was obtained to convict army personnel. The case of Hon. Ssebugwaho, the Democratic Party MP who was killed by soldiers, is a case among a myriad of similar cases. The fear of consequences was aggravated by corruption. The police were demoralised by the treatment they received, especially from the Minister of Internal Affairs during the second Obote regime. Promotion was based on party affiliation.

The authority and dignity of the judiciary were further severely undermined as the public lost faith in the administration of justice. People found it dangerous to report crimes against the army and powerful citizens because of the possibility of being victimised. The police took no serious note of much reporting for various reasons. Murders, robberies and other serious crimes were thus often committed with impunity simply because the public would neither report nor participate in the restraint of offenders. Because of economic hardships as well as other reasons, some magistrates became prone to bribery just like their counterparts in the civil service and in parastatal bodies.

There are a number of lessons that should be learned from this for the future. The administration of justice in a country is the very foundation of social order. If the wrong are not punished, and the right rewarded, the incentive for social living is destroyed. An executive head of state should not be above the law, for his actions can be dangerous to the state. The independence of the judiciary in the administration of justice is a cardinal value which should both be enshrined in the constitution and daily encouraged in the practical administration of justice. The direct interference of the state in the judiciary makes it impossible to maintain the integrity and the rule of law.

CONSTITUTION

A constitution is the system of laws and customs established by the sovereign power of a state for its own guidance. On looking at national constitutions throughout Africa, one cannot help but be amazed at the absence of African content. Indeed these constitutions were constructed just before self-government began in African countries at meetings in the imperial capitals. In the first place, therefore, we are faced with a situation in which a constitution has no cultural content for the country in which it is supposed to be the source of guidance. At the same time, and this has alredy been implied above, national leaders in Africa do not respect these constitutions. The history of Uganda since independence is littered with the manipulation of the constitution by national leaders for personal aggrandisement.

That Uganda did not have a constitution during the period 1900-62 underlines its dependence as a colonial state. It is therefore not surprising that the written constitution which was inaugurated at independence has taken such a long time for incorporation into the values of the country. The country's leaders themselves have regarded constitutions as simply political formulae which have been arrived at around a table and can be contravened with impunity.

Without going into the details of the main articles of the Ugandan Constitution, its first major amendment was made in 1963 when the position of head of state was created. Along with the creation of the ceremonial presidency—and contrary to the unitary government that was Obote's proposed formula for the country—constitutional heads were created throughout Uganda. The position of president was filled by Edward Mutesa II, the *Kabaka* of Buganda. That he could not combine two roles— the role of the *Kabaka* of Buganda and the role of the presidency of Uganda—at the same time, led to the events of 1964-66 and, eventually, to his escape to Britain. In the state of emergency that was then declared by Obote, the constitution was at first suspended, then abrogated. In turn, a new constitution was put into place during a hushed ceremony with no debate in parliament. This act introduced a major new dimension into Ugandan politics. That the head of state could abrogate a constitution and replace it with one of his own choice was the severest blow at the working of the state. It showed that the constitution was not a sacred and respected document, and that the power of the president was in a sense limitless. The 1967 Obote constitution is not only coloured by the immediacy of the situation at the time but also by Obote's personal interests and ambitions. Ugandans have never had the chance to work out a constitution and formula germain to the conditions of Uganda. That remains a target for the future.

ECONOMY

Colonies in general provide markets for the goods manufactured, and raw materials for industrial production, in the imperial power. Whether or not inimical to local interests, colonies must engage in activities which are acceptable to the imperial power. A colony, therefore, cannot produce what it wants, even if it has the capacity to do so, nor trade with countries other than those identified as "acceptable". Like all colonial economies, the Ugandan economy was built to service colonial interests and encourage the dependence of Uganda on Britain. The introduction here of coffee, cotton, tobacco and tea as crops to be exported to Britain is clearly illustrative of this.

After over sixty years of the entrenchment of dependency, Uganda's economy at the time of independence seemed to have visible signs of growth even though the ultimate beneficiary continued to be the metropolis. As is almost automatically the case throughout Africa, new projects were introduced to expand economic activity soon after independence. There was a drive to develop new acreage for tea, coffee, tobacco and cotton; there was also an effort to develop sugar cane, tourism and other programmes. Marketing boards and cooperatives expanded in their scope and activities.

Yet one thing remained a stark reality. Though the Africans were now in control, they continued to manage a colonial economy! They were operating an economic system which was established to exploit Ugandans for the benefit of an external system! So, like in all other sectors of Ugandan society, independence meant an intensification of the activity that enhanced the inequities of the colonial system.

The collapse of Uganda's economy became most demonstrably noticeable during the Amin era, with the allocation of businesses to Africans following the 1972 expulsion of the Asians. The Asians had been beneficiaries in a system which was racially based. Their position in the economic structure had also been a hindrance to the emergence of African business entrepreneurship. Certainly their expulsion from the country in ninety days introduced disequilibria into the economy with consequences which became dramatic by 1977 (see Kabwegyere, 1974b, and Jamal, 1976).

It would be incorrect, however, to attribute the total economic collapse of the 1970s to the mere expulsion of the Asians. Many other factors were also involved. Those who took over from them were not equal to the task. The establishment of political terror through organs of the state forced thousands to flee into exile. Those who could not flee were subjected to direct personal harassment or forced to live in a state of panic and uncertainty. Planning for the proper utilisation of human and material resources could not be undertaken. Through mismanagement and the lack of direction, the negative forces of corruption, nepotism and personal greed took root. The Ugandan economy had been depleted of investable resources over the years. Instead of investments in productive sectors like industry and agriculture, scarce resources over the years had been spent on the army and other oppressive organs of the state, and on ostentatious ceremonies like Obote's Bushenyi annual event. Foreign exchange earnings had been used to purchase consumables instead of machines which could produce other machines. On the whole, Uganda's economy over the years became more dependent and weaker than it was at the time of independence, because of failures in management.

The war of liberation of 1978-79, and the guerrilla war of 1981-86, were conducive neither to agricultural production nor investment of any other kind. The Ugandan elite during these periods instead tended to invest abroad, adding to the capital haemorrhage to developed countries. Obote's economic policies of the early 1980s, together with his political failures, did not help the situation. In fact the involvement of the International Monetary Fund and the World Bank to almost unprecedented levels during this period perhaps made the nation's economy more vulnerable to outside forces than it was at independence.

The collapse of Uganda's economy has had wide-ranging consequences, even in sectors that normally would not be associated with the economy. The future of Uganda lies in the reduction of its economic dependencies, and the conquest of backwardness, through the proper and meaningful utilisation of its own resources.

A SENSE OF HOPE

The old saying, "If it were not for hope the heart would break," is a major commentary on social living. Humans without hope in the future are worse off than wild animals. It is not possible to put a quantitative value to the importance of hopefulness in society, but it cannot be denied that the working of society depends largely on hopeful conceptions of the future.

The independence movement unleashed a sense of hope. The political message of the time implied that oppression was to dissipate with the coming of independence. Yet by the late 1960s the euphoria instead had dissipated. The constitution was abrogated in 1967, following political turmoil. The 1967 elections were suspended, and the say of the masses in their governance evaporated. In the twenty-four years of independence between 1962 and 1986, Ugandans participated in only two elections, in 1962 and 1980, and in the 1962 elections Buganda did not even participate directly beacause of the indirect election here that followed the UPC/KY (Uganda Peoples Congress/Kabakka Yekka) alliance. In 1969 there was an attempt to ban political parties other than the UPC. In the same year an attempt on the president's life was made at Lugogo Stadium. Previously the vice-president had narrowly escaped assassination. Meanwhile political opponents were continuously being herded into Luzira prison.

The army which had mutinied in 1964 continued to take a more and more significant role in public affairs. Amin, the army commander, became increasingly vocal in public. By the end of the 1960s all sorts of allegations had become rife at home and abroad. The General Service Unit, a multifarious institution, had come to exercise prevalent and pervasive influence. The omnipresence of the oppressive agents of the state made private life an open secret.

The Amin era (1971-79) set in with the intensification of fear and hopelessness. Thousands upon thousands of Ugandans were killed. Many more—professionals, the young as well as the old, businessmen as well as soldiers—ran for their lives into exile. Others ran from towns to rural areas to hide from Amin's killers.

The war of liberation in 1979 came with a sigh of relief. The foundations of the UNLF seemed to bring back hope to Uganda. But the coming to power of the Military Commission Government in mid-1980 once again drowned the hopes of the people.

The promises of the December 1980 elections restored a measure of the people's confidence. Their results, however, brought despair instead and led to the founding of guerrilla movements.

The second Obote term must be remembered as a period of hopelessness. It was a period during which murder became an almost legitimate daily occurrence. The insecurity of life and property became the rule of the day. National Security Agency (NASA) and UPC youth wingers terrorised people in towns and villages alike.

Serious observers did not see hope in the overthrow of Obote on 27 July 1985. The system had not changed. The same army which had been Obote's tool against the people was now in power and the same atrocities continued unabated. Nor did the peace talks in Nairobi and the signing of the peace accord (on 17 December) prove a firm basis for hope. Instead more and more people began to look to guerrilla efforts in the country as the only source of hope, a look which has been vindicated so far by what has happened since the NRM took over on 26 January 1986.

The implications of the state of anomie through which Uganda has gone have been many. Uganda has lost many professionals through death or exile.

This has led to a shortage of manpower in certain areas, while countries and organisations abroad have benefited. It is estimated that there are some two hundred Ugandan medical doctors in Britain alone, and around eighty in southern Africa. Many other doctors live in Kenya and elsewhere.

Without an estimation of what the future can bring, humans cannot plan. The pursuit of short-term gains and results cannot be the basis for a stable society. The restoration and re-creation of confidence in existence and in the country is a task of primary concern for the future. Otherwise, the abundant world of nature with which Uganda has been provided will remain underutilised. Necessary changes can only come about if meaning in life and a firm sense of direction are provided and are in answer to the basic needs of Uganda's people.

CONCLUSION

This brief survey has covered different aspects of Ugandan society with comment on the state destruction process. Destruction has been considered more in terms of the perversion rather than the deracination of the state. The little good that was left at the departure of the colonial rulers has been lost as the state has become an increasingly anti-people machine involved in the creation of untold human misery.

The challenge of today and tomorrow is to be very familiar with what has happened in the past and to chart a new path for the future so that the people can determine their own destiny. This will require a new sense of direction which focuses on human dignity and welfare as its primary objectives.

The NRM seems keen on pursuing this new direction. Though it is a direction full of obstacles and challenges, it is a direction worth pursuing.

REFERENCES

Jamal, V. 1978. "Taxation and Inequality in Uganda, 1900-1964." *Journal of Economic History*, XXXVIII, 2 (June).
Jamal, V. 1976. "Asians in Uganda, 1880-1972: Inequality and Expulsion." *Economic History Review*, 29 (November).
Janowitz, M. 1962. *The Military in the Political Development of New Nations*. The Hague: Mouton.
Kabwegyere, T. B. 1974. *The Politics of State Formation: The Nature and Effects of Colonialism in Uganda*. Nairobi: East African Literature Bureau.
Kabwegyere, T. B. 1974b. "The Asian Question in Uganda, 1894-1972." *Kenya Historical Review*, 2.
Kabwegyere, T. B. 1972. "The Dynamics of Colonial Violence: The Inductive System in Uganda." *Journal of Peace Research* (Oslo), 4.
Lenin, V. 1933. *The State and Revolution*. London: Martin Lawrence.
Uganda, Government of. 1977. *Three-Year Action Programme*. Entebbe: Government Printer.

THE HISTORICAL BACKGROUND TO THE UGANDA CRISIS, 1966-86

W. Senteza-Kajubi

Uganda is a country of great natural beauty and great diversity in ethnic composition, indigenous cultures and social and political institutions. Generally at independence in 1962 the country projected an image of a peaceful and prosperous territory.

The post-independence history of Uganda, however, has turned out to be a story in which one government after another has entered at gunpoint, then left behind a record of bloodshed, misrule, corruption and human-rights abuse. Indeed, in many ways Uganda falls in a class of its own in terms of the human brutality and waste, unrelieved armed conflict and suffering its people have had to endure.

How did this tragedy come about? And how can it be abated? This paper examines the historical and socio-cultural background against which the crisis of recent years in Uganda has occurred, identifying factors which have contributed significantly to national disunity and, therefore, to questions around political legitimacy and national integration.

THE COMING OF FOREIGNERS TO UGANDA

Uganda as we know it today began to take shape towards the end of the nineteenth century as a direct creation of nineteenth-century European imperialism. Outsiders began to penetrate the area from both the north and the southeast in the middle of the nineteenth century with similar motives: intellectual curiosity, trade, conquest, colonisation, evangelisation or some combination of such interests. By about 1849 the first Arab traders had reached Buganda from the eastern coast of Africa in search of slaves and ivory. The challenge of the age-old quest by Europeans for the source of the Nile was resolved in 1862 when Captain J. H. Speke reached its source at Jinja. Colonel Chaille Long visited Buganda in July-August 1874 as an envoy of Colonel Gordon, Governor of Equatorial Province, in an attempt to bring Buganda under the suzerainty of Egypt. In 1875 H. M. Stanley visited the Court of Mutesa I (1856-84), the thirty-fifth *Kabaka* of Buganda. Stanley was followed by Ernest Linant de Bellefonds, a French Calvinist also in Gordon's service (Stanley, 1878: 205-07).

Stanley and Linant described Western civilisation and what they considered the superiority of Christianity over Islam to the curious *kabaka*. In Christianity and the power associated with it, Mutesa thought that there might be an answer to the Muslim threat which was coming from the north to infiltrate his dominions. So he urged his chiefs to accept Christianity when it was preached to them.

The making of modern Uganda was initiated by Mutesa when, through Stanley, he invited the first missionaries to come to Buganda to evangelise his people. In response to a letter of appeal written by Stanley and published in the *Daily Telegraph* of 15 November 1875, the first Protestant missionaries arrived in Buganda from Britain in 1877. They were followed by Catholic White Fathers from France in 1879. Both groups were hospitably received by Mutesa who allocated them land on which to begin their work.

THE BEGINNING OF POLITICO-RELIGIOUS CONFLICTS

At first Mutesa was very desirous of becoming intimate with Europe and of introducing European religion, goods and coined money to his realm, and in employing European technicians to teach his people. Soon after their arrival in Buganda, the Anglicans and Catholics began to rival one another and the Arabs, not only for converts but also for political power. This made Mutesa very suspicious of—and ultimately antagonistic to—foreign influence. He himself embraced neither Christianity nor Islam and let the rival groups compete with each other for his shifting favours, while ensuring that none grew strong enough to threaten his throne (Rowe, 1985: 5).

The two Christian groups brought two versions of the Bible and two versions of the political, economic and cultural rivalries of the time between England and France. Protestant converts were known as *Abangereza* (the English), Catholic converts as *Abafalansa* (the French) and those who continued to believe in indigenous gods as *Abakaafiiri* (from the Arab word *kafir*, meaning infidels or pagans). Like the Christians, the Arabs were interested both in economic advantages and in furthering their own religious and ethnic influences in the area.

Mutesa died on 19 October 1884, a disappointed and disillusioned person, to leave his son Mwanga to face the political turmoil which was to follow because of political rivalries. Mwanga started by ordering the killing of Bishop James Hannington (the first Anglican bishop of Eastern Equatorial Africa) who was executed in Busoga in October 1885. Then he turned to the Christian "readers", and some thirty-two Protestant and thirteen Catholic youths suffered martyrdom at Namugongo in June 1886. In all, two hundred victims are said to have perished in religious persecutions at the time.

The Christians and Muslims rebelled against Mwanga when they discovered that he was determined to destroy all those who believed in foreign gods, and eventually installed Prince Kiwewa as *kabaka* instead. But Kiwewa also turned against Islam and Christianity and sided with those who believed in autochthonous gods (*balubaale*), and was able to remain as *kabaka* for only seventy-two days before he was killed by his brother Kalema with the support of the Muslims. Kalema accepted circumcision and took the Qur'anic name, Nuhu. He ruled for only one year, however, before the Christians were able to put Mwanga back on the throne. Then the Christians fought each other—Protestants against Catholics.

The association between religion and the national divisions of Europe was so close at the time that although the politico-religious wars in Buganda were fought by Baganda against other Baganda, they were in fact wars between foreign interests. When Christians fought Muslims it was European versus Arab interests, and when Protestants fought Catholics it was in fact a war between British and French interests. When the *Abakaafiiri* fought against the Muslims it was because of their concern for the cultural destiny of Buganda in the face of Arab interests.

A step was taken in 1895 to ease the tensions then existing in Buganda when the first representative of the Roman Catholic Mill Hill Mission in Britain (not France) arrived in order to try and dispel the association between religion and national origin which had been fixed so firmly in the minds of the Baganda through the presence of the Church Missionary Society Protestants from Britain, and the Roman Catholic White Fathers from France. But the arrival of the Mill Hill Missionaries does not seem to have abated the religious rivalry. If anything, it only strengthened British interests.

In the midst of the fighting among Protestants, Catholics, Muslims and "pagans", Captain (later Lord) F. Lugard, the first British imperialist agent in Uganda, marched into Buganda ostensibly "to save the country from itself." On 26 December 1890 Lugard signed a formal treaty with *Kabaka* Mwanga and his chiefs, according to which Buganda was brought under the administration of the imperial British East Africa Company. Gradually and bit by bit the neighbouring kingdoms of Bunyoro, Ankole and Toro, and other parts of the region, were brought under British suzerainty.

Many of the problems of national integration and conflict Uganda has had to face since independence are rooted in the conflicts of pre-colonial times and in the manner in which the country was administered during the colonial period. Some of the salient factors are traced below.

THE 1900 BUGANDA AGREEMENT

Of all the peoples of what is now Uganda, the Baganda, who constitute about 25 percent of the country's fifteen million people and inhabit its geographical heartland, were in the forefront in shaping the future of the region. Buganda was the first part of Uganda to be annexed by the British. It gave Uganda its name. It also gave the country much of its history and emergent culture.

The birth of modern Uganda can therefore be rightly dated from the year 1900 when the British government concluded an agreement with the *Kabaka* of Buganda which was to influence the subsequent history of Buganda and the entire protectorate. The 1900 Agreement, formerly regarded by the Baganda as their "Magna Charta", not only governed relations between Britain and the Kingdom of Buganda for the next fifty years or so, but also set forth new developments in the internal political structure of Buganda and thus had a profound and continuing effect on economic and political developments throughout the country.

Among other things, Buganda was declared a province of the Protectorate of Uganda *equal* in status to any other province. As long as the *kabaka* and his people cooperated loyally in the organisation and administration of the protectorate he was to be recognised by the British as the native ruler of Buganda. By this *quid pro quo*, in short, the *Kabaka* of Buganda surrendered his military power, the jurisdiction of his kingdom and his land settlement policy to the British, and his sovereignty and his people became agents of the Crown in bringing other parts of the protectorate under British suzerainty. About half of the land in Buganda was distributed among 1000 notables (mainly chiefs) under private ownership arrangements, and popularly became known as *mailo* land; the other half, including forests, swamps and wasteland, was left in the hands of the British Crown in order to safeguard the interests of the Africans against the interests of white settlers who had already begun to encroach on African interests in Kenya.

So satisfactory did the Buganda arrangements appear at the time that the British decided to adopt them in general as a model for native administration throughout the protectorate.

WEAKNESSES OF THE 1900 AGREEMENT

Satisfactory as the 1900 Agreement seemed to be to the British—and sacrosanct as it was to the Baganda—it contained a number of serious weaknesses. For one thing, it recognised the Kingdom of Buganda as a separate unit with its own parliament (*Lukiiko*), while at the same time making it a province of the protectorate. The size of Buganda and its political and cultural solidarity set it apart from the other political units of Uganda which were ethnically, culturally, linguistically and politically fragmented.

Secondly, certain parts of Bunyoro Kingdom which historically came to be known as the "Lost Counties" were ceded to Buganda as a reward for Buganda's assistance to the British in bringing Bunyoro under subjugation. The issue became a constant source of friction between Buganda and Bunyoro for the next six or seven decades.

Thirdly, the privileged position which the Baganda continued to enjoy under the terms of the 1900 Agreement incited envy and hatred among other ethnic groups. The Baganda were naively proud of the fact that they had invited (or rather thought they had invited) the Europeans and the Christian missionaries to Uganda, that their country was not being ruled by the British as a result of conquest but by negotiated agreement, and that Uganda was a protectorate (whatever that meant) in contrast to Kenya which was a colony. They were proud of the fact that they could possess *mailo* land which was not the case in Kenya and other parts of Uganda—not knowing that Ugandans from other parts of the country could buy land in Buganda, but that the reverse was not true (see Kajubi, 1965:141).

Indeed, Buganda's continued claim to a privileged position even up to and after independence generated so much ill-will and opposition in the rest of the country that the rest of the country became united on the "Buganda issue". The fear of domination by Buganda as a province among other things propelled A. Milton Obote to form the Uganda People's Congress—a multi-ethnic party, in 1960, and to dismantle the provincial level of local administration in 1966. The fragmentation of the country into districts later not only removed the name and hence the spectre of Buganda from the map of Uganda, but also left political units too weak financially to challenge the centre, and therefore much easier to control.

Fourthly, in Buganda itself the 1900 Agreement upset traditional sociopolitical structures by dispossessing clan heads from their traditional clan estates. Each clan had traditionally had its family estates to which it acquired exclusive rights when three or four generations of its dead had been buried there. When half of the land in Buganda was distributed among 1000 notables, the rights of the clan heads to the *butaka* or clan estates, were ignored. This planted seeds of political discontent in the minds of the *bataka* (clan heads) and the peasants against the landed chiefs, and eventually against the *kabaka* himself.

THE POLICY OF INDIRECT RULE

Faced with the problem of administering peoples of widely divergent backgrounds, the British at first considered the possibility of abolishing the various traditional offices in Buganda as opportunity arose, in this way paving the way for the introduction of British laws and customs. But the grave shortage of British officials, let alone those with any experience in native administration, made this proposition unfeasible. Moreover, the British had chosen not only to govern Buganda through the *kabaka*, his chiefs and his parliament, but also to extend this system of indirect rule even to those areas where traditionally there had been no system of chiefs.

This "system of indirect rule", as it was called, was based on the premise that the indigenous people would obey their traditional leaders more easily than they would accept British officials directly, and that the traditional autocracies would be gradually transformed into modern and democratic local administrations.

THE POLICY OF DIVIDE AND RULE

The policy of indirect rule would have been all right in the long run if the whole of Uganda, like Lesotho or Swaziland for example, had been composed of only one homogeneous ethnic nation. But Uganda consisted of many ethnic and cultural nations, each with its own system of values and aspirations. The British approach was, in the first place, to play one ethnic group against another, such as the Sudanese soldiers against the Baganda and the Baganda against the Banyoro. Within a given ethnic group they also played one political subgroup against another. When the British reached an area they sought first to influence the uppermost strata of the traditional political and social hierarchy by aligning themselves with the king as in Buganda. If the king resisted, as in the case of Kabarega of Bunyoro, they sought to overthrow him and find a "more reasonable" substitute. Secondly, the British made no effort to create a national ethos among the various ethnic groups they had brought together under one territory by force, and which they administered separately by design. There was, for example, no provision in the 1900 Agreement in Buganda, or in similar pacts concluded elsewhere, for traditional rulers to meet together in some kind of national forum where they would get to know one another and their British overlords better, and in which they would be able to play some role at the national level. Even when the legislative and executive councils were eventually established in 1920, they remained for an unduly long time the exclusive preserve of Europeans, with the result that the Asians, and particularly the Africans, for the same period viewed them only from a respectful distance and as "foreign" institutions. In this way the policy of indirect rule, and the manner in which it was applied, only encouraged the development of ethnic sub-nationalism, which tended to perpetuate rather than resolve ethnic and regional conflicts. Indeed, instead of modernising traditional autocracies and other indigenous political structures, the policy of indirect rule only helped to "freeze" and render them temporarily impervious to the normal processes of change (see Tilman and Cole, 1962: 4-5).

In short, under the policy of indirect rule ethnic groups were set against one another and the indigenous people were encouraged to be steeped in local and religious politics—Roman Catholics against Anglican Protestants, Christians against Muslims, all of these against the *Bakaafiiri* and so on—at the expense of national institutions which were monopolised by Europeans and Asians. As a result, a kind of ethnic sub-nationalism, which later made the process of national integration particularly difficult, was encouraged.

THE INSTITUTIONALISATION OF RELIGION

Another phenomenon which complicated the political scene and the process of national integration in Uganda from the very beginning was the penetration of religion into indigenous political and social systems. Religion became part and parcel of the life of Buganda to the extent that the converts of one sect no longer referred to the others as Baganda.

After the wars of the 1890s, in which the Protestants or English faction (later to be organised as the Native African Church, and ultimately as the Church of Uganda) emerged as the victors, religion in Buganda was institutionalised as a major factor not only in the appointment of chiefs of all ranks but also in granting British recognition to traditional rulers. The 1900 Agreement established the tradition that the *kabaka* and his chief minister (*katikkiro*) and minister of finance (*muwanika*) should always be selected from the Protestant faction, the minister of justice (*mulamuzi*) from the Catholic faction. Thus, of the three principal ministers, none was to be a Muslim. Of the twenty administrative counties (*masaza*) into which the country was divided, ten were allocated to Protestants, eight to Catholics and only two to Muslims. In each of the eight counties administered by Catholic chiefs there was to be at least one sub-county administered by a Protestant chief. The appointments of other civil servants in the ministries, counties and sub-counties, as well as the distribution of the population in the country, also tended to encourage Protestant strengths. Thus Uganda, a country with a Catholic majority, was essentially turned into a Church of England state.

Primary and secondary schools were started by Christian missionaries for their own converts; the government did not even establish a department of education until 1925. Even then it did not build or manage schools directly, but only gave grants-in-aid to voluntary agencies that had taken the initiative to build their own schools. There were thus no government schools in which children of different religious sects could interact with one another.

Political leadership training, which in Buganda had been traditionally carried on in the homes of chiefs and the *kabaka's* palace, shifted to the school classroom. Schools like King's College Budo (British CMS), St. Mary's College Kisubi (French White Fathers) and Namiryango College (British Catholic Mill Hill Fathers) were established to train the children of Baganda chiefs in Christian and political leadership. And each system prepared its students with values appropriate to the political and religious reality. According to F. Welbourn (1965: 10), King's College emphasised responsibility and initiative, St. Mary's College nurtured obedience and submission, while Namiryango College combined the Anglo-Saxon idea of initiative with the Catholic insistence on obedience.

The Muslims who did not have foreign missionaries to build schools for them were educationally disadvantaged and were until recently generally looked down upon by other people. Their mode of dress in turbans or turbushes, their mode of burying their dead, their insistence on greeting each other with the Arabic "Salaam alaikum" instead of a local greeting, and other such traits, singled them out as "strangers" in their own country.

The expression "Si Muganda, Musiramu" (He/She is not a Muganda, but a Muslim) is still common in many Buganda villages (Rowe, 1985: 7-8). Unable to find a way into clerical jobs, the civil service or teaching, the Muslims have found their identity in trade, the butchery business and taxi driving. Only during Idi Amin's time was it possible for them to emerge from their position as third-class citizens and to claim an important share in the politics of the country.

In conclusion, religion added a new dimension to the problem of identity in the area. In the olden days, if you asked an individual the question, "Who are you?", he might reply that he was a Muganda, of the grasshopper clan, an Acholi, a blacksmith, a bark-cloth maker or a fisherman. Today he might say he is a Protestant, Catholic, Muslim, an agnostic, a doctor or a teacher. Religion properly conceived can play an integrative role by expanding an individual's circle of identity and community boundaries beyond those of the family, clan and ethnic group. The situation in Uganda has been made more complex not only by the fact that Christianity and Islam here compete with each other, but also by the fact that the two versions of Christianity offer different answers to questions of identity and correct ethical behaviour, and have historically come into conflict with each other. Furthermore, religious leaders sought first to influence and control the uppermost reaches of Ugandan society—the kings and their chiefs, then have their teachings trickle down to the common people. The result of this approach was that in Buganda and in other places religion became inextricably bound up with the politics of the palace, and cleavages between the religious sects, particularly the Catholics and Protestants, persisted and left many scars. Religion, in short, failed to provide an overall integrative force, an over-riding philosophy or mythology which would have allowed Uganda to move from tribalism to modern nationalism, and even to pan-Africanism and world citizenship.

THE TRADITIONAL SOCIO-POLITICAL SYSTEMS

Citizenship has to do with the norms and values which guide the thoughts and actions of individuals in their roles as members of the larger society (Prewitt, 1971: 1). Value integration is concerned not only with long-term agreements on mores and morally binding customs, procedures and institutions for resolving political conflict (Nsibambi, 1986), but also with ideas of what is socially acceptable and worth striving or dying for. A crisis of national integration arises when different groups—be they religious as in Northern Ireland, racial as in South Africa or ethnic or tribal as in many parts of Africa—do not accept each other as fellow citizens. Members of such groups do not understand each other because they do not have a common "language", let alone a shared universe of ideals and values.

According to C. Wrigley (1985: 2), small and compact as it is, Uganda is "an arbitrarily delimited, culturally heterogeneous, historically shallow collection of peoples with none of the attributes of a nation." Uganda was an artificial creation of British imperialism bringing together a conglomeration of peoples of diverse cultures, political systems and customs within the confines of one territory without due regard for their differences. From the standpoint of political organisation the traditional societies of Uganda ranged from those that lacked any political integration beyond the level of the extended family, clan or local village, to highly centralised political kingdoms and empires of great complexity unparalleled anywhere in Africa.

John Stuart Mill (as cited in the *International Encyclopedia of the Social Sciences*, 1968, 2: 7) saw a nation as a "portion of mankind . . . united among themselves by common sympathies . . . which make them cooperate with each other more willingly than with other people, desire to be under the same government, and desire that it should be a government by themselves or a portion of themselves exclusively."

If we accept Mill's definition as identifying the adequate criteria of nationhood, then before colonisation there were many, albeit small, nations in the region which is now Uganda. In addition to the centralised political nations, fixed within well-defined territories like the Bantu lacustrine kingdoms of Buganda, Bunyoro-Kitara, Ankole and Toro, and the princedoms of Busoga, there were also nations consisting of ethnic groups which lacked central political institutions though they were united by a common language and cultural bonds, particularly in times of adversity.

The Baganda offer an example of a highly centralised political nation. They had built up a national consciousness and a long tradition of administration, law and order. They lived under a highly centralised and hierarchical socio-political system, the pinnacle of which was their *kabaka*. Below the *kabaka* were the *bakungu* (or ministers) as well as chiefs and sub-chiefs. Chiefs owed their authority not to hereditary or dictatorial claims, but to appointment by the *kabaka* who, in turn, was selected from among the princes by the ministers and a council of elders.

Side by side with the political hierarchy of chiefs was the clan structure, and the clans of Buganda have always played an extremely important role in the social structure of the nation. The Baganda are organised in a number of patrilineal, exogamous, totemic clans. Members of each clan trace their origin to a common ancestor through the male line and have totems, animals or plants which are held sacred by all clan members. No one should marry a person of the same clan.

The *kabaka* was the head of all the clans; below him was a hierarchy of clan heads and sub-clans and sub-clan heads all the way down to the household level. The clan system running side by side with the political hierarchy of chiefs was very important as it provided a system of checks and balances against the powers of the chiefs and, at times, of the kings themselves.

The traditional system of education in Buganda emphasised *obuntubulamu* (humaneness and decency) and followed the above hierarchical system. The homes of chiefs as well as the *kabaka's* palace were centres of learning and social decorum. Thus the *kabaka* was the fountainhead of the values of the Baganda.

In contrast with the political and social systems of the Baganda and many of the other Bantu-speaking and sedentary agricultural groups south of Lake Kioga—which number more than seventy rulerships all together (Low, 1985: 11), the political and social systems of the Nilotic, Nilo-Hamitic and Sudanic peoples to the north of Lake Victoria—consisting of ethnic nations such as the Langi, Alur, Karamojong and Lugbara—were, in general, not politically centralised.

Then too, even among the southern Bantu-speaking peoples certain groups did not have centralised authorities. The Bakiga of Kigezi in southwestern Uganda, for example, had neither a king nor chiefs but were organised along the *amuryango*, or lineage, which was composed of several households which traced their origin to a common ancestor. Internal conflicts among the Bakiga were settled by members of families and sometimes by the people of the village acting democratically. In their eagerness to implement their system of indirect rule, the British imported Baganda chiefs and their feudalistic system into Kigezi, to the great resentment of the Bakiga.

THE KARAMOJONG

Karamoja represents another example of the problems of culture conflict and value integration. Karamoja is a semi-arid region in the northeastern quadrant of Uganda, which is inhabited by the Karamojong people, a resilient and strong people who have retained strong cultural traditions over the years. The Karamojong do not participate much in crop agriculture, trade and other aspects of the national economy; rather they are nomadic pastoralists who derive much of their livelihood in cattle husbandry.

Unlike the Bantu sedentary agriculturalists, the Karamojong do not have kings or chiefs. Their social system is organised in a series of groups based on age, in which elders as members of a group make decisions and settle disputes. Some elders are more influential than others, but all decisions are made as group decisions.

The Karamojong have traditionally observed definite codes of rights and obligations which have kept their society together. These centre around the possession, rearing and protection of cattle and include the right (1) to graze and water their herds in any part of Karamoja without interference from other members of the political community, (2) to immediate assistance by members of the community in case of conflict or competition with outsiders, (3) to seize the cattle of non-members of the Karamojong community without being questioned by other members of the community (Gukiina, 1972: 28-29).

When the British colonised Karamoja they were interested in establishing efficient administration, law and order. They spent large sums of money on the development of local government through the introduction of a system of chiefs, police posts and so on, not on cattle development. The Karamojong, on the other hand, were interested in their traditional rights of unrestricted grazing and the seizure of foreign stock in order to maximise or maintain their cattle assets.

Since independence, the philosophy of administrators with reference to Karamoja has been the same as it was before, and has continued to conflict with the over-riding concern of the Karamojong with the maximisation of their cattle assets. Another problem of modernisation here has been the introduction of automatic weapons. Cattle raiding which once centred around the use of spears and knives has, in recent years, taken on an increasingly deadly nature (see Alnwick, 1985).

THE PROBLEM OF VALUE INTEGRATION

In order to survive, every society tries to socialise its members into those views, values and behaviours which favour the perpetuation of the society's mores. To most people in Uganda, *society* still means the local ethnic group, and each ethnic group regards its own culture to be the norm if not the ideal culture, and all others to be deviations.

The consequences of the differences in socio-political systems and the customs and traditions related to them in Uganda are very important. They have made integration difficult, for many of the problems related to the crisis of political legitimacy and national integration here, as indeed in most parts of Africa, stem from such cultural roots. There is a growing intermingling and assimilation in schools, colleges, universities, churches and mosques, clubs, the work place, political parties and so on, and people increasingly move from one district to another (and particularly to Buganda) in search of economic opportunities. But ethnic factors have continued to make themselves felt with unfailing tenacity. Each Ugandan has attitudes and options which are coloured by cultural background: what is or is not eaten, the way a language is spoken, what is to be strived for, and what will gain allegiance.

During the colonial period in Uganda the British exploited ethnic and cultural differences by playing one group against another. Successive regimes after independence, from Obote through Amin and Okello, perpetuated and aggravated related conflicts by trying to concentrate military, political and economic power within their own ethnic groups, and to kill members of rival groups. During his first period in power Milton Obote concentrated military and economic might within the Langi and Acholi alliance, and killed Baganda. Amin relied on his Kakwa and Nubian kinsmen, and killed Langi and Acholi as well as Baganda intellectuals. When Obote returned from exile in 1979, the people of West Nile, Amin's home area, became the victims of revenge. Obote now concentrated military power within his own ethnic group, the Langi, and to a certain extent within their cultural neighbours and military compatriots, the Acholi. At the same time he continued to kill Baganda, and ultimately turned on his compatriots, the Acholi, forcing Commander Tito Okello and Bazilio Okello to sound the call for the Acholi as well as other northerners, principally the Lugbara and the Madi of the West Nile region, to come together in arms, which led to Obote's second downfall in July 1985.

THE IDENTITY CRISIS

To be an "American", a "Briton" or a "Russian" means adhering to certain social, political and cultural values. Accordingly, in the words of Kenneth Prewitt (1971: 210): "Rules of political conduct are recognised, friends and enemies can be identified, goals and aspirations are formed, clues are available for selecting from among competing values; in general, one knows how to relate to the political collective."

In Uganda, as in most African countries, there are no general patterns of political and cultural norms and values that can be internalised by young people beyond the slogans of fighting "disease, poverty and ignorance". There is no national culture as yet, no *we*-feeling of national identity and no universe of ideals and values shared by all citizens.

Humankind, according to A. N. Whitehead (cited in Harper, et al., 1977: 27), can survive in the lower stages of life with merely barbaric flashes of thought. But as society develops, the absence of "a coordinating philosophy of life, spread throughout the community" spells disaster. In a society which does not have a "coordinating philosophy", and in which legitimacy and authority are low, political leaders must depend either on the gun or bribes and corruption in order to secure and maintain compliance. And this has been the problem in Uganda. Successive ethnic dictatorships from the first Obote regime through the Okello regime have relied on ethnic armies, murder and terror in the attempt to maintain civil order. Such alternatives are costly in terms of resources and the quality of life. They are particularly costly to nations like Uganda which are still in the initial stages of building social and political order (see Prewitt, 1971: 11).

Unfortunately, unlike many other African countries, Uganda does not have at least one major unifying factor on which to build a national ideology. It has lacked a charismatic father figure liker Kenyatta or Nyerere, one who could be trusted by all and who could inspire confidence and a sense of national identity. There is none of the pride here which in places such as Kenya and Zimbabwe has come out of the overthrow of colonial oppressors. There is no unifying national language or *lingua franca*, such as Kiswahili or Kichewa. There is not even an official national language policy. Above all, there is no national economic or social policy to match Tanzania's *ujamaa* or Zambia's "humanism".

Because there are no clearly articulated national ideals it is difficult to know which values to emphasise in Uganda's schools. As a result, teachers are forced to tip-toe rather precariously between two conflicting cultural worlds—the world corresponding to traditional tribal life and the world corresponding to Western ideals (see Kajubi, 1965).

Plato suggests in his *Republic* that problems of national unity can be overcome with the "right" programme of political education. Yoweri Museveni seems to share this view. Since coming to power he and the NRM Government have started to build a national ethos by a programme of political education which puts emphasis not on parochial loyalties and differences, but on the interdependence of the various parts of Uganda and the advantages which can accrue to all if each part contributes its best to the national culture and economy.

The concern on the part of Uganda's new leadership to evolve a national identity must go hand in hand with an attempt to reconcile and synthesise the drive towards modernisation with the conservation of the cultural matrix both as a means of channelling the energies of the people in constructive directions through appealing to their pride in their unique cultural identity and as an attempt to ensure that the new national society will have the stability, strength and confidence which can be derived from a link with the past and a sense of belonging and identity (see Thompson, 1981: 77-78).

ECONOMIC FACTORS

Economic factors at times have also had a close bearing on the problem of national cohesion. For example, the disproportionate success of one ethnic group in a given field such as education, trade or the armed forces, has generated intense and disruptive conflict between ethnic groups over access to opportunities and the allocation of resources.

In the area south of Lake Kioga, particularly in the crescent around the northern shores of Lake Victoria, rainfall is abundant and reliable and the soils are fertile. These conditions made settled agriculture and a higher level of development possible and profitable in contrast to the situation in the northern part of the country, where, in a more arid environment, only shifting agriculture and nomadic pastoralism were practised. It was also in the south rather than the north that mission schools, hospitals and teachers' colleges were first established.

The colonial policy was to encourage peasants in the south to grow cotton and coffee—the cash crops the cosmopolitan market needed—and the peasants in the north, through a system of taxation and administrative pressure, to provide recruits for the security forces and migrant labourers for the plantations and the peasant farms in the south. A situation therefore developed whereby the southern Bantu peasant farmers produced not only the country's cash crops for export, but also its teachers, clerks, middle-level civil servants and semi-professional workers, while the north—particularly Acholi, Lango and West Nile—almost exclusively provided the recruits for the army, police and prison services. The resultant dichotomy naturally tended to sharpen the jealousies that grew out of other differences.

Meanwhile, the marketing of cash crops was entirely in the hands of Asian middlemen. The African peasants who grew the cotton and coffee were paid a pittance for their labour. Profits went to the middlemen and of course the protectorate government. In the same way the retail and wholesale trade, the marketing of food crops (such as beans and groundnuts) and the developing industries and building trades of the country were entirely in Asian hands.

Africans resented the dominance of Asians in the retail and wholesale trades and manufacturing, and expressed their resentment in a populist movement known as the "Uganda National Movement" which first erupted on the scene in February 1959. Among other things the UNM aimed at "removing Asian traders from the villages into big towns and bringing trade into the hands of Africans." In 1960 its leaders declared a boycott of Asian shops and foreign goods such as beer and milk from Kenya, and Coca Cola. The boycott was so effective, particularly in Buganda, that the UMN was banned. In 1969 cooperatives and coffee and lint marketing boards took over the marketing of cash crops.

Like the policy of indirect rule, the continued dependence of Uganda on a system of peasant agriculture based primarily upon small individual holdings of not more than two hectares had also its debit side in economic as well as political terms. There is little or no doubt that Uganda could produce much more than was the case under small peasant producers. In spite of the praises sung of the Baganda by early missionaries and travelers, the response of the Baganda to forces of economic and social change was in many ways disappointing. Farming continued to be regarded by the peasants as a way of life rather than as a means of making money. The Baganda continued to pursue a subsistence mode of existence, growing cash crops only to pay taxes, buy sugar and tea and pay for school fees for some of their children. The individual who wanted to escape the drudgery of subsistence farming did so by aspiring to become a chief, clerk, taxi driver or shopkeeper rather than by improving his farm (Kajubi, 1965: 141). Indeed, historian Wrigley (1957: 60-80), in reviewing this part of the economic history of Uganda, arrived at the paradoxical conclusion that "one of the consequences of British rule and economic development in Buganda was a rustication of the Baganda."

The agrarian policy of the government, based primarily on the small individual and usually illiterate peasant holder rather than on the progressive developer as well, was therefore an important limiting factor. Development dependent on an agglomeration of small individual holders could not move any faster than the rate at which the peasants themselves were willing and able to adopt new methods. This, plus the fact that the peasants were exploited by both the Asian middlemen and the government, meant that no African entrepreneurial class with a large economic and political stake in the development and stability of the country was able to grow. Thus, even at the time of independence, there was no substantial class of successful African businessmen or large farmers to act as a catalyst in encouraging developmental change.

Even after independence, business enterprise in the country continued in the hands of Asians, a matter which Amin tried to redress or exploit in his own style when he expelled the Asians in 1972.

None of this should be taken to suggest that either the north or the south in Uganda is economically homogeneous. It is just that both British colonial, and post-independence economic policies, generally continuous as they were in certain respects, favoured certain groups over others, with the result that the inequitable distribution of military, economic and bureaucratic privileges by successive minority military regimes has had the effect of reinforcing parochial ethnic and religious loyalties. Consequently, the history of Uganda has turned out to be a sorry tale of conflicting groups each trying "to survive" by promoting and protecting its own interests at the expense of nationalism. Successive generations of politicians in Uganda have sought political office not to get power to direct the development of the country, but to amass wealth for themselves and to invest such wealth, not in Uganda, but in foreign countries, just in case there was another coup d'etat!

THE POSITION OF THE POLITICAL PARTIES

The political parties which have developed in Uganda since independence have been inspired primarily by parochial factors. The Uganda People's Congress (UPC), for example, a predominately northern-based multi-ethnic Protestant party founded in 1959-60, and led by Obote, was essentially the product of an anti-Buganda movement in which disparate ethnic groups were held together only by their common opposition towards Buganda. The Kabaka Yekka (KY) party, which cropped up in Buganda shortly before independence, was started to fight for the interests of Buganda. While the Democratic Party (DP)—which at the time of independence was led by Benedicto Kiwanuka, a devout Catholic Muganda and a prominent advocate in Kampala—vehemently opposed the parochialism of Kabaka Yekka, its own following was predominantly Catholic.

The UPC, a republican anti-monarchy party, and the KY, a traditionalist-feudalist party, joined in an alliance which led to their victory in the pre-independence elections in which Obote emerged as the executive prime minister, and Sir Edward Mutesa (Mutesa II) as the ceremonial president. On the surface, the cohabitation seemed to be a remarkable feat in the politics of negotiation. It could now be said that Uganda had a widely based government drawn from all of the country's major ethnic groups.

But that was only part of the story. The sharing of power and prestige between Mutesa II, a hereditary monarch from the hitherto powerful and favoured kingdom of Buganda, and Obote, a commoner from the republican north, was a tenuous one. Mutesa, on the one hand, was still *kabaka* and had the charisma of the hereditary ruler in the kingdom in which the capital was situated, though he did not have the formal and political power of the elected chief executive. Obote, on the other hand, had the formal power but not the charisma and prestige of the head of state. Neither Obote nor Mutesa was content, however (Low, 1985: 19-20), and it soon became clear that the bastard alliance of convenience between the UPC and the KY would not endure for long. In fact the alliance broke up in 1964, and in 1966 Obote's forces, under the command of Amin (then Obote's chief of staff), attacked the *kabaka's* palace at Mengo and Mutesa was forced to flee to Britain (where he died in exile in 1969).

In turn, Obote turned Uganda into a dictatorship by abolishing the kingdoms and other traditional rulerships, and centralising all power around himself. Thereafter he used the army to suppress political opposition until he was ousted by Amin in January 1971. In the end he left the country to face the fiasco and bloody turmoil of the eight years of the Amin military regime, as well as the bloody turmoil of his own second coming in 1980.

TOWARD NATIONAL INTEGRATION: THE PROBLEM AS PART OF THE SOLUTION

The process of creating a new nation out of a conglomeration of disparate entities is as complicated as putting together a jigsaw puzzle. Ali Mazrui (1972: 4) has coined the term "cultural engineering" to describe the role of culture as a catalyst in the process of nation-building. The making of new nations has so much in common with the process of constructing a new building that the term "nation-building" has been most appropriately used. As sturdy columns and beams are essential to keep a building up, and strong, so it is with a nation. Pillars have to be erected out of the strengths of different cultures, and beams built across them to keep the new nation strong.

National integration is a process which has just begun in Uganda. As in many African countries it will take many years to accomplish. What our leaders can do to the centrifugal cleavages in order to evolve a viable nation out of the different ethnic nations is still the big question. They can, however, either choose to ignore or destroy all cultural differences in order to attain a homogeneous new Ugandan culture, or elect to nurture indigenous cultures in order to build a nation based on pluralism and inter-cultural harmony.

Political scientists have distinguished between two main approaches to national integration, namely the mobilisation approach and the consociational model (see Apter, 1961: 24-25). Under the mobilisation approach, the regime in power, in its attempt to bring about national unity, engages in a drastic and far-reaching reorganisation of the existing society or societies, the argument being that in order to build a nation out of different ethnic subcultures, indigenous political and social structures must be drastically altered or destroyed and a new system built in its place.

The consociational approach, on the other hand, places a high premium on give-and-take among the various groups that make up a society. Rather than seeking to throw pre-colonial ethnic groups and cultures into a melting pot in order to produce a monolithic and homogenised society, it seeks unity through variety and complementarity. Its emphasis is on compromise and concession as well as the willingness to accomodate groups of divergent views in order to evolve national unity.

It seems to me that the problem of ethnicity and cultural heterogeneity in Uganda can only be abated effectively by accepting and encouraging heterogeneity in the sense of extracting from each culture its best elements in the formation of the new national culture. In this way the problem is indeed part of the solution.

CONCLUSION

The post-independence history of Uganda has been disappointing and tragic. Although poverty, disease and ignorance are important enemies in Uganda, as they are in all developing countries, the greatest problem is one of lack of unity. There is no doubt that the most important single task facing leaders, educators and, indeed, all Ugandans today is not only some method of enabling a large number of ethnic and ethnocentric cultures to live together, but also the development of a means of integrating the production and application of new knowledge into the fabric of the country's traditional systems.

REFERENCES

Alnwick, D. J. 1985. "Background to the Karamoja Famine." In Dodge, Cole P. and Paul D. Wiebe (eds.), *Crisis in Uganda: The Breakdown of Health Services*. Oxford: Pergamon.

Apter, David. 1961. *The Political Kingdom in Africa*. Princeton, New Jersey: Princeton University Press.

Gukiina, Peter M. 1972. *Uganda: A Case Study in African Political Development*. East Bend, Indiana: University of Notre Dame Press.

Harper, William, Donna M. Miller, Roberta J. Park and Elwood C. Davis (eds.). 1977. *The Philosophic Process in Physical Education*. Philadelphia: Lea and Febiger.

Kajubi, W. S. 1965. "Coffee and Prosperity in Uganda: Some Aspects of Economic and Social Change." *The Uganda Journal*, 29, part 2.

Low, D. A. 1985. "Uganda: The Dislocated State." Uganda Seminar, Institute of Political Studies, University of Copenhagen, Denmark, 25-28 September.

Mazrui, Ali A. 1972. *Cultural Engineering and Nation Building in East Africa*. Evanston, Illinois: Northwestern University Press.

Nsibambi, Apolo. 1986. "Failure of State to Provide Security to All." *The Star* (Kampala), 7 March.

Prewitt, Kenneth. 1971. *Education and Political Values*. Nairobi: East African Publishing House.

Rowe, John. 1985. "Islam Under Idi Amin: A Case of Deja Vue?" Uganda Seminar, Institute of Political Studies, University of Copenhagen, Denmark, 25-28 September.

Stanley, H. M. 1878. *Through the Dark Continent* (Volume 1). New York: Harper Brothers.

Tilman, Robert and Taylor Cole (eds.). 1962. *The Nigerian Political Scene*. Cambridge University Press.

Thompson, A. R. 1981. *Education and Development in Africa*. London: Macmillan.

Welbourn, F. 1965. *Religion and Politics in Uganda, 1952-62*. Nairobi: East African Publishing House.

Wrigley, Christopher. 1985. "Four Steps Towards Disaster." Uganda Seminar, Institute of Political Studies, University of Copenhagen, Denmark, 25-28 September.

Wrigley, C. C. 1957. "Buganda: An Outline of Economic History." *Economic History Review* (Second Series), 10, No. 1.

ACHOLI AND NUBIANS: ECONOMIC FORCES AND MILITARY EMPLOYMENT

Dennis R. Pain

The nature of military recruitment from Uganda has frequently been interpreted as a combination of prejudicial selection and political machination, without regard to the economic imperatives at work. This is understandable coming from those politicians wishing to decry the ex-colonial power or post-independence leadership for creating an ethnically unbalanced army, but further academic analysis is required. This article calls for a radical reappraisal of the historical military realities of Uganda, and therefore for a positive and progressive answer to the dilemma of an unrepresentative army, rather than a negative populist solution.

The Acholi and the Nubians have each at various periods dominated the various Ugandan armies (or units of the King's African Rifles, KAR). However, they have done so for quite different historical, cultural, political and, above all, economic reasons. They have nothing in common culturally and indeed have remained staunch enemies throughout their 120 year contact. Although the Nubians originate far to the north among various Sudanese groups, they have more in common culturally and economically with perhaps the Baganda than the Acholi. On the other hand, the Acholis could better be compared with the westerners in Uganda.

NUBIAN MILITARY PARTICIPATION

The Nubians originate in the phenomenon of Arabic-speaking northern Sudanese operating as slave traders in what is today southern Sudan, in the middle of the last century. Many of these Sudanic slaves were co-opted into this slaving network, and women from these southern areas were taken as wives and concubines, thus contributing genetically, culturally and linguistically to the pure northern Nubian ethnic stock. Among the Nubians encountered by the early European administrators under the *Khedive* of Egypt, Samuel Baker and Emin Pasha, were Bari, Azande, Kuku, Moru, Monbuttu, Mittu, Banyoro, Ethiopians and Nigerians who were identifying with the Nubians. In time these accretions themselves passed as Nubians. Today, whether in Bombo around the former 7th KAR Barracks in Uganda, or in

Kibera, a similar Nubian enclave in Nairobi, the Nubians have recognised "clans" of Bari, Kakwa and Kuku Nubians who may now be fourth or fifth generation, along with some first generation accretions.

For over 100 years, this broad Nubian entity has found itself shifting between regular and irregular military employment and legitimate and illegitimate trade, and Islamic proselytisation joined with the role of *fakir* or healer. Sir Samuel Baker's men included Nubians, as did Emin Pasha's and the Mahdi's. The Nubian slaving network operated throughout southern Sudan, but the Nubians who reached Acholi and west across the Nile were too extended to attempt to gather slaves, especially against the powerful Acholi chiefs. However, they had a camp at Patiko from where they gathered ivory and raided cattle to carry ivory north, surviving by playing off one Acholi chief against another.

In 1872 Baker arrived in Acholi, and in the battle of Patiko he totally defeated the Nubians who far outnumbered him. As a result he was faced with a dilemma since he could not hold the Nubians prisoners for logistical reasons and realised that to send them home without guns would lead to their death, whereas to re-issue them with guns would lead to their restarting operations. The option he chose was therefore to co-opt them into his own force, a move that puzzled the Acholi who were nevertheless indebted to him for his military action. Baker built the fort which remains to this day, and left an officer in charge to collect a corn-tax and encourage the introduction of various crops including, hopefully, bananas and coffee. Acholi at the time was so fertile and productive in millet, sorghum and other crops that Baker saw it as "the granary of Africa".

Baker was followed by Gordon who in 1876 left behind him a series of forts in Uganda manned by Nubians. When left to their own devices in the various stations, they quickly reverted to their former techniques, and the next governor of the province, Emin, found that such events had again alienated the powerful Acholi chief, Rwotcamo. On the other hand, the marginal, then "Madi" now "Acholi", clans at Pabbo and Paloro, on the marches of Madi and Acholi, actually asked Emin in 1878 for Nubians to be allowed to return to the stations there, possibly to support them against more dominant neighbouring Acholi clans. Even the Padibe seem to have wanted Nubian support. But, under Emin's weak ineffectual leadership, the behaviour of the Nubian forces under his command left a bitter folk memory among the Acholi.

In 1887 it appears that Rwotcamo, chief of the Payeera and therefore a close ally of King Kabarega of Bunyoro, was killed by Nubians sent by the Padibe of East Acholi. Emin claimed that at the time his Nubian Suleiman Aga attacked Rwot Ochama, Kabarega's people were there exchanging ivory for ammunition, powder and percussion caps (see Gray, 1964). Casati (1891: 30) reported that the incident was part of an uprising against the Nubians instigated by Kabarega. In the vacuum after Emin's departure in 1889, until the arrival of the British, the remnants of Emin's force who remained in the area and did not join the Mahdi, caused havoc between the clans. In one notable event the east Acholi clans combined to drive out the Nubians from a strongly established fort in Kalongo. Rwotcamo's successor, Awich, also attacked the Nubians when they started raiding for food, and it seems that the Nubians were largely driven out of Acholi during the 1890s and moved west across the Nile. Here they remained until re-introduced by the British under Lugard in Buganda in 1891 as part of the pacification of Uganda in general and Bunyoro in particular.

In the whole upper Nile area we can estimate 30,000 to 40,000 persons claiming allegiance to this emergent ethnic entity—the Nubians—although with fighting, enslaving, inter-marriage, accretions and reversions, everything was fluid. Only a small percentage could claim to be "real", core Nubians deriving from the Danagla-Ja'aliyyin Nubians north of Khartoum. As a well-armed military community, the Nubians were a force to be reckoned with. Occupying a structurally dominant position in the area west of the Nile, they attracted many from the surrounding ethnic groups, but not the powerful Banyoro and Acholi.

When Lugard, that opportunist mercantile British administrator, arrived in Uganda in 1890, he found himself part of a triangular struggle in Buganda, with the Catholic and Protestant parties generally opposed to the Muslim party, and traditionalists sometimes opposing all three. The Catholics were particularly suspicious of Lugard because of the English-Protestant association. When the Muslim party joined forces with Kabarega in Bunyoro, Lugard marched against them with a combined Buganda army of 25,000. After temporarily defeating them, Lugard decided to stabilise his tenuous position by increasing his meagre forces, totaling less than 250, through seeking out the remainder of Emin's troops, under the command of Selim Bey, as he understood them to have a reputation for being the "best material for soldiery in Africa".

Lugard found the Nubians scattered all over the country west of Lake Albert in batches of fifty to seventy, for the sake of food. They were mostly in poor dress, but the officers were well dressed in coats and trousers of cotton cloth made by the Nubians from their own production. Lugard learned from Selim that the Nubians had over 1000 Remington rifles and any amount of ammunition, and that three companies of the original troops were left, others having deserted with the rebel Fadl-el Mula and been replaced by raw recruits. On 24 October 1891 the Selim section of the Nubian community crossed the Semliki River into what is now part of Toro. Having come to terms with Lugard regarding pay and status, just over 2000 soldiers and a total of 13,000 including women and children crossed over, and the Nubian community walked into Uganda's history. From the signing of the agreement onwards, they were to be treated as a composite community, variously referred to as "the Sudanese" or "the Nubians". Lugard records how this Nubian horde, traveling through populated areas, caused considerable headaches by their continual capturing of women. On his return to Buganda, Lugard found himself effectively dismissed, and early in 1892 he left Uganda ignominiously. The same year the Khedive of Egypt disowned the Sudanese soldiers and the only solution seemed to be to settle the Nubians in Uganda in what were referred to as "colonies".

In 1893 fear that trouble was about to break out amongst the Nubians stationed in Kampala and Entebbe resulted in these being disarmed and Selim Bey deported to Kenya. In 1894 some of Fadl-el Mula's men, hearing of the arrangements with Lugard, came south to Wadelai where they joined the British forces, and 10,000 men, families and followers were ferried across to Bunyoro. Other Nubians were recruited by the Belgians as administrators in what is now the West Nile part of Uganda, and were later taken on in that role by the British.

For the next fifteen years or so, the Nubians were at the height of their power and notoriety, a position they were not to regain until the coup of 1971. No book written around the turn of the century about Uganda could fail to mention them. The Nubians were continually used against that masterly guerrilla warfare exponent, Kabarega of Bunyoro, with whom they had many fierce encounters. As Kabarega obtained more arms and ammunition from Arab/Swahili traders, it was decided to enlist more Nubians from among those settled in Uganda. The War Office in London considered it to be undesirable for the Nubians in Uganda to be taken over as regular troops, but in 1895 the Uganda Rifles were constituted. These Nubian refugee mercenaries had become the foundation of the Uganda Rifles.

In 1897 a Nubian mutiny erupted and disaffection continued until about 1900. Their women were said to have been excessively avaricious and the troops indulged in looting, but they did have a genuine grievance about the method of pay and arrears of such things as clothing allowances. In some circles the aim became to replace the Nubians with local Ugandan recruits, and some Sikh troops were brought over temporarily to improve discipline. In 1901 the last of the Nubian mutineers, with a few Lango and Banyoro, were finally defeated in the Lango campaign by a combined force of Nubians and Baganda, with some Acholi, Madi and Bari reacruits. In the four-year punitive campaign against the Nandi of Kenya from the end of 1895, over half the medals went to Nubians and nearly one-third to Indian troops and most of the balance to Baganda. By 1904 there were five and a half companies of Nubians, one company of Swahilis and a half company of Baganda. It was said that the Baganda proved not to be satisfactory soldiers, but that the number of volunteers was practically unlimited, and they were found to be good in the police where they formed the majority. Given this dominance in the army of the Nubians, it is not surprising to find that non-Nubians from small groups identified with the Nubians and sought to adopt their culture and language.

However, the special commissioner, H. Johnston, gave a vivid description of the Nubians in 1902. He considered that from the time the Nubians were introduced into Uganda, trouble with them began. "Themselves mostly exslaves, they had all the cruelty and unscrupulousness of the Nubian slavetraders, whose name, principles and religion they had inherited." In Toro, "their ravages, robberies, and rapes were more terrible even than the misdeeds of Kabarega's warriors. After the greater part of them and their locustlike wives and followers were removed from Toro and placed under better control in (Buganda), they rendered very efficient service in fighting the Banyoro and the rebel Baganda in the years which followed Lugard's departure. ... The ease with which the brave and steady (Nubians) encountered and defeated larger bodies of Banyoro, Baganda, and Bahima inspired them with a great contempt for the pagan or Christian natives of the Protectorate. They were fanatical Muhammadans; they secretly despised the white man as an unbeliever, and they hankered continually after the founding of

Muhammadan kingdoms of their own in these fertile, easily conquered countries" (Johnston, 1902: 237-38).

In 1908, with the forming of the barracks at Bombo and the later gift of land to the Nubians by the *Kabaka* of Buganda, the Nubians began to settle there and elsewhere in separate *mulkis* or communities. They developed a pattern within families of the first son joining up with the King's African Rifles "voluntarily", with the second son becoming a Muslim leader and the third son going into trade. Their last action within Uganda almost entirely took place in Acholi between 1912 and 1914, starting with several punitive raids into Acholi where government runners from Lango had been attacked, assisting the police in disarming the Acholi of about 5000 guns, and finally in suppressing the 1912 Lamogi rebellion in the Guruguru hills and caves. In 1914 they helped in rounding up the cattle of several Acholi chiefs who seemed most likely to give trouble to the British at the start of the war. From the beginning there was Acholi distrust of the new British administration because of its use of Nubian troops and their past memories of them.

Thus by 1914 the role of the Nubian co-colonisers with the British in the task of "pacification" had ended, and the fight for the maintenance of their special status and privileges was begun. British militarists wished to bestow special privileges upon the Nubians to place them above "native" Ugandans in recognition of their alien origin and military support of the British. They were to be free from rendering the *luwalo* labour tax and to be free from the jurisdiction of local (eg. Buganda) courts. Written instructions were issued by the soldier turned governor, Archer, in 1923 to accord these privileges which were later revoked to the anger of the Nubian leaders in the mid-1930s. By that time, with the joint military service established with Kenya, the importance of the Nubians in the new KAR was diminished. It had been one of these British officers who wrote the chorus of the KAR song, "The Sudi" (see Archer, 1963: 150).

> It's the Sudi, my boy, it's the Sudi
> With his grim-set ugly face.
> But he looks like a man and he *fights* like a man
> For he comes of a fighting race.

Another problem for the administration was the number of "marginal" Nubians eager to identify with the Nubians and to share in their privileges. By taking a strict definition of the Nubians essentially on linguistic grounds, the 1931 Census identified only 5528 Nubians. At about the same time a committee set up to look at the question of the status of the Nubians, took another strict criterion for recognising a Nubian, as one descended from the armed forces of Emin Pasha and his predecessors or associated with them over that time. The possibility of moving the Nubians to their own district carved out of Acholi was rejected on the grounds of expected Acholi hostility. Finally, it was determined in 1939 to record the names of recognised Nubians "in a book of the Nubis which will be kept by Government." They were to be moved from Buganda, against their expressed wishes, and set up in *mulkis* near Gulu, *Kitgum* and Arua townships on Crown land. The proposals were totally rejected by the Nubians, with petitions to the British king, demonstrations and boycotts of taxation.

However, the start of the second world war at the time gave a renewed military role to the Nubians, and left the status of the Nubians ambiguous in the light of their rejection of the government proposals. They remained ambiguous even in terms of their nationality.

The 1967 constitution of Obote introduced a definition of "African" in relation to Ugandan citizenship, which left open the possibility of discriminatory legislation and action against non-Ugandan Africans, especially in trade. Action was taken by Obote against the Kenyan Luos in 1969, and the Nubians believed that Obote might be intending to send them back to the Sudan, and that, if thwarted by the U.N., he would resettle them in Acholi. Such a step, the Nubians claimed, was intended to remove their influence completely from the army and other occupations. The Nubians acted accordingly, through the 1971 coup, to pre-empt such a move (Wanji, 1973: 177). Yet there is no evidence that such action was planned, but that the reports were simply a ploy to generate Nubian dissatisfaction with the government.

The Nubians had been imposed from above by the colonial power. The Nubian myths of origin are rooted in their colonial past and have yet to be rewritten appropriately for participation in an independent open society. Their interest in trade and the military encouraged their formulation as an ethnic community, viewing itself as a corporate entity, which hindered their progress and participation in Uganda as citizens.

It was in protection and furtherance of their corporate interest in the military and trade, at the periphery of the Asian trading network, that Nubian action in 1971-72, following the Amin coup, sought to eliminate the Acholi in the army and the Asians in the economy.

At a series of *mauledis* (ostensibly Islamic teaching functions), in the north restricted to Nubians, the idea of taking over the Asian trading network, as well as direct control of the government, was expounded. Those privy to the Nubian aspirations were aware that the Asians were to be expelled, and several censuses of Asians were undertaken in preparation for the event. Essentially the bureaucrats followed the Obote plans of 1970 for a rapid phasing out of non-citizen Asians. However, the distinctive contribution of the Amin regime was the elimination of *citizen* Asians in trade, professions and government, in many cases allowing non-citizens to remain if in key professional jobs. Those Ugandans taken by surprise when these plans for an expulsion were announced, were generally jubilant in the opportunistic hope of benefiting from the subsequent allocation. Few were aware that the expulsion was planned to enable the takeover of the economy by the Nubians which then took place, reinforced by the power of the Nubian military. Most Nubian traders were themselves in the army or at least were supported by immediate relatives in the army. The army also took over the lucrative coffee trade, either informally through controlling the smuggling or formally through the control of the Coffee Marketing Board. With the collapse of Brazilian coffee production, Uganda's foreign exchange earnings, legitimate and illegitimate, soared above all previous records while real prices to coffee farmers dropped. The principal beneficiaries of those boom years were the Nubians (see Twaddle, 1985).

The Nubians had been totally eclipsed in the army as a result of the second world war and the massive recruitment of Acholi as a consequence of the particular economic conditions prevailing in Acholi in 1939 and 1940. In 1948 the Acholi formed 50 percent of the Ugandans in the KAR, which may have risen to 75 percent through the 1950s, before falling markedly after independence. The Nubians did not regain their ascendency until the 1971 coup which, in restoring the old colonial structures, also revived the Nubian association with fighting. Once more it became advisable for those who could to pass as Nubians, in the army or when dealing with the army. Thus more and more, what might be called "potential Nubians" from the Sudan were recruited into the Uganda army in large numbers after 1971, culminating in the heavy recruitment of 1978 which led to divisions within the regime as established Nubians saw their slice of the cake being divided up. This, at a time of falling coffee prices and available resources, in turn led to the externalisation of the problem through the device of invading Tanzania. The repercussions of this led to the fall of the regime and the collapse of all Nubian influence.

Nubian hegemony lasted from 1973 until the collapse of the Amin regime in 1979. By 1973 virtually all army units were controlled by rapidly promoted Nubians, some of whom were in civilian occupations such as that of taxi drivers at the time of the 1971 coup. About one-third of the Defence Council which ostensibly ran Uganda were Nubians, but the secrecy which surrounded its full membership made it difficult to ascertain precisely.

ACHOLI MILITARY PARTICIPATION

Whereas the Nubians were originally recruited as a group into the early Uganda administration, and continued to participate and settle in urban areas as such, the Acholi have been recruited and participate as individuals. Although there is a pattern of Acholi recruitment and employment, it has its roots in economic pressures and statistical rather than cultural norms. The large number from Acholi in the army until 1971 was primarily economically, rather than culturally or politically, determined. Thus it must be understood why more soldiers came from east Acholi (Kitgum District) rather than west Acholi (Gulu District), and why, for instance, all the males of one extended family living on poor land in northeast Acholi could be in the army and so be totally eliminated in the 1971 massacres.

The Acholi are a Nilotic-speaking Luo people occupying Gulu District (the *lo-piny* clans) and Kitgum District (the *lo-maalo* clans). In addition there are a few Acholi living over the border in the Sudan, and two former Madi-speaking clans in Gulu District (the *lo-Madi* clans). To the west on the Nile are the Jonam, the people-of-the-big-river, and the Alur, both closely related culturally, linguistically, politically and mythically with the Acholi. To the south, across the Nile, are a small group of Luo people known as Jo-pa-Luo or Chopi, and the large and formerly powerful kingdom of Bunyoro. Kingship in the western kingdoms of Uganda is thought to originate with the Luo migrations south. The Babitu dynasty of Bunyoro kings has always been closely linked with Acholi and has traditionally exercised a certain political suzerainty over the western Acholi clans, at least, in particular, settling chiefship succession disputes (Girling, 1960: 172). To the east are the quite distinct Karamojong as well as the Labwor group who now speak Acholi. To the southeast are the Lango who are widely thought to be a Karamojong people who have adopted Luo language and culture ("Lango" meaning "foreigner" in many Luo languages).

The Acholi are organised in patrilineal localised clans. Traditionally there was no individual land tenure, and the right to cultivate was held by all clan members. Outsiders could be given the right to settle and cultivate by the clan head of the *won paco* (the village head or "owner"), if spoken for by a village member. In a system of generally shifting cultivation, crops planted by a cultivator are his property, but not the land on which they grow. There is no land shortage, but a dearth of capital to develop viable marketable agricultural production. Since 1970 elite Acholi have been using modern national laws to register title to land, potentially creating an artificial land shortage.

The Acholi have been involved in the Uganda national economy in two ways—through cash crop production and through migration to the urban areas. However, these two patterns of participation are part of the same overall picture. Between 1948 and 1971 a key factor had been education, especially of males, as an avenue to remunerative urban employment with the potential for reinvestment in agriculture at home. The collapse of urban incomes in the 1980s, together with the collapse of cotton and tobacco prices and marketing in the 1970s, has left the Acholi in the 1980s in the deepest depression they have known, following after the politically imposed depression of the 1970s.

The economic history of Acholi can be divided into seven periods since the establishment of the British administration. The inter-war period up to 1939 was one of a low level of participation in the cash economy of the nation. This was followed in the war years by a period of crisis and transformation. The third period after the war, from about 1946 to 1952-53, was one of economic boom. From then until 1966-67 the Acholi economy settled to an equilibrium plateau, followed by a period of depression until 1971 when disaster struck, compounded in 1977 with the elimination and exile of the majority of educated Acholi. Finally, from 1979 as Uganda has generally seen a shift of access to resources from the towns to the rural areas, Acholi have been unable to benefit significantly due to lack of capital and infrastructure.

The most dramatic events for Acholi, affecting both the social and economic orders, have been initially external events. The second world war, compounded by drought and locusts, was the catalyst for a positive transformation in Acholi. Had the 1971 coup only led to the massacre of Acholi soldiers in July 1971 (Martin, 1974), Acholi might have been able to profit indirectly by transforming its agricultural base and increasing its participation in those sectors of the economy requiring education. But the attacks on Acholi educated elite and a regressive agricultural policy effectively halted the progress seen in Acholi from about 1950 to 1970.

Until 1939 there was little economic incentive for Acholi to migrate. Labour recruitment for the south of Uganda did not take place in Acholi, where the response would have been minimal, since the Protectorate Poll Tax could be met by the sale of cotton introduced before 1914 after the founding of Gulu. In the late 1930s cotton produced a total income to Acholi of about one and a half million shillings per annum, of which nearly 40 percent was given over in tax.

The unpopular grain taxes of Baker and Emin to support their forces had long since given way when the British introduced tax and labour obligations in 1912. The resentment this caused resulted in the burning down of some temporary station buildings and encouraged the Lamogi rebellion (Postlethwaite, 1947: 58, and Adimola, 1954). By 1938 the vast majority of Acholi had taken up the option of converting their annual month's *luwalo* labour obligation into a cash payment.

By this time some Acholi were working outside the district. In the first world war, after initial government objection to recruiting Acholi due to their oppostion to the British administration, they "took to soldiering like ducks to water, and nowadays are the tribe from which a large portion of both the KAR and the police are drawn" (Postlethwaite, 1947: 70-71). In 1938 there were still Acholi serving in the KAR and 23 percent of the Uganda police force were Acholi, a percentage which fell to 15 percent by independence, partly due to strong recruitment in Teso and Lango in the 1950s (in the Annual Reports of the Uganda Police). At this time only about 1000 children attended the church-founded elementary schools.

In the cotton season of 1938-39 disaster struck, which was to prove a turning point for the Acholi. In 1937 a good season in the United States resulted in the Uganda cotton price being halved, and disappointed farmers left up to 25 percent of the cotton unpicked. On the basis of the fall in prices, Acholi farmers reduced their acreage in 1938, received a low price and suffered a massive loss of income, a reduction of 57 percent on the 1937 low income. Great efforts were made by the administration to collect taxes and, as a result, 91 percent of the value of the cotton of Acholi in 1939 was given over in taxes.

There was worse to come. In 1939 there was a drought followed by locusts, resulting in the failure of 90 percent of the millet in east Acholi. Famine relief was needed for 100,000 people and maize was obtained from Kenya to supplement the food in the famine granaries. Though west Acholi had been the worst hit in the northern province by the cotton disaster, east Acholi was the worst hit by the drought and locusts.

With the start of the second world war in 1939, and in the light of prevailing economic conditions in Acholi together with their past history, it was not surprising that the Acholi sought to join the army in large numbers. Sixty percent of adult males sought to join up and recruiting officers were able to be selective in recruiting only 20 percent of adult males—by far the largest proportion of recruits from any district although numerically far less than those from Mengo, and less than those from Mbale, Teso and Busoga (see Second Progress Report on Civil Reabsorption, 1948). In the heart of the famine area, at Adilang, a great Bwola was performed to inaugurate the intensive recruiting of war-time soldiers for the KAR (see the Annual Reports of the P.Cs. for Northern and Western Provinces).

The Acholi soon had a reputation as soldiers. Though the most over-represented group in the army, this reputation was not just because of weight of numbers. Of the honours and awards given after the end of the war, easily the most disproportionate number, in relation even to their numbers in the army, were awarded to Acholi who received nearly 40 percent of the total. The Nubians were also undoubtedly rated highly, but no figures are available as to their numbers in the army, nor is it clear just how many awards they received, because of their marginal status by this period as a category in the official records. Just over 17 percent of those who died in active service were Acholi.

There is general agreement that the war was a period of traumatic social change in Acholi. Experience of travel abroad, the army education services and promotion to higher ranks in the army being restricted to the better educated, together with demobilisation grants and higher post-war prices for cotton, promoted an intense interest in education immediately after the war. The question was no longer one of fees, but of places in the existing schools (Adimola, 1962: 71).

In the demobilisation period there was an increased volume of money in circulation. Demobilised soldiers were exempt from paying poll tax for one year, and something like three million shillings was paid out to Acholi in terminal cash benefits during the years 1945-47, some to cover travel and other expenses. It was estimated that, during the war, payments made actually in Acholi totaled ten million shillings. Thus army service generated nearly twice as much income through the 20 percent of the men who left home, as the remaining 80 percent and the women generated through cotton production in their absence.

A pattern, begun with the first world war, had been established by the second. After the completion of demobilisation, the regular army included 2101 Ugandans, after recruiting 1043 of whom 222 were ex-soldiers. About 50 percent of these Ugandan soldiers were Acholi. "The two recruiting parties during the war had no difficulty in obtaining the recruits required, and in fact requirements were greatly oversubscribed, even though virtually no infantryman, which is the most common role for the Acholi entering the Armed Forces, were called for" (Civil Reabsorption Second Progress Report, 1948, and Annual Report of the P.C. Northern Province, 1947: 10).

The government hoped that the majority of demobilised soldiers would return to the land, with some setting up as village craftsmen and shopkeepers, and a few being offered retraining and urban employment. Few Acholi seem to have secured such employment directly through the agencies, but nearly 25 percent of those seeking training were Acholi, far above the number of vacancies available. In Uganda as a whole, less than 8 percent of ex-soldiers applied for training of any sort, whereas 20 percent of the Acholi ex-soldiers did so. Many ex-soldiers joined the police and prisons especially, and others became medical assistants, social welfare assistants, road headmen with the PWD, or agricultural and other department assistants. But the majority were content to return to the land.

However, many Acholi were reluctant to return to the vagaries of cotton production, or to start as labourers in the south at the low pay obtaining. Some of the uneducated did take up employment in the south as night watchmen and security guards. Because of the nature of the work, outsiders are preferred, and the physique and background of these Acholi were seen as an added advantage. By 1949 labouring jobs for the uneducated and unskilled produced an annual wage equivalent to only two acres of cotton. So Acholi aspirations turned towards paid employment as teachers, clerks and so on, but for which there was a shortage of openings even for the educated.

For the less educated, the "security services" also provided higher wages and prospects for promotion and a career structure which factories and plantations lacked.

With the Asians and Nubians controlling the post-war retail trade, few Acholi who invested their gratuities in shops made them pay. It had been hoped that much of the newly acquired wealth would be invested in post office savings accounts, housebuildings and setting up in crafts and commerce. Though many accounts were opened, they were often mostly drained within a short period, leaving a little in to keep the account open. There were problems over the availability of materials and a general shortage, especially of *bati* for roofing. A large quantity was specially imported into Uganda, and house improvement became an essential aim of most Acholi. It became one of the first rural home improvements carried out by a successful urban employee, before he would consider improving the land. This conformed with traditional attitudes, whereby a young man had to build his own house before he was recognised as an adult by others. Inlaws might require a young man to help in constructing a house in order to prove his worth. It is seen as a traditional measure of status. To have one's own house emphasises that individuality so essential to the Acholi. Such a house should be built at one's father's home place, and this attachment to home is said to have prevented the successful introduction of rural resettlement schemes.

Much of the wealth apparently was redistributed by the much inflated marriage-wealth payments, in spite of an official maximum rate. The suggestion that much of the cash was thus being withdrawn from circulation implies that the senior males were benefiting. In fact, the official maximum rate was effectively interpreted by Acholi fathers of girls to be a *minimum* rate.

By far the most important investment of Acholi at this time was in terms of education. The effect of the war on patterns of education and the long-term consequences of this provided the major feature of the post-war period. This investment in education did not extend to girls on the grounds that any investment in their education would be lost at their marriage. The local administration decided to compete with the missions in provision of education, and demobilisation grants and some of the Cotton Fund Grant were invested in building a number of primary schools and a secondary school.

The ideal type contrast between Acholi and Nubians in this period is of Acholi investing their war gratuities in the *education* of their children, while Nubians invested theirs in *trade*. What the Acholi learnt from the war was that increased participation in the national economy and society required education. The only asset Acholi had was manpower and land, and they chose to invest in their manpower which promised better terms for the limited outlay which was available from cotton production. The Nubian's asset was their past history and special status which constricted their investment to traditional avenues.

As a result of all this investment, Acholi *men* became more highly educated than most Ugandan groups with 59 per 1000 acquiring S.1 or higher by 1969, lower than that of West Mengo males, but higher even than other districts in Buganda (1969 Uganda Census Report, III, Table 6). Even more so, employed Acholi had well above average education compared with the total labour force, the latter including, as it always has done, 30-40 percent less-educated non-Ugandan Africans. The estimated income of employed Acholi rose faster than cotton incomes up to 1964, and then up to 1972 exceeded total cotton income for Acholi (Pain, 1975: graph 3). Yet the Acholi had the lowest migration rate of any group in Uganda. Few Acholi were migrating without having urban formal employment prospects.

It is primarily in the sphere of cotton production that there are two points of marked discontinuity in the Acholi economy, around 1952-53 and 1966-67. In the intervening period of economic equilibrium, cotton acreages and production increased. In these boom years the Acholi became used to a rapid rise in real rural incomes, which did not require an increase in effort in terms of cotton acreages planted. In a number of these years the unenforceable British law compelling most adult males to cultivate a minimum of two acreas of cotton, was fulfilled on average. Agricultural experts consider Acholi an extremely marginal cotton producing area, whose usefulness as a cash crop depends entirely on prevailing prices in relation to the cost of living and alternative crops and avenues of employment. Agricultural advice, pre- and post-independence, has been notorious for its neglect of the production of food crops and local social factors—such as the existence of *rwodi kweri*, the traditional "hoe chiefs", the seasonal distribution of labour and the level of risk due to climatic conditions. The capital required in Acholi for a breakthrough into capitalist farming, not dependent on family labour, was provided out of urban incomes from professional employment as a result of the earlier investment in education. For those who failed to obtain the necessary education, the only acceptable income-earning opportunity was military employment.

The period of Acholi economic stability and prosperity ended in 1966-67. From a peak income from the sale of the 1965 crop, cotton incomes dropped to less than half the following year as a result of drought combined with a reduction of the buying price when the Cotton Price Assistance Fund ran out. At the same time the price index rose sharply, and real rural incomes fell to those of twenty years earlier, while wages of urban employees kept pace with rising prices. This period coincided with a national increase in military recruitment, which provided an outlet for the little-educated rural poor as a result of the state of emergency in Buganda. However the proportion of Acholi never regained its immediate post-war level of nearly 50 percent of Ugandans in the KAR. Although no official figures were available for the army, police or prisons, it is widely accepted that the tradition of Acholi serving in the security services was maintained right up to 1971, even if their proportion had fallen to about 30 percent of an estimated 9000 in the army up to the 1971 coup. It is thought that not more than 2000 Acholi soldiers were killed in the massacres of July 1971 and earlier in that year, and that less than 1000 escaped. About 17 percent of formally employed Acholi must have been soldiers, and a higher percentage are understood to have come from the more economically depressed east of Acholi. After the 1979 war, Acholi again made themselves ready to be recruited into the UNLA, an army which was ill-disciplined and underpaid and which became under Obote as rapacious in living off the people and ultimately as notorious in carnage as its predecessors. In many eyes its reputation was worse as it confronted and exploited individual peasants rather than systematically extracting the surplus and killing any organised leadership as in Amin's days.

SUMMARY AND CONCLUSION

Like others in Uganda, Acholi, as an area and a people, was incorporated into the nation from *below*, being drawn up into the higher levels by the integrating pressures of the central economy. In contrast, the Nubians were incorporated from *above*, or were, in other words, *imposed* from above by the British administration.

Military recruitment per 1000 population from any particular area may provide one of the best indices of economic underdevelopment for the country as a whole. Kitgum, Moyo, Koboko, north Soroti, Gulu, Rukungiri, Kisoro, Lira and Apac, rating high on military recruitment, are also areas high in terms of underdevelopment. Luwero, Mpigi, Mukono, Masaka and Mubende, traditionally rating low on military recruitment, have had the highest levels of economic development. Karamoja, although well represented in the army, would rate lower in terms of military recruitment than its level of underdevelopment might suggest. This may be due to the specific nature of the area's incorporation into the Uganda polity or could reflect a measure of economic wealth and development in terms of cattle which is often overlooked. To counter this imbalance requires economic, not political, solutions.

In particular, four out of the five major periods of military recruitment, namely 1939-40, 1966-67, 1981 and 1985, but excluding the 1972 Sudanese recruitment, have coincided with drought and food deficit in Acholi, particularly in the east. To avoid labouring for wealthier farmers, considered humiliating by Acholi, any number from one to a whole family have in these periods joined the army. The economic weakness of Acholi, with a lack of government support for traditional grain production and profitable food crops, has led to a dependency on military recruitment in the interests of ruling elites. This has made the Acholi vulnerable to manipulation and exploitation and resulted in instability for the whole nation. The Acholi in particular have paid a heavy price for their underdevelopment.

We live by myths, whether true or false, which influence the paths of our actions. Such myths may become redundant, or even anti-social, as a result of social change. The British recognition of "martial races" was available to be adopted by the Nubians and the Acholi to create a boundary to the particular economic niche of military recruitment. It also enabled post-independence politicians to find sources of ready recruits. Yet such a myth could not continue to live without the fertile ground of economic underdevelopment in Acholi in which it germinated.

Another myth, that of Nubian hegemony under the British, created the basis of their action in the 1970s in taking over the government and the army of Uganda and later the economy, but ultimately led to the alienation of the Nubians from other Ugandans, paralleling the Asian position. This exposed the Nubians and made them an identifiable target with the overthrow of the Amin regime. During the military regime of late 1985, there was a disastrous return of FUNA troops, the soldiers of the Amin era associated with the

Nubians. After the NRA took over in January 1986, the Nubian community of Bombo addressed a memorandum to the new government seeking once and for all to remove the military association with Bombo and the Nubian community. Fortunately for the Nubians a new myth of the "Anyanya" diverted attention from them. The Anyanya were the southern Sudanese guerrilla movement of the 1960s and forerunners of the Sudan People's Liberation Army. With the 1972 settlement in southern Sudan, some elements on the fringe of the Anyanya movement found themselves jobless and ready recruits for Amin's 1972 recruitment of mercenaries from southern Sudan. However, many Ugandans mistakenly believed the Anyanya (the "Scorpions") to be a Sudanese tribe. With the NRA takeover a new community witch hunt burst out in which even Acholi were pointed out by children as "Anyanya" and risked losing their lives. Such criminal acts died out as order was established.

The myth in Buganda that all UNLA soldiers were Acholi, even if from Lango or elsewhere, led to a temporary focus on the Acholi and "Okellos" as the target in the war. As the war drew to a close in February/March 1986, such a myth became dangerously subversive of national unity, and the new president, Yoweri Museveni, had to stress to his men that Acholi had to be recognised as brothers and sisters. It is yet to be seen whether new myths expressing national unity rather than the old myths associated with "divide and rule" tactics can be forged which measure up to the new realities.

The Acholi cautious welcome of the new NRM administration, and the hope for an era of rural development to become once again "the granary of Africa", may provide the basis for Acholi reintegration into the mainstream of Uganda's polity and economy. That will require the reality of economic development on which to build a new myth and a new future.

REFERENCES

Adimola, A. M. 1962. *The Development of Primary Education in Acholi.* Nairobi: East African Literature Bureau.
Adimola, A. M. 1954. "The Lamogi Rebellion, 1911-12." *Uganda Journal*, 18.
Archer, G. 1963. *Personal and Historical Memories of an East African Administrator.* London: Oliver and Boyd.
Casati, G. 1891. *Ten Years in Equatoria, and the Return with Emin Pasha.* London: Warne.
Girling, F. K. 1960. *The Acholi of Uganda.* London: H.M.S.O.
Gray, J. M. 1964. "Diaries of Emin Pasha." *Uganda Journal*, 28.
Johnston, H. 1902. *The Uganda Protectorate.* London: Hutchinson.
Martin, D. 1974. *General Amin.* London: Faber and Faber.
Pain, D. R. 1975. "Incorporation, Participation and Division in Northern Uganda." Unpublished Ph.D. thesis, Cambridge University.
Postlethwaite, J. R. P. 1947. *I Look Back.* London: Boardman.
Twaddle, M. (ed.). 1975. *Expulsion of a Minority: Essays on Ugandan Asians.* London: Athlone.
Wanji, B. 1973. "The Nubi Community: The Dynamics of Ethnicity and Minority Status." Unpublished M.A. thesis, Makerere University.
Uganda Census Report. 1969. Entebbe: Government Printer.

THE PROBLEMS OF INSTITUTION BUILDING: THE UGANDA CASE

Dan Mudoola

Uganda has been independent for twenty-four years. Over this period she has had nine governments. In the normal course of events this would not be out of the ordinary. But only one of these governments, the first independence government in 1962, was formed by peaceful constitutional means. Uganda's first independence government ended in 1966 when the Milton Obote faction, assisted by the army, overthrew the 1962 constitutional arrangements and introduced the Republican Constitution of 1967. Obote was overthrown in 1971 by his military commander, Idi Amin. The Amin regime was overthrown by a combination of Tanzanian and Ugandan forces, while the second short-lived post-1979 government was overthrown by a military commission which subsequently organised the controversial 1980 elections, which returned Obote to power. Obote was overthrown in July 1985 by the army. The next government, which was headed by Tito Okello, was overthrown in January 1986 when the National Resistance Army, the military wing of the National Resistance Movement, took over under Yoweri Museveni. The peaceful handover of power by constitutional means has evaded the Ugandan political process for the past twenty years.

S. P. Huntington (1969) once worked out a model to account for political instability in developing countries. Accordingly, instability is attributed to the absence of political institutions which are able to domesticate power. The attributes of developed political systems—namely complexity, coherence, autonomy and chronological and generational age—are lacking. By Huntington's criteria a political system may be modernised (where modernisation is measured in terms of material and social development) without being developed if there continue to be no generally accepted political formulae for the resolution of conflicts short of the use of physical force.

Ugandan political processes since independence rather neatly fit the Huntington model. Measured in material and social terms, Uganda was more highly developed at the time of independence than were her neighbours. Yet her political institutions remain so underdeveloped today that even the physical infrastructures she inherited at independence are in a state of decay. The purpose of this paper is to examine the characteristics and nature of the problems of political institution building in Uganda.

ELITE FRAGMENTATION

Ugandan political life has not remained deeply troubled and marked by repeated violence because the Ugandan economy has been fragile. Indeed the country's agriculturally based economy was strong during the political upheavals that occurred both in 1966 and 1971. Rather, the problematic characteristics of Uganda's political institutions can be attributed to the problems which face highly fragmented political elites as they seek to operate in social contexts that are highly polarised. Force in Uganda has not been institutionally coordinated under the state. It has been used as a means by which groups have sought to establish hegemony over competing groups. While Uganda's political elites are reflections of various political traditions—monarchist, liberal and republican, for example—they have not outgrown the local social forces they represent. Their political formulae are used not to resolve conflicts for the ultimate good of the political system, but as tactical weapons to be used in protecting particular interests.

This is not to say that constitutional formulae should not be vehicles for advancing particular interests. Such interests are always important. The problem in Uganda lies in the fact that political elites over the years have adhered to political formulae only to the extent that their own interests have been served. If they have felt disadvantaged, and have been strong enough to operate outside established boundaries, they have been only too ready to do so.

The period between 1962 and May 1966 was one of relative peace, not because the leaders of the time were committed to the "politics of reconciliation", but because none of them felt strong enough to question independence constitutional arrangements (see Mazrui, 1967). In fact, because the arrangements in existence served well the faction he represented, Obote was an ardent constitutionalist during this period. He and his supporters invoked the constitution to hold the referendum they called during the "Lost Counties" controversy. In his confrontations with the *kabaka*, he frequently referred to the "sanctity" of the constitution.

At the time of the Obote-Mutesa showdown and the breaking of the UPC-KY (Uganda Peoples Congress-Kabaka Yekka) alliance in the middle 1960s, Obote had the majority in parliament. Discovering that their interests could no longer be cared for under normal constitutional procedures, the anti-Obote forces and *kabaka* supporters joined together and vied for support within the army. Obote moved fast enough to purge the army of pro-*kabaka* officers, however, while effecting the replacement of Brigadier Opolet by Colonel Amin, and the ensuing power struggle was eventually resolved in favour of his faction.

Obote then proceeded to introduce his own rules into political life through the 1967 Republican Constitution and the subsequent "Move to the Left" documents. The new rules were introduced in the attempt to regularise and legitimise Obote's seizure of power. Their net effect was to bring the army to the center-stage of politics. Hereafter, parliament, political parties and other civilian institutions that had served as arenas within which disputes could be resolved were relegated to the background and used simply to legitimise courses of action already undertaken. When Amin stormed the political stage in 1971, civilian institutions were simply too weak to contain him.

COLONIAL LEGACIES

Political problems in Uganda may be attributed to imbalances in the socio-political context. They may also be attributed to colonial legacies. Institutional arrangements in colonial Uganda, like in other colonial contexts, subordinated the interests of local institutions to the interests of external metropolitan institutions wherein lay real colonial sovereignty. Unlike in other colonial settings—for example, Kenya, Rhodesia, Algeria and Mozambique, where the colonial presence was directly and painfully felt by local populations through settlerdom, land alienation and forced labour—the central institutions of the colonial government in Uganda following colonial conquest and the establishment of regular administrative and other infrastructures, remained relatively remote. The colonial government certainly stepped in with force when its authority was threatened—for example, during the riots of 1945 and 1949, and at the time Sir Andrew Cohen exiled the Kabaka of Buganda, Sir Edward Mutesa. But, in general, it served more as an arbiter in inter- and intra-ethnic disputes than as a direct participant. Thus it stepped in to settle conflicts between groups within the same administrative boundaries—for example, stepping in to settle the historic Buganda/Banyoro conflict over the "Lost Counties", the Bamba/Bakonjo bid to secede from Toro and the Baira/Bahima conflict in Ankole. But more commonly it governed from a distance. Buganda was given a meaningful degree of autonomy in the 1900 agreement; so were the kingdom areas through various agreements; and so were the districts through the African Local Government Ordinance of 1949. In short, the colonial situation in Uganda did not provide a background in relation to which central political institutions in the future would be able to generate loyalties among divergent national forces, or create bases for the emergence of viable political institutions that enjoyed a wide degree of acceptance.

The drawing up of internal political and administrative boundaries during the colonial period also in general followed the lines of culturally and politically homogeneous groupings. They thus tended to encourage separate political identities within the country, a fact that was noted in the Wallis Report (Wallis, 1953: 13-14).

> All Standing Committees made plain that they were bent on reaching the status of a Native State. Their object is to achieve a constitution as like that of Buganda and they believe that they will eventually supplement the Protectorate Government as the government of their areas in nearly all affairs. In short, they aim at Home Rule and think that this was the Protectorate Government's intention in handing over, as they say, the power to govern their areas.

However, internal political and administrative boundaries acquired permanence for the kinds of reasons suggested, and soon came to identify the arenas within which various socio-political forces separately defined and articulated their own interests. T. Kabwegyere (1974), S. Karugire (1979) and G. Ibingira (1969) have argued that the polital and administrative arrangements that developed in no way gave meaningful power to local kings or chiefs, that "indirect rule" was in fact "direct rule" and that colonial sovereignty impaired or undermined local authority. But such arguments are tautological, for the very logic of the colonial presence meant that sovereignty, the ultimate power to make politically binding decisions, lay with the colonial power. The fact of the matter is that the arrangements that were established were important in so far as they had significant consequences for the behaviour of Uganda's political elites and the forces they represented, and because, ultimately, they shaped the characteristics of the Ugandan political system both after as well as during colonial rule.

On the eve of independence the political boundaries already in effect were reinforced by independence constitutional stipulations which provided federal and semi-federal status to the kingdom areas and the territory of Busoga respectively, and provided for the administration of the rest of the districts under the watchful eyes of district commissioners. The basic units in the allocation of resources and for political action remained the kingdom areas and the districts, and all political leaders of significance during the independence period used their own districts or kingdoms as their power bases. The negative consequences of all of this for the building of central political institutions lay in the fact that such central political institutions as there were in the making—parliament, the civil service, the army and so on—were simply regarded as fora for power bargaining, means to be used in the accumulation of the resources necessary in strengthening local power bases or as instruments for the allocation of rewards to supporters and the denial of rewards to opponents. They were not regarded as important in terms of what they could do in the building of a new nation.

It is not simply suggested here that there should be no meaningful local power centres within political systems. Such centres do not necessarily exist at the expense of central institutions, and examples of local political autonomy abound in many parts of the world. The tragedy in Uganda lies simply in the fact that the country has never been able to work out a formula in relation to which divisive forces and tendencies might be balanced.

Finally, the heirs to leadership positions in Uganda after independence flouted political rules to their own advantage, even as their predecessors had done. Colonial rule had been authoritarian. So was local rule after independence, however different and responsive to participatory forms local leadership had been in different regions of the country before independence.

UNBALANCED RESOURCE ALLOCATION

A political order is threatened if groups of people within the order fail to acquire a commitment to the system or internalise constitutional rules, but simply look at the formal rules that exist as weapons to be used to preserve what they have, or gain what they do not have. Here political formulae are not regarded as sacrosanct or as a means to be used in the peaceful resolution of conflicts, and groups operate within or outside the rules to the extent their own interests are served. In a situation of extreme imbalance, where a generally disadvantaged group has access to resources it can convert into political capital, it may choose to operate outside the formal rules to redress the imbalance, or, if it has the chance, to overthrow them altogether. In a situation where a formerly disadvantaged group finally does gain access to power, the formerly advantaged group will invoke the old or seek to establish new rules in the attempt to reassert its strengths.

The above model in which the unbalanced allocation of resources can have negative consequences for the development of central political processes is applicable both to colonial and post-colonial Uganda. Imbalances were reflected along regional, ethnic, religious and class lines during the colonial period. They are still so reflected today. Now as then there are advantaged groups which feel a sense of psychological, material and political security and seek constitutional arrangements that will guarantee their positions. There are also disadvantaged groups whose material or political sense of deprivation has generated a sense of material and political insecurity.

Uganda may be broadly divided into two regions, the North and the South, in terms of economic development. In the colonial period the changes and developments introduced in the two areas were not uniform. The South, especially Buganda, benefited in the establishment of socio-economic infrastructures in the form of social services, communication networks, a cash economy and attendant material goods. Despite the attempts by various post-colonial governments to "restore" the balance by building roads, schools and hospitals in areas that had been developmentally left behind, the general imbalance between the North and the South has remained.

The sense of regional deprivation has long been reflected in the parliamentary speeches of leaders from the North. Such was the economic plight of Acholi soon after independence that Alexander Latim introduced a notion urging the Uganda Development Corporation to establish cattle ranches in Acholi, arguing as follows (as recorded in *Uganda Parliamentary Debates* (UPD), 20: 284-85):

> Acholi District is poor. It has remained poor for a long time for various reasons. It is far away from the cattle trade and money circulation. There is a lack of employment in the district. This has been illustrated in many ways. In the past we did get a lot of people coming down here (to Buganda) in search of work. ... Most of these people went back worse than when they came and this did not help them very much. ... In the past very many Acholi found their way in the forces. This was not because they were very fond of being *askaris* but it was because they were in search of work. But this source of employment is now becoming more difficult because other tribes which used to despise this type of employment are now interested in it. ... Acholi District is one of those areas in Uganda which has lagged behind economically.

When opposed in this statement by Felix Onama, Latim explained that he could not understand why a fellow northerner could not understand the economic plight of the North, as follows (UPD, 20: 308-09):

> I was particularly annoyed when, during his speech, the Minister had to be advised all the time privately by the Minister of Internal Affairs against this motion of mine. This I felt was extremely shocking. This Minister, coming from the North and knowing our problem, the man who should now support me very strongly to see that the wealth of the nation is distributed justly, is the man who hinders the distribution of wealth to the North. ... Selfishness towards one district is destroying Uganda. The wealth of this nation is all of ours and does not belong to any particular Minister alone.

Similarly Okello was concerned about the economic circumstances of West Nile (UPD, 35: 3135-36).

> What I know the government does think about West Nile is to keep it as a human zoo, and get cheap labourers from it to work in places like Kakira, to work in places like Kawolo and in places where new industries will be started.... Because I do believe that government does think that if one, two or more industries are started in West Nile, the flow of labour from that district to other districts will be stopped.

The sense of possessiveness on the part of southern leaders is not as well documented. When Obote tore up the 1962 constitution, however, members of the Buganda Lukiiko (Parliament) passed a resolution calling on Obote to remove the capital from Bugandan soil. Over the past twenty-five years southerners have repeatedly expressed the opinion that northerners have had a disproportionate share of the country's power, considering their contribution to the nation's wealth.

The unbalanced allocation of resources has also characterised relationships within the political boundaries of Uganda. Some groups have benefited politically and materially, while other groups have been marginalised. The Bamba and Bakonjo in Toro have at times reacted strongly to the overlordship of the Batoro. Banyoro lived in the "Lost Counties" that were transfered to Buganda. Soon after independence the Bamba/Bakonjo/Batoro conflict culminated in the Ruwenzururu Movement, and the central government had to send in troops to contain it. The Obote government invoked the constitution over the "Lost Counties" issue, and through a subsequent referendum the "Lost Counties" were returned to Bunyoro.

Again, in the allocation of resources in the colonial period and in the post-colonial period, certain ethnic groups—for example, the Banyarwanda and the descendents of Lugard's troops, who today are frequently referred to as "Nubians"—did not have their own geopolitical administrative boundaries and so did not have their positions provided for in constitutional definitions. While other groups were able to claim "constituencies" for themselves, because of traditional or administrative identifications with particular territories, such groups could not, with the result that they were not seriously considered to be part of the political equation in independence constitutional arrangements and allocations.

In short, the economically marginal groups within ethnic constituencies, plus the groups without legitimate channels of political communication, were potentially destabilising factors. Thus it is not surprising that Obote effectively made use of troops from the economically disadvantaged North to consolidate his own position in power during the 1960s, and not surprising that Amin recruited persons from certain marginal groups for his intelligence and armed services. Because of their positions within Ugandan political and social life, members of more marginal groups have generally been willing to serve any "Lugard" seeking to tilt the balance of power in his own favour.

Another factor in the unbalanced allocation of resources in Uganda has to do with religious membership. The earliest political "parties" in the country were defined along religious lines (see Senteza-Kajubi's article in this book). From the mid-1880s through the 1890s the major issue among these "parties"—the Bangereza, Bafalansa and Baisiramu (generally Protestants,

Catholics and Muslims, respectively)—was over which group would gain power within Uganda under the overall control of the British. Patterns differed in different places. The Protestant oligarchy, however, eventually gained ascendancy in Buganda, and while various attempts were subsequently made to find balances in the allocation of resources among the different religious groups, the Catholics and Muslims hereafter had little difficulty in understanding where real power lay. Thus, on the eve of independence, the raison d'etre of the Democratic Party was the interest among Catholics in challenging Protestant hegemony at Mengo. The Muslims remained the most disadvantaged of the three groups over the years, which helps explain why many of them followed Amin's lead when he championed their interests.

The overall political significance of the unbalanced allocation of resources in Uganda—between the North and the South, within political boundaries and between various major religious and other groupings, and, of course, between the Ugandans themselves and their colonial masters—lies in the fact that it encouraged separatism and the pursuit of particularistic interests. Deprived groups felt they could only set right their grievances through political confrontation, and sought to upset whatever arrangements existed. Advantaged groups sought to defend the status quo. As a result independence constitutional arrangements were put under severe strain.

Such was the imbalance of resources that groups placed at some advantage over resources which they could translate into political advantages rationalised such advantages in a kind of "doctrine of ethno-functionalism", according to which particular ethnic groups are endowed physically and historically to perform specific functions and should be left to perform them. Thus Gaspar Oda (UPD, 35: 3135-36) during the 1960s subscribed against the principle of evenly spreading recruitment into the Ugandan army:

> There is one thing which should be taken into consideration, that not all tribes, not only in this country but throughout the world, are born warriors or warlike people. Some tribes are warlike people, and others are intellectuals, and are not prepared to face warlike people.

Similarly, Felix Onama (UPD, 35: 3205), when Minister of Defense during the 1960s, argued that it was the manifest destiny of Northerners to defend Uganda:

> Thousands of Northerners died in the two world wars to defend Uganda against Nazism and Fascism and if the young generation or their children who have grown up in the North would like to follow in the footsteps of their fathers, nobody is going to stop me recruiting them into the army. . . . In colonial times some tribes believed that the life of a soldier was a very low job unfit for people from certain tribes and that is why you find in the army the Northerners. . . . Now because people think there is no war and these young men wear a very smart uniform, they want their weaklings from certain tribes also to wear this uniform.

The "doctrine of ethno-functionalism" was widely held. At the same time it was challenged. Ali Kisekka (UPD, 23: 955-56), for example, argued against selective recruitment on the grounds of the need for creating a national army:

> We want to know whether the Minister is prepared to bring a new outlook that portrays national unity to our army. At the moment things seem to be very much northern-sided. Even the Military Council . . . is composed of only Northern

people. They say the Chairman is the Prime Minister. . . . The Prime Minister comes from the North. The Minister of Internal Affairs is from the North. Now another member and the Secretary is the Permanent Secretary of Internal Affairs. . . . Because they want people from the North to be the only people to deal with military affairs they have gone to the extent of bringing in a doctor to be Permanent Secretary in the Ministry of Internal Affairs and this doctor happens to come from the North. . . . Even the Parlimentary Secretary comes from the North. . . . When we have this lopsided arrangement, one expects that any mutiny can be organised in one night because people are of the same understanding. They are of the same stock. They can plan anything at night and the next day the whole country would be in trouble. If they want stability in our army, the army must project a national outlook. It must not be regional or tribal. . . . Today when they (army recruiters) go to the North they spend there two or three months, but when they come to Kampala they spend here one day, and do you know, Mr. Speaker, they recruit mainly those whom they have directed to come to Kampala because they failed to recruit them in the North.

When Kisekka was interrupted in his presentation by a member who said that whatever his arguments, the Baganda could not fight, Kiseka retorted (UPD, 23: 955-56):

It was because the Baganda were great fighters that the British people feared to recruit them in the King's Rifles. They knew that if they had recruited Baganda in the army the British people would not have ruled this country for fifty years' time.

Arising as it did out of the historically unbalanced allocation of resources, the "doctrine of ethno-functionalism" has had far-reaching negative consequences for building national institutions in Uganda. It has generated a sense of possessiveness among those leaders who are beneficiaries of a particular institution, and a sense of alienation among those who are not. Institutions which are supposedly national institutions have over the years come to be regarded as resources to be allocated to groups or individuals as rewards in the political balancing game. The doctrine is invoked when it serves the interests of a particular group, challenged when it is to the disadvantage of that group.

CONCLUSION

I have set out in this paper to account for the political institutional problems and disruptions that have pervaded the post-colonial political scene in Uganda. Fragmented political elites, colonial institutional arrangements and the unbalanced allocation of resources have provided a setting for political institutional normlessness. Political leaders have only made use of political formula to the extent particularistic interests have been served. Groups have not hesitated to use extra-legal means to overthrow factions in power, and have generally considered power to be a resource useful in the service of parochial ends rather than the common good. The Ugandan tragedy lies in the fact that there has so far been no sovereign individual, structure or ideology with ultimate importance in the affairs of state. Instability has persisted. The use of force in the resolution of conflicts has remained commonplace.

Such a situation prevailed after the July 1985 coup, with government forces and allied groups ranged against the forces of the National Resistance

Movement. The parties involved, hoping to tilt balances in their own favour, called in external allies to the potential extreme disadvantage of Uganda as an entity. Then the National Resistance Movement gained national power. Perhaps now a new political ethos and new viable central political institutions will emerge to the advantage of the nation as a whole.

It may be argued historically that many political systems have been established despite the local inability to resolve conflicts peacefully. In such situations one group or a political "heartland" has been able to impose its own rules upon others. These rules in turn become the core political values of the system. In such situations "marginalised" groups have at times internalised the values of the dominant group if these are not associated with the interests of the "heartland" people alone. Thus one cannot think of Britain without England, the USSR without "White Russia", Kaiser's Germany without Prussia or the United States without the "Wasps".

One might wonder why stability has not so far been established in Uganda through the "normal" imbalance of forces. Accordingly, Anthony Low (1985) has wondered why Buganda did not "Prussianise" Uganda.

A number of factors mitigated against this. Firstly, Buganda's natural political growth was interrupted by colonial intervention. Secondly, Buganda's creative political potential was undermined under colonialism. Without colonialism, and with Buganda's political and cultural affinities for certain other areas and her military strengths, Buganda could have become a Prussia. With colonialism, it was in the interests of the colonial power to prevent the emergence of a Bugandan Prussia. With colonialism Buganda also had her interests defined for her, and Bugandan leaders came to understand that their own interests could not be well served by embracing all-Uganda causes. Buganda thus courted "encirclement" by the rest of Uganda (see Mudoola, 1985b). The UPC, for example, was formed to "contain" Buganda. With Buganda marginalised politically following independence, the groups that later sought to establish hegemony through a "normal" imbalance of power were not successful in doing so because they were unable to evolve a core of values acceptable to the groups "marginalised". At the same time the groups that have attempted to establish hegemony have themselves been historically, economically and culturally marginal to the mainstreams of life in Uganda.

It is by now entirely clear that Buganda cannot be left out of any equation for establishing stability in Uganda. A politically marginal Buganda is not in Uganda's interests.

REFERENCES

Huntington, S. P. 1969. *Political Order in Changing Societies*. Yale University Press.
Ibingira, G. 1969. *The Forming of an African Nation*. New York: Vintage Books
Kabwegyere, Tarsis B. 1974. *The Politics of State Formation*. Nairobi: East African Literature Bureau.
Karugire, S. 1979. *The Political History of Uganda*. Nairobi: East African Literature Bureau.
Low, Anthony. 1985. "Uganda: The Dislocated State." Uganda Seminar, Institute of Political Studies, University of Copenhagen, Denmark, 25-28 September.
Mazrui, A. 1967. "Violent Constitutionalism in Uganda." *Government and Opposition*, II, 4.
Mudoola, Dan. 1985. "The Pathology of Institution Building: The Tanzanian Case." In Kiros, F. (ed.), *Challenging Rural Development*. New Jersey: Africa World Press.
Mudoola, Dan. 1985b. "Post-War Politics in Uganda." Uganda Seminar, Institute of Political Studies, University of Copenhagen, Denmark, 25-28 September.

Wallis, C. 1953. *Report on an Inquiry into African Local Government in the Protectorate of Uganda.* Entebbe: Government Printer.

THE AGRICULTURAL COOPERATIVE MOVEMENT AND THE EMASCULATION OF PRODUCER MEMBERS IN UGANDA

J. M. A. Opio-Odongo

INTRODUCTION

The purpose of this paper is to examine the manner in which the cooperative movement in Uganda has failed to ensure that the benefits for which it was established accrue to members. The promotion of cooperatives in Uganda by producer-members and government has been based on the belief that the cooperatives would:

1. Enable the producer members to gain control of the business of agriculture;
2. Provide producer-members with effective training in democracy and self-government;
3. Provide channels for transmitting government information and assistance to rural people;
4. Maintain economic and social considerations in proper balance;
5. Promote regional development and hence improve rural life (Digby and Gretton, 1968; Brett, 1970; Okereke, 1970).

But available evidence suggests that the cooperative movement in Uganda has not been effective in meeting these expectations (Brett, 1970; Okereke, 1970; Opio-Odongo, 1978 and 1980; Vincent, 1976). The basic thesis advanced here is that this failure derives from the fact that having liberated the local agricultural producers from alien oligopoly power in the early 1950s, the cooperative movement henceforth failed to safeguard itself from predation by vested interest groups who viciously sought financial benefits accruing from the new marketing structure. A logical consequence of that predation has been the powerlessness of producer-members over the affairs of the cooperative movement.

Appeals to lack of spontaneous origin of the cooperative movement in developing countries in explaining this kind of crisis (see Nash and Hopkins, 1976) are certainly deficient in the Ugandan case, where the genesis of the movement was spontaneous (Opio-Odongo, 1978). As illustrated below, the origin of the cooperative movement in Uganda represents a reform commodity movement (see Paige, 1975), because the movement's genesis was prompted by a protracted conflict between alien non-cultivators who were dependent on income from commercial capital and native cultivators who were dependent on land as a source of income and livelihood. However, in exercising countervailing power and in pursuit of greater control of the market in agricultural commodities, the movement failed to understand fully the texture of its environment and its implications for strategic offensive against vested interest groups. It failed to devise effective tactics, operations and strategies to meet challenges from such groups, and thus could not reap the benefits generated by the new marketing structure.

THE GENESIS OF THE COOPERATIVE MOVEMENT

The introduction of export agriculture (based on cotton) in Uganda in the early 1900s, especially within the traditional feudal agrarian structure of Buganda, where the 1900 Buganda Agreement had created a class of landlords, fostered growing social inequalities based on the power of landlords to exact heavy tributes from their tenants producing cotton (see Wrigley, 1959; Mamdani, 1976). The Buganda traditional political structure was propagated throughout Uganda in the wake of imperial territorial expansion, resulting in similar social inequalities. Consequently, chiefs outside Buganda conscripted labour from their subjects for deployment in their cotton fields. Excessive application of such power led to agitation, which in conjunction with the so-called Bataka Movement of 1922, prompted the colonial government to formulate legislations ushering in the emancipation of local producers from excessive feudal and patriarchal exploitation.

Within Buganda, tenants were protected from exploitation and illegitimate eviction by landlords. The enactment of the 1927 law limiting the amount of rent payable to landlords exemplifies this. Similarly, chiefs outside Buganda were denied freehold titles and the retention of feudal dominion over their people indefinitely. Salaries henceforth were paid to the chiefs thus making conscription of local labour unnecessary. The local producers were also granted security of tenure. Thus by the late 1920s local producers in Uganda became increasingly masters of their own time and labour which they could deploy in the production of export crops (see Wrigley, 1959). More importantly, a strong sense of efficacy which had begun to develop in them subsequently enabled them to acquire the rights to participate in the processing and marketing of export crops.

But the social organisation of export agriculture in the 1920s was strongly characterised by a racial division of labour. Colonial administrators encouraged the natives to specialise in the production of export crops and the European and Indian aliens to concentrate on the processing and marketing of the crops. It was a division of labour not based on known efficiency criteria. Understandably it fostered imperfect competition in the domestic market for export agriculture, and hence racial conflict between Africans and the aliens. Both of the racial groups resorted to organisational strategies and tactics aimed at gaining ascendency over the other as each one of them sought to defend and expand its niche.

The competition between the two groups became more imperfect when interventions by the colonial government, purportedly geared to conflict resolution, favoured the aliens. The interventions invariably protected the vested interests of the aliens, enabling them to exercise oligopoly control over the processing and marketing of export crops (see Opio-Odongo, 1983). In response to the deliberate alliance between the colonial government and the alien vested interest groups, the African producers tactfully adopted a cooperative strategy in seeking redress. They did this in alliance with their kindred in business and civil service. Thus 1923 witnessed the beginning of a cooperative strategy when three farmers organised the Baganda Growers Association with the object of forming "a body through which the views of the African growers could be voiced to government in the face of powerful vested interests which were springing up in the cotton industry" (UCA, 1971: 32). Many other small cooperative groups subsequently emerged but suffered serious setbacks resulting from a series of government legislations which instead protected the interests of the alien commercial interest groups (Opio-Odongo, 1978 and 1983).

The strength of the alien commercial interest groups was clearly demonstrated in 1937 when a cooperative bill introduced by the colonial government was killed at first reading because of severe opposition from the unofficial members of the Legislative Council who represented Asian and European interests in the protectorate (Gee, 1961). These interest groups established and maintained oligopoly power through buying associations and ginning pools without any legal restraints from the colonial government (see Yoshida, 1970). Nevertheless, fears that a further promotion of imperfect competition within export agriculture would foment severe racial strife similar to that which was being experienced in Kenya, eventually forced the colonial government to consider institutionalising the cooperatives so that Africans could participate in the marketing of export crops. Accordingly, the colonial government invited W. H. K. Campbell, a League of Nations advisor on cooperatives, to determine and advise on the suitability of establishing cooperatives in Uganda.

Campbell's report urged that immediate action should be taken to control and assist the numerous quasi cooperative societies already in existence by the enactment of legislation and the appointment of a registrar (Horace Plunkett Foundation, 1949). Consequently, a new bill was introduced to the Legislative Council in 1945 and passed. This bill was enacted into the 1946 Cooperative Societies Ordinance effective from September 1946, and the rules under it were promulgated the following year. But the enactment of this ordinance and the attendant formation of the Department of Cooperatives, coupled with the power vested in the Registrar for Cooperatives, were interpreted by the leaders of the African cooperative groups as a political tactic to control those who challenged the political and economic status quo (Shepherd, 1955). Henceforth many African cooperative groups refused to register with the Cooperative Department, demanding that the regulations under the 1946 ordinance be liberalised.

THE EPITOME OF THE COOPERATIVE MOVEMENT'S VITALITY

Post World War II cotton and coffee booms made export agriculture in Uganda very profitable, especially for those who controlled the marketing and processing of the two major export crops. African cooperative groups were aware of the enormous profits accruing to alien commercial oligopolies and were interested in having a share. But the texture of the environment within which export agriculture was being promoted had begun to change from a domestic oligopoly market to a turbulent one characterised by vicious competition between vested interest groups. There was a need for a shift in strategy if a competitor was to survive. Hence, rather than just confining itself to the need to come to terms with the other(s) and to know when not to fight to death, a competitor also had to recognise the salience of the political facet of what seemingly was an economic or commercial issue (see Emery and Trist, 1965).

The salience of the political dimension of the competition within export agriculture was evoked by two factors. First was the ongoing collusion between the colonial government and the alien oligopoly firms (Yoshida, 1970; Opio-Odongo, 1978 and 1983). Second was the 1947 dispatch from the Secretary of State for the Colonies in London to all governors of British colonies urging the development of efficient and democratic systems of local government (Burke, 1964). In recognition of these factors, the African cooperative groups, especially the Federation of Uganda African Farmers, resorted to petitioning the governor and the Secretary of State for the Colonies as well as rioting (e.g., 1949 riots). They resorted to using whatever means that could enable them to put a break to the alien oligopoly control over the processing and marketing of export crops.

The African cooperative groups welcomed the appointment of a new and more liberal governor (Sir Andrew Cohen) to Uganda in the very early 1950s. They interpreted the appointment not only as a positive response by the British government to their countervailing power, but also one providing an ideal opportunity for them to exercise that power fully for the benefit of the cooperative movement. Accordingly, the leaders of the Federation of Uganda African Farmers effectively negotiated with the new governor soon after his arrival in Uganda. They presented the grievances of their members regarding the imperfections within the cotton and coffee industries as well as their antipathy against the Cooperative Department, particularly against the authoritarian power vested in the Registrar for Cooperatives by the 1946 Cooperative Societies Ordinance (Shepherd, 1955). The governor consequently appointed three Commissions of Inquiry to investigate fully the complaints by African cooperative groups regarding the cotton and coffee industries as well as the 1946 ordinance.

The ultimate recommendations by these commissions ushered in a new era for African cooperative groups because they led to some reform measures. The colonial government decided on immediate plans to:

1. Take over and scrap fifty or more ginneries which were deemed inefficient;
2. Acquire at least twenty ginneries in the next five years to be sold on long-term credit to African cooperatives;
3. Strip the cooperative registrar's office "of all authoritarian powers over the cooperative societies" and establish a "Cooperative Council on which would sit representatives from the various cooperative organisations throughout Uganda" (Shepherd, 1955; Opio-Odongo, 1978).

Supporting legislations such as the 1951 Acquisition of Ginneries Ordinance were enacted. Overall, the victory was decisive for the cooperative movement because (a) the movement henceforth could participate effectively in the processing and marketing of export crops and (b) it restored one of the basic cooperative principles of democratic control.

EMASCULATION OF COOPERATIVE MOVEMENT

Even if many of the African cooperative groups subsequently registered with the Department of Cooperatives, the future of the movement was fraught with difficulties. These difficulties arose from three sources. First was a shift in enemy orientation from alien to indigenous groups, especially after independence, which undermined corporate solidarity. Second was the growing disruptive effect of vulgar competitive commercialism which weakened the basis of so-called African communalism and complicated the propagation of the virtues of selfless service and community spirit among members of the movement. Third was the liability of newness (Stinchcombe, 1965) resulting from the grave inexperience of leaders and members of the movement with organisational techniques and methods. This liability arose partly from the unfavourable policies of the colonial government which tended to deny Africans the opportunity to acquire organisational and commercial skills (Opio-Odongo, 1978) and partly from inadequate socialisation within the movement. As M. Digby (1965: 5) has pointed out, heads of cooperative departments "often knew nothing about cooperatives or even ordinary commercial methods". The cooperative movement consequently became more vulnerable to predation, cooptation and powerlessness as vested interest groups penetrated it.

The performance of the first few cooperative unions between 1952 and 1962 illustrates this vulnerability quite well. For instance, Bugisu Cooperative Union Ltd., which was the largest in the country (with ninety primary societies), had by 1957 begun to show signs of stress. Most of the other unions later experienced similar stress (Young, Sherman and Rose, 1981). The stress in the case of Bugisu Cooperative Union arose from the nascent resentment by Bagisu of the alien control of their coffee industry. For instance, following the resignation of an expatriate (but experienced) coffee manager from the services of the union, the leaders of the union demanded that all matters regarding the coffee industry and the management of the union should be handled by Bagisu. While this demand seemed consistent with the newly regained principle of democratic control and the pre-independence fervour of national self-determination, meeting it became difficult. The leaders of the union had (a) to learn new roles and skills, (b) to evolve an effective reward-sanction system, (c) to learn to trust non-organisational employees and (d) to forego extra-organisational relationships which undermine corporate principles and solidarity.

Unfortunately, these requirements were frivolously met. The gaining of control over the union, rather than leading to strong self-management, fomented crisis. For instance, poor market intelligence and the desire for popular support prompted the leaders of the union to pay a high price for coffee despite the lower price trend worldwide for the commodity. Furthermore, money was embezzled irrecoverably and the union became "dominated by an unscrupulous and politically minded board, which started to interfere more and more with the day-to-day management of the business" (Uganda, 1968: 19; Young, Sherman and Rose, 1981). Such problems prompted the Commissioner for Cooperative Development to set up a commission of inquiry into the working and financial conditions of the union. On the basis of the commission's recommendations the union lost its monopoly of the Bugisu coffee crop and was subjected to serious supervision by government.

The turbulence of the environment within which the cooperative movement operated tended to exacerbate this kind of vulnerability to predation by vested interest groups. That turbulence was characterised mainly by relentless partisan politics that eventually engulfed the cooperative movement. Bugisu Cooperative Union, just like other unions, became a victim of partisan politics soon after the withdrawal of the supervising manager in 1961. Capitalising on the broken monopoly of the Bugisu Cooperative Union Ltd., the then ruling Democratic Party (DP) sanctioned the establishment of an alternative marketing organisation—Bugisu Coffee Marketing Association (BCMA)—mainly as a political gesture to the promoters of DP. In response to this challenge, the Bugisu Cooperative Union Ltd. declared a price war against BCMA. It set up too high a price for the 1962 coffee crop which resulted in a trading loss of over Sterling Pounds 60,000. But BCMA had to be dissolved the following year by the new Uganda Peoples Congress (UPC) regime. Nonetheless, this type of competition between local vested interest groups became widespread as is documented by the reports of all commissions of inquiry into the affairs of cooperatives in Uganda (Uganda, 1952, 1965 and 1968). The result was a rapid deterioration in the autonomy of the cooperative movement.

In all, three factors have been responsible for the rapid deterioration in cooperative autonomy and vitality. First was the competition between vested interest groups. Second, the inertia of fundamentalist cooperativism demanding strict adherence to cooperative principles and practices even if they were not necessarily congruent with the existing social organisation of local communities. Third, the failure by the cooperative movement to foster adequate organisational methods and techniques in order for it to dispense with excessive governmental control and supervision. The effects of these factors are examined below.

Effects of Vested Interests

Mention has already been made of the vested interests pursued by alien commercial firms in the control of the domestic market for export agriculture. The colonial state independently, and in alliance with the firms, also pursued vested interests in the appropriation of surplus value from export agriculture. For instance, it established statutory organisations such as the Cotton Export Group (1942), which later became the Lint Marketing Board (1949), in order to meet that need. Similarly, the institutionalisation of price assistance funds for cotton and coffee as a means of stabilising producer prices of export crops was an effective means of appropriating surplus value. When the funds were operative, the agricultural producers could not receive a substantial proportion of the value of export crops (Alibaruho, 1975).

In consequence membership in the cooperative movement did not enable agricultural producers to improve their welfare or promote community development (see Opio-Odongo, 1980). This was because only a very small proportion of the final sale price of export crops accrued to them. S. Carr's 1982 data which are reproduced in Table 1 illustrate the situation in the case of cotton. As for coffee, the data in Table 2 indicate that Uganda producers tended to receive prices much lower than the prices received by their counterparts in Kenya and Tanzania. While it is true that some of the funds were diverted to industrial and social development (see Walker and Ehrlich, 1959; Haring, Christy and Humphrey, 1969), the allocation of such funds did not duly reflect the contribution made by agricultural producers to national development. Instead industrial and social development were restricted to urban centres.

The involvement of parastatals (Lint and Coffee Marketing Boards) as the main exporters of the main crops is part of the problem. It has had three debilitating consequences for the cooperative movement. First, due to the movement's lack of business acumen, its unions have rarely got favourable terms from the marketing boards in fixing profit margins. In consequence, the unions have often made less profit potentially transferable to producer-members in the form of bonuses. The capability of the Lint Marketing Board, at least up to 1972, to appropriate for itself most of the value of cotton seed attests to the weaker trade position of the movement (see Alibaruho, 1975). Second, the marketing boards have often operated inefficiently, especially by incurring higher administrative costs. The ultimate consequence of this has been an additional burden on the farmers, especially in terms of lower producer prices, which essentially are residual items that have been depressed by tax-levies and administrative and other costs (see Alibaruho, 1975). Third, the primary producers, through their cooperative unions, have been denied the opportunity to learn and acquire the art of export marketing. As one African legislative councillor who was opposed to the idea of continuing indefinitely with the marketing boards once argued, if the opportunity had been provided to the cooperative movement, time would have come when the country could have done away with marketing boards (Uganda Protectorate, 1958). This certainly remains a contentious issue given the kinds of vested interests at stake.

Within the cooperative movement itself, vested interests have been exercised in several forms. According to the 1968 report of the Committee of Inquiry into the Affairs of All Cooperative Unions in Uganda, the following methods have been employed (Uganda, 1968: 45):

1. Restrictions on the admission of fresh members;
2. Avoiding the holding of general meetings for the election of office bearers and for an open discussion about the finances and general working of the society;
3. Manipulating elections;
4. Employing near relations in the paid service of the society;
5. Granting liberal loans to friends and relatives;
6. Non-recovery of overdues from friends and relatives.

Table 1.
The Proportion of the Final Sale Price of Lint Passed on to Ugandan Cotton Growers, 1929-70

	Price to grower seed cotton cts. per lb.	Sale price of lint cts. per lb.	Price to the grower as a percentage of sale price
1929	16.0	81	19
1930	10.7	60	18
1931	10.7	40	15
1932	8.4	38	22
1933	9.0	45	20
1934	12.0	51	23
1935	9.0	56	16
1936	12.5	52	24
1937	8.0	63	12
1938	7.6	42	18
1939	11.0	47	23
1943	12.0	141	8
1945	16.0	132	12
1946	18.0	125	14
1947	20.0	155	13
1949	23.0	222	14
1950	43.0	239	18
1951	48.0	417	11
1952	48.0	396	12
1953	50.0	251	20
1954	60.0	265	23
1955	54.0	267	20
1956	55.0	256	21
1957	57.0	259	22
1958	46.0	234	20
1959	47.0	206	23
1960	54.0	205	26
1961	56.0	262	21
1962	56.0	194	29
1963	50.0	197	25
1964	56.0	238	23
1965	54.0	172	31
1966	57.0	171	33
1967	38.0	174	22
1968	43.0	217	20
1969	47.0	215	22
1970	50.0	204	24

*Source: Carr (1982: 83).

Table 2.
Average Producer Prices for Coffee — Uganda, Kenya and Tanzania, 1974-79

		1974	1975	1976	1977	1978	1979
A.	Producer prices (US cts./lb. green bean equivalent)						
	Uganda	15.20	15.90	15.20	27.20	40.40	42.43
	Kenya	62.90	59.70	121.40	218.60	149.60	n.a.
	Tanzania	38.80	31.80	59.30	101.00	76.50	n.a.
B.	Producer prices (National currency Shs./kg.)						
	Uganda	1.19	1.25	1.40	2.50	3.50	3.50
	Kenya	9.82	9.40	22.30	40.14	26.06	n.a.
	Tanzania	4.80	4.00	8.40	14.90	11.00	n.a.
C.	Producer prices in constant terms (Shs./kg. July 1975 = 100)						
	Uganda	1.55	1.29	0.99	1.11	1.04	0.86
	Kenya	12.12	9.90	21.04	34.60	20.04	n.a.
	Tanzania	7.00	4.30	8.20	13.20	8.90	n.a.
D.	Average of export value (US cts./lb.)						
	Uganda	53.20	49.10	88.30	188.00	125.10	n.a.
	Kenya	68.10	63.80	131.80	237.30	170.50	n.a.
	Tanzania	58.20	52.20	119.70	223.10	153.30	n.a.
E.	Proportion of export value paid to producers (A/D)						
	Uganda	28.60	32.40	17.20	14.50	32.30	n.a.
	Kenya	92.40	93.60	92.10	92.10	87.70	n.a.
	Tanzania	66.70	60.90	49.50	45.30	49.90	n.a.

*Source: Belshaw and Stent (1979, Table 4.3: 62).

However, as the 1968 committee's report convincingly remarked, one has to examine the political climate of the country, the social traditions and the general levels of educational development in order to understand the problems of vested interests within and without the cooperative movement. These aspects of the political economy have made a mockery of the claim that co-ops operate on the basis of the Rochdalean principles and practices.

Effects of Inflexible Adherence to the Rochdalean Cooperative Model

Three basic principles characterise Rochdalean-type cooperatives. These include (a) democratic control, (b) non-profit operations and (c) limited returns on dividends upon ownership capital. Additional principles and practices exist, but they vary from country to country. In Uganda these additional principles and practices include (1) open membership, (2) neutrality in political and religious matters and (3) promotion of member education (see UCA, 1973). But effective execution of these principles and practices depends on (a) corporate solidarity in order to achieve organisational goals, (b) a minimum level of technical and managerial skills required to run a cooperative and (c) a strategic handling of systemic linkages with other organisations capable of providing assistance if autonomy is to be safeguarded.

Available evidence suggests, however, that these basic conditions necessary for upholding cooperative principles and practices have rarely been met. Mechanical rather than organic solidarity has characterised most cooperative societies. This has been the case mainly because "social relationships based on kinship and other local institutions are still more important than mutual loyalty between peasants in different village communities" (Hyden, 1970: 65). So-called cooperative principles and practices have tended to provide a facade behind which clan, village and religious functionalism are fought out. Similarly, given the low levels of literacy and cooperative organisational leadership skills in the rural areas, those elected to lead and manage the co-op have rarely served the interests of producer-members (see Young, Sherman and Rose, 1981). The businessmen and teachers in rural areas who usually provide such leadership "belong to cooperatives because these institutions in the rural areas offer a convenient platform for political campaigning and the maintenance of social control over the population in the area" (Hyden, 1970: 67). Furthermore, rural elites have sought cooperative leadership in order to (a) derive material benefits, (b) control cooperative operation and resources so as to further private ends and (c) amass wealth through embezzlement for which many have gone unpunished (Young, Sherman and Rose, 1981). T. Vincent's (1970, 1976) study in Teso provides an excellent example of a country-wide crafty alliance between the agricultural producers and rural elites which invariably has robbed the cooperative movement of its vitality and autonomy.

The absence of effective organisational solidarity and strong leadership within the cooperative movement prompted government to assume the control and supervision of the movement. The enactment of the 1963 Cooperative Societies Acts and Rules has been the hallmark of this intervention in postcolonial Uganda. "Under these (Acts and Rules) the Cooperative Council was abolished and the office of the Registrar of Cooperatives was combined with that of the Commissioner of Cooperatives and some of the powers lost in 1952 were restored" (Uganda, 1968: 15). Henceforth the autonomy of the cooperative movement has been gradually but considerably eroded. While it may be argued that government control and supervision protects the members of the cooperative movement from exploitation by some unscrupulous leaders, the mere exercise of control and supervision has had no remarkable effects on the performance of cooperatives (see Opio-Odongo, 1978). Instead, increasing government paternalism has promoted laxity in management and destroyed the co-op's unique organisational integrity. Furthermore, continued supervision by government is "an admission of the failure in achieving the goal of educating the mass of cooperative members to a degree of informed activism capable of guaranteeing responsible and capable performance by cooperatives' elected leadership and hired professional staff" (Young, Sherman and Rose, 1981: 153).

Effects of Inadequate Organisational Methods and Techniques

The weakness of inadequate organisational methods and techniques has been with the cooperative movement right from its birth (see Shepherd, 1955; Brett, 1970). Right from the inception of cooperative marketing in Uganda, leaders of the movement have never had a clear vision of how to "replace (the alien) system of exploitation of man by man with a system of cooperation which distributes the profits to all justly" (Shepherd, 1955: 28). Consequently, serious managerial and leadership problems followed the establishment of co-ops. As the expatriate adviser to the Federation of Uganda African Farmers once remarked, "To operate an organisation while at the same time educating the participants in how to operate it promises to be a herculean task" (Shepherd, 1955: 41), more so if the educational programme is poorly organised.

That herculean task has been the responsibility of the Department of Cooperatives and the Uganda Cooperative Alliance Ltd. (an apex organisation). And in executing the task, an assumption seems to have been made that a well-known model already exists and hence the need to design education and training programmes based on that model. Cooperative societies were, therefore, allowed to mushroom in the 1960s, and crash programmes were organised to educate and train officials (see Opio-Odongo, 1978). For instance in 1971, 510 one-day courses were conducted and these were attended by 26,183 members, 5804 committee members and 6204 non-members. Similarly, in 1970-71, 1500 film shows were staged, 120 radio talks were broadcast and 300,000 copies of *Cooperative News* were circulated (see UCA, 1975). The recent rehabilitation programme sponsored by the United States Agency for International Development seems to have been based on the same assumption.

But the educational and training programmes have produced no remarkable improvements in organisational methods and techniques. Rampant managerial and leadership difficulties in many co-ops in the country have attested to this (see Okereke, 1970; Opio-Odongo, 1978). Fundamentally, the main problem has been caused by inadequate socialisation within the cooperative movement such that no new value system has been fostered in the marketing system to differentiate it from the one it superceded. While expecting cash from the cooperative, many producer-members have been ignorant of the unique features of this marketing system and their obligations to it (see Vincent, 1976; Opio-Odongo, 1979). For instance, the results of a 1975 study conducted among sixty-five secretaries of cotton marketing co-op societies belonging to the Lango Cooperative Union Ltd. revealed a situation of management with little or no organisational knowledge. While 93 percent of them were absolutely ignorant of how shares had to be managed, 57 percent did not know who had to exercise supreme authority over the co-op. Furthermore, a considerable degree of uncertainty existed over some basic issues: while 53 percent of them had some vague ideas on the procedures to be followed in bonus disbursement, 85 percent had the same problem regarding membership qualifications (Opio-Odongo, f.c.). Help from the staff of the Cooperative Department has not been effective mainly because work scheduling at the primary society level has all along been left to the energy and initiative of the ill-informed local staff. Indeed crises, "rather than periodic reviews, tended to draw staff's attention" to the managerial difficulties facing cooperative societies (Young, Sherman and Rose, 1981: 155).

REVITALISATION OF THE COOPERATIVE MOVEMENT

The ongoing concern with the rehabilitation of agricultural cooperatives in Uganda is ample evidence that some vested interests exist in the survival of cooperatives. Whatever those vested interests may be, and whatever purposes they are meant to serve, they permit one to assume that despite the ongoing crisis within the movement, it has advocates who defend its existence. Assuming the desirability of the movement in national development, its revitalisation would require the following:

(1) A critical assessment of the existing cooperative system given the apparent disharmony between the cherished Rochdalean principles and practices and the basic logic of cooperation permitted by the social organisation of agricultural communities in Uganda. Rather than continue to encounter managerial crises with the imposed Western model of cooperation, it may be useful to assist producer-members to develop their own organisational model. Experience in Niger indicates that this alternative is feasible (Gentil, 1974). Its attractiveness lies in the possibility of promoting organisations, the nature of which members fully understand and with which they strongly identify and depend upon for the protection of their vested interests.

(2) Existing methods of cooperative education and training should be reexamined with the view to making them relevant to the realities of the local rural economy. As a unique method of conducting agricultural business, cooperation has its specific value system (ideology) that needs to be properly inculcated, especially in a society where alternative value systems for the same line of business exist. Certainly a country that values the cooperative form of agricultural business cannot afford to have its educational curricula at nearly all levels devoid of the sub-

ject of agricultural cooperation. But in seeking to introduce the subject, a considerable degree of creativity would have to be exercised if the socialisation in agricultural cooperation is to be effective.
(3) Further government paternalism will be detrimental to any revitalisation effort. It is necessary that a gradual disengagement of government control and supervision be done systematically in order to allow the Uganda Cooperative Alliance Ltd. and the cooperative unions to assume their rightful advisory roles (see Opio-Odongo, 1978). Furthermore, the managerial capability of the cooperatives could be fostered through exposing them to some competition with private buyers. This could help to eliminate inefficient cooperatives and hence ensure marketing efficiency. The government's role would then be basically that of ensuring that unnecessary restrictions are not brought into the market place by any of competitors. In any case, does not the granting of cooperatives monopoly contravene the democratic practice of free entry and exit?

However, on relaxing the assumption on which the above three suggestions have been based, there would be a need for launching a National Commission on the Conditions of Rural Life. That commission, among other things, would examine the claims often made that cooperatives contribute significantly to the welfare of rural people. The commission would have to determine the manner and extent to which cooperatives in collaboration with marketing boards have promoted or hindered rural welfare and hence recommend how best rural welfare could be promoted through or without the cooperatives and/or marketing boards. Short of such an inquiry, the claim that cooperatives play a major role in the socio-economic development of the countryside would be a mere expression of vested interests in the extraction of surplus value from export agriculture rather than a genuine concern with the welfare needs of agricultural producers.

REFERENCES

Alibaruho, G. 1975. "The Impact of Marketing Board Policy on the Level of Variability of Cotton Producer Prices in Uganda, 1945-69." Discussion Paper No. 199, IDS, University of Nairobi.
Belshaw, D. G. R. and W. R. Stent. 1979. "An Overview of the Agricultural Sector." *The Rehabilitation of the Economy of Uganda*. Commonwealth Secretariat Report, Paper No. 2
Brett, E. A. 1970. "Problems of Cooperative Development in Uganda." In R. Apthorpe (ed.), *Rural Cooperatives and Planned Change in Africa*. Geneva: UNRISD.
Carr, S. 1982. "The Impact of Government Intervention on Smallholder Development in North and East Uganda." ADU Occasional Paper No. 5, Wye College, University of London.
Digby, M. 1965. "Cooperative Training in Africa." In the Horace Plunkett Foundation for Cooperative Societies (ed.), *The Yearbook of Agricultural Cooperation*. Oxford: Basil Blackwell.
Digby, M. and R. H. Gretton. 1968. *Cooperative Marketing for Agricultural Producers*. Rome: FAO.
Emery, F. E. and E. L. Trist. 1965. "The Causal Texture of Organizational Environments." *Human Relations*, 18.
Gee, T. W. 1961. "Uganda's Legislative Council Between the Wars." *The Uganda Journal*, 25.
Gentil, D. 1974. "The Establishment of a New Cooperative System in Niger." Paper presented at the Second International Seminar on Change in Agriculture, Reading University, England.
Haring, J. E., S. Christy and J. F. Humphrey. 1969. "Marketing Boards and Price Funds in Uganda, 1950-60." *Journal of Agricultural Economics*, XX (No. 3).
Horace Plunkett Foundation (ed.). 1949. *Yearbook of Agricultural Cooperation*. London: Routledge.
Hyden, D. 1970. "Cooperatives and their Socio-Political Environment." In C. G. Widstrand (ed.), *Cooperatives and Rural Development in East Africa*. New York: Africana Publishing Corporation.
Mamdani, M. 1976. *Politics and Class Formation in Uganda*. New York: Monthly Review Press

Nash, J. and S. Hopkins. 1976. "Anthropological Approaches to the Study of Cooperatives, Collectives and Self-management." In J. Nash et al. (eds.), *Popular Participation in Social Change.* The Hague: Mouton.

Okereke, O. 1970. "The Place of Marketing Cooperatives in the Economy of Uganda." In C. G. Widstrand (ed.), *Cooperatives and Rural Development in East Africa.* New York: Africana Publishing Corporation.

Okereke, O. 1974. *The Economic Impact of Uganda Cooperatives.* Nairobi, East African Literature Bureau.

Opio-Odongo, J. M. A. 1978. "The Cotton Cooperatives as an Institutional Innovation in Uganda." Unpublished Ph.D. Thesis. Cornell University.

Opio-Odongo, J. M. A. 1979. "The Determinants of Organizational Knowledge among Members of Rural Cooperatives." *Agricultural Administration,* 7.

Opio-Odongo, J. M. A. 1980. "The Contribution of Agricultural Cooperatives to Member Welfare and Community Growth: The Case of Lango Cooperative Union." *Journal of Rural Cooperation,* 8 (Nos. 1-2).

Opio-Odongo, J. M. A. 1983. "The Poverty of Agrarian Intervention in Uganda." Paper prepared for the Annual Meeting of the Rural Sociological Society, Lexington, Kentucky, U.S.A.

Opio-Odongo, J. M. A. f.c. "The Determinants of Managerial Knowledge among the Committee Members of Agricultural Marketing Cooperatives." *The Uganda Journal of Public Administration and Management.*

Paige, J. M. 1975. *Agrarian Revolution: Social Movements and Export Agriculture in the Underdeveloped World.* New York: The Free Press.

Shepherd, Jr., G. W. 1955. *They Wait in Darkness.* New York: The John Day Company.

Stinchcombe, A. L. 1965. "Social Structure and Organizations." In J. G. March (ed.), *Handbook of Organizations.* Chicago: Rand McNally and Co.

Uganda, Government of. 1952. *Commission of Inquiry into the Progress of the Cooperative Movement in Mengo, Masaka and Busoga Districts.* Entebbe: Government Printer.

Uganda, Government of. 1965. *Report of the Committee of Inquiry into the Affairs of the Busoga Growers Cooperative Union Ltd.* Entebbe: Government Printer.

Uganda, Government of. 1968. *Report of the Committee of Inquiry into the Affairs of all Cooperative Unions in Uganda.* Entebbe: Government Printer.

Uganda Protectorate. 1958. *Proceedings of the Legislative Council.* Entebbe: Uganda Argus Ltd.

Uganda Cooperative Alliance Ltd. (UCA). 1971. *Inside the Cooperative Movement in Uganda.* Kampala: UCA.

Uganda Cooperative Alliance Ltd. 1973. *Duties and Functions of the Department for Cooperative Development.* Kampala: UCA.

Uganda Cooperative Alliance Ltd. 1975. *Brief Activities and Achievements of the Uganda Cooperative Alliance Ltd., 1971-75.* Kampala: UCA.

Vincent, T. 1970. "Local Cooperatives and Parochial Politics in Uganda: Problems of Organization, Representation and Communication." *Journal of Commonwealth Political Studies,* VIII.

Vincent, T. 1976. "Rural Competition and Cooperative Monopoly: A Ugandan Case." In J. Nash et al. (eds.), *Popular Participation in Social Change.* The Hague: Mouton.

Walker, D. and C. Ehrlich. 1959. "Stabilization and Development Policy in Uganda: An Appraisal." *Kyklos,* XII.

Wrigley, C. C. 1959. *Crops and Wealth in Uganda.* East African Studies No. 12. Kampala: EAISR.

Yoshida, M. 1970. "Government Intervention in Agricultural Marketing in East Africa, 1900-65: A Historical Study." Unpublished Ph.D. Thesis. Makerere University.

Young, C., N. P. Sherman and T. H. Rose. 1981. *Cooperatives and Development: Agricultural Politics in Ghana and Uganda.* Madison: University of Wisconsin Press.

CHANGES AND CONTINUITIES IN THE POSITION OF WOMEN IN UGANDA

H. M. K. Tadria

The picture of the advancement of women in Uganda is a picture of change. In most cases, however, the changes underway have had a negative impact upon women, particularly in rural areas and at lower socio-economic levels. There are success stories to be sure, but these are too few in number and individualised to leave a generally positive image.

Women's roles in Uganda have not diminished in importance or changed in nature in recent years. Nevertheless, their social interpretations have changed and women's tasks are now conceived of as subsidiary to the tasks of men, not as complementary or crucial to survival and development. As a result, women's roles are today often performed under stifling circumstances, and women are frequently left open to the possibility of further exploitation and oppression.

The data reported in this paper were collected during eleven months of field research in two villages in 1983 and 1984. They are unique to these villages. But they also enable more general understandings of the gender structure of Uganda as a whole. Among the 100 village households observed in detail, fifty were "poor peasant" households, twenty "rich peasant" households, the remainder in-between. Thirty of the "poor peasant", two of the "rich peasant" and ten of the households in-between (a total of forty-two households altogether) were headed by females.

My main task here is to show how women continue to make critically important socio-economic and political contributions in Uganda even though they are not now rewarded reasonably in either ideological or material terms. I will proceed in describing the existing division of labour in household maintenance and how this relates to differential gender resource control and ownership. I will then show how the existing gender ideology derives from and in turn maintains the existing subordinate position of women in different spheres of life. Finally, in a review of the history of women's organisations, I will show why, despite continual efforts to establish national machineries for the expression of women's interests, there is still no effective national forum for women in Uganda.

This essay concentrates on women. It is important to emphasise, however, that household gender and economic relations are interconnected in the wider economic sphere. In the villages studied, as in most of Uganda, there are many problems peasant men and women experience together. Their activities can only be understood in relation to each other.

WOMEN IN THE PERI-URBAN HOUSEHOLD ECONOMY

The most typical pattern in the two villages studied is that women produce the bulk of the food, while men provide most of the cash necessary in the purchase of food and other items. The dominance of women in household subsistence production involves them in various types of decisions. But the nature and significance of women's responsibilities can only be appreciated if one understands the conditions under which subsistence activities take place.

In every household studied, women were expected to collect basic staple carbohydrate foods from the fields as needed. Men were mainly responsible for earning the cash necessary for the purchase of protein-rich foods and luxury items such as sugar. At one time women grew even the beans, sim-sim and groundnuts used in the preparation of sauces. Recently—because of land shortages and soil depletion—men have had to provide the cash necessary for such purchases as well.

The fact that men provide most of the cash used in households, while women are responsible for planning and preparing meals, presents certain problems. This is the case, for the women cannot proceed with their cooking until their menfolk bring home the necessary items or provide the money with which to purchase them. Secondly, it is still considered an indication of negligence for a woman to serve her husband a meal without sauce (*emere enume*), whether or not her inability to do so is because of his inability to bring home enough cash to purchase the necessary items. Finally, the woman's dependence on the cash brought into the home by her husband or male friend is not limited to the purchase of food items alone, for today people must often purchase even firewood. They no longer have access to nearby public or scrub-bush lands on which to gather their own.

Noticeable differences were observed in the actual dependence of different households on men's versus women's contributions to the food supply. Among poor peasants there was a total dependence on household food production, with the result that there was a greater dependence on female provision at this level. Because there was some dependence upon purchased foods among those who were richer, there was a noticeably greater female dependence upon the provisions of men among richer peasants. Groups differ in that women among the poor peasantry are more often at starvation level than are women among the rich peasantry. Overall, the differences in food supply are not so much in the types of food the villagers all basically depend upon—cassava, pumpkins, yams, beans, maize, soybeans and groundnuts—but on the quantity and regularity of the foods available.

Though the two villages studied are less than thirty miles from provincial agricultural headquarters, they were never visited by an agricultural officer during the period I was in the field. In fact many of the villagers said they had not seen an agricultural officer since the late 1960s. This means that women have had to be their own agricultural experts and advisers. The effects of this on agricultural production were visible in the low levels of food available in many of the households. One thus cannot isolate the stagnation in the subsistence production sector from governmental indifference to this sector and those who are involved in it—mainly women and poor peasants.

Besides the various problems women face as food producers because of local environmental conditions and the absence of expert assistance, women also face difficulties which are imposed by the land tenure system of the region. Women have to decide not only what to grow and when to plant, but also where to grow their crops. The land holdings of most households are very limited, and land shortages and land disputes arise frequently.

In many cases women use kin and neighbourhood networks to borrow pieces of land they can use freely. In all such cases they negotiate the arrangements made, and the only payment they commonly have to make in return is perhaps a basket of food. However, they do not regard this kind of borrowing as a permanent solution to their land—and consequently their food—problems. Considering the constant borrowing and renting it involves, it is only a procedure by which they are able to keep their families supplied with food at a subsistence level.

Another significant dimension of gender differentiation is that while women's responsibilities as major food producers keep them largely within the boundaries of their villages, the responsibilities of men for cash often take them away from the villages, at least during the day. This places added responsibilities on women in day-to-day decision-making and activity that affect the well-being of their households. Most of the clients of local medicinal specialists are women who bring their children for healing or come for consultation on behalf of other household members. Women are generally more frequently involved than men in providing for the security of their households and in making contacts with local chiefs who represent political administrators. Chiefs sometimes contact each household separately. They sometimes call for public meetings at which each household is expected to be represented. Since men are often gone during the day, such meetings tend to be dominated by women.

It is generally observable, then, that women have become embedded in the household subsistence economy with primary responsibilities for tasks associated with food production and preparation, and for household and health maintenance. Their "embeddedness" here was in large part imposed in the early years of colonial rule when a dual economy was established. As in certain other colonial systems, men took up the new economic opportunities that emerged while women became increasingly important in the production of food crops. But unlike in certain other countries (Cameroon, for example), where women were subsequently able to improve their situation (see Byson, 1981), the position of women in Uganda has deteriorated.

WOMEN IN THE CASH SECTOR

The pattern of gender differentiation that pervades the subsistence sector in Uganda also pervades the cash sector, but here men rather than women are dominant. The exclusion of women from the cash sector, however, has very serious implications. This is particularly so, not because the cash sector makes more contribution to household survival, but because, since colonial times, the cash sector has become more highly valued than the subsistence sector. Today the differences between men and women in access to cash produces and maintains significant gender inequities. A man who earns cash is highly regarded even if he cannot feed his family, whereas a woman who is "merely" a subsistence producer (*omulimi wabulijjo*) is undervalued even if she feeds her family. It follows, in general, that with the existing division of labour, a man is highly regarded because he is essentially a cash earner (even if he is not earning cash) whereas a woman is underrated because she is regarded essentially as a dependent (even if she is earning cash).

Subsistence-related activities affect the pattern of cash-generating activities. Since all households are essentially dependent on subsistence production, only those people not directly involved in agriculture leave the area to pursue other economic activities during planting and harvesting seasons. The structure of the cash economy is also shaped by the proximity of the villages to Kampala. Although the villagers say they are too far from Kampala to benefit directly from urban services and facilities, the Kampala suburbs in fact offer them ready markets for their food and labour.

The traditional cash crops of Buganda (cotton and coffee) are no longer the cash crops in the general area investigated. The peasants here generally get their cash by selling a variety of food crops in addition to their labour, and it is the pattern of this cash economy that must be understood if we are to grasp the different implications of the peasant cash economy for men and women in the villages.

If one stands alongside the roads that lead from the villages toward Kampala at any time of the day, it is possible to observe the types of commodities taken into Kampala. Men almost exclusively transport their commodities by bicycle or wooden cart, or by carrying them. The most common items are bags of cassava, baskets of fruit (mainly jackfruits and mangoes), loads of sugar cane, banana leaves and firewood. The volume and variety of commodities decreases as the day progresses. Sometimes a man who carries a load of sugar cane in the morning carries firewood in the afternoon. Another man might work in a garden in the morning and carry banana leaves to town in the afternoon.

The signs of a cash economy in operation are also observable within the villages. One may see a few canes of sugar on someone's veranda, or a few heaps of cassava, or occasionally a homemade mat or basket. The verandas are usually unattended, but if one calls out, a child or woman will come to sell the commodity. Late in the evenings one can observe individual men moving from one household to another while collecting cassava or bananas to sell later. At all households a little of anything produced is sold in order to meet immediate cash needs. This means that an individual might sell cassava one day and beans the next. In contrast, a cassava "middleman" will go from household to household until he has collected enough to take to town. No one in the villages specialises in the sale of just one commodity or in selling only labour. In short, individuals tend to sell whatever they are in a position to offer.

In an effort to specify and compare the nature of men's and women's cash-producing activities, I asked people to identify their "occupation" (what they did to get cash) for me. The primary source of income for women is derived from the sale of food and handicrafts made and sold within the household. Men get cash through the sale of goods produced in the household or within the neighbourhood, but sold away from the villages, and from the performance of wage labour. That is, there are actually two sectors in the cash economy: a local sector dominated primarily by women, and an "external" sector dominated by men. Most men leave their homes in the morning and typically spend the whole day engaged in a variety of cash-generating activities.

Though women do not identify themselves as occupational "specialists", they do sell alcohol, foodstuffs, baskets and mats to neighbours and relatives, often selling on credit or at reduced prices depending on their customers. Because men are not responsible for subsistence production, they are able to engage in economic activities away from the villages. Those who refer to themselves in some contexts as "common cultivators" (*omulimi wabulijjo*), also classify themselves as carpenters, builders or brokers, rather than as food sellers or middlemen, despite the fact that they often sell food and goods produced in the household when they go to the urban centre.

The major consequence of the male/female (or local/external) division in the cash economy is that men are able to generate more cash than women. This is due to the amount of time they spend in cash-producing activities, and because they are able to sell their goods and labour at higher prices in Kampala. Women have become increasingly dependent on men for cash, especially as cash becomes increasingly essential in securing goods. The dependence of women on men is true even in female-headed households. Women in such households report that their main source of cash is men, even though there are no husbands in their households.

Another interesting point is that women in the rich peasant group tend to describe themselves occupationally as housewives, while women in the other peasant groups tend to refer to themselves either as cultivators or housewives who are also cultivators. The difference in self-perception indicates that although all women are in general dependent on men for cash, women among the rich peasantry tend to be more dependent than the others.

To learn more about how the "bifurcated" cash economic structure works among peasants, I looked at several specific cases comparing men's and women's activities. One case involved a middle peasant household where members depended largely on subsistence activities—that is, work done primarily by women—for food. Their main source of income was from selling sugar cane. Every evening when the man of the household came back from town—or early in the morning before he went to town—he cut enough sugar cane to carry along for sale, plus enough for his wife to sell at home. According to his wife, he took along more than half of what he cut and never failed to sell all of it, while she could never sell all that he left for her to sell at home.

I watched her sales one day and noticed that the majority of her customers were school children who came to buy sugar cane at lunch time. Each child would ask if she had a piece of cane worth a certain amount, thereby setting the price he or she could afford. Most of the children lived in the neighbourhood and she called them by name. I never saw her refuse a school child a piece of sugar-cane, either on credit or at the price set by the child. Although her husband did not expect her to give him the money she made, she really did not make much. In contrast, he made enough from the sale of sugar cane in town to build a permanent block house for himself. She told me that the income from her sales was used only in making the minor purchases necessary in the day-to-day running of the household.

In another case, I asked a widow who sold alcohol to give an account of how much money her household spent and how the money was used. I then compared this with men's accounts of the money they received from their fish sales.

Namwandu is a popular beer seller. She says she gets all of her money from the beer she brews locally (*amalwa*). She sells beer only once a week because it takes her that long to get everything ready. Nakyeyombekedde, a neighbour in whose compound Namwanda sells her beer, encourages women beer sellers who want to make money to use her home and compound for their sales. In the kind of relationship which is typical of the women's sector of the economy, Nakyeyombekedde does not charge rent for this, though it could prove a reliable source of income. She gives priority to social ties of kinship and neighbourliness.

Namwandu sells beer on Wednesdays. In order to have her beer ready for Wednesday evening, she starts to prepare it on Monday. She can never predict how much people will drink, but that is not her most important consideration. Since she depends solely on her own labour, she has to consider how much beer she can prepare and sell. Initial preparations do not take much labour, but the day of the sale does, and if she had the money she says she would employ a young girl to help her.

For one evening's supply of beer, Namwandu must buy three cups of millet flour at Shs. 1050, and one cup of yeast flour at Shs. 350. Transport costs her Shs. 200. This means that on Monday mornings she must have Shs. 1550 in order to start. If she doesn't, she must wait to start until the following day. On Wednesday, after her sales, she has between Shs. 1800 and 2000, which means that her profit for the *entire week* is around Shs. 450. And she is only able to make this much because she fetches her own firewood and water!

Namwandu admits that selling beer makes her feel like a slave. Customers sometimes shout at her and order her around. But without any education she does not see any options for herself. Like many other poor women in the villages studied, she feels that her economic opportunities in life are limited to what the village has to offer. When not selling beer, Namwandu cooks for a sickly relative, which at least guarantees her free meals when her own food runs out.

Fishmongers, in comparison, all of whom are male and claim that they do not make much money, earn much higher incomes. The most commonly used local fish, Nile perch (*mputa*), have to be obtained from lakeshores. The fish sellers always go in groups of at least seven people, which helps to pay the fare of the taxi hired. To hire a special taxi, the men require a total of Shs. 15,000. Each person may buy six pieces of fish at Shs. 1800 each, which he expects to sell for at least Shs. 2100 each. When the men get to the fishing area they commonly find others who seek transportation back to the village, which reduces their costs of transportation.

To cover expenses, then, a fishmonger needs about Shs. 12,500 a day. At the end of a day he will have at least 12,600 or, if he was able to get a very good price for his fish, as much as Shs. 12,700. This means that he will have a profit of between Shs. 100 and 200 a day, as compared with a woman beer brewer's profit of around Shs. 450 a week. Even if a woman supplements her income with food cultivation and in bartering her labour in cooking food, a man's activities are clearly more profitable.

Since fishmongers do not go to the fields, they can make fish selling a daily activity. I asked one fishmonger whether or not he was making enough money to live on, and he replied that he wasn't and that if it was not for the fact that he didn't have to buy the basic foods needed in his household, he didn't know how he would be able to keep it together. When I asked him why he continued to fish, he said: "If one day law authorities come looking for thieves, my neighbours will be able to say, he sells fish, he is not a thief."

Illustrations such as these highlight several features of the cash economy as it operates in the villages. Women tend to generate less cash through their efforts than do men in large part because their cash-producing activities are carried out in addition to their subsistence-related tasks, and because these activities are confined within local environments. Within the broader economic system, women produce primarily for household use while men produce primarily for exchange. The work of men rather than the work of women is seen to allow for the purchase of major household goods—for example, houses, cows and bicycles. Such purchases are more and more commonly considered important, and are generally considered to be the possessions of men alone.

The devaluation of women's work both within the cash sector and the subsistence sector has repercussions in other areas of life, particularly those related to women's mobility, marriage customs and overall household organisation. The peasant's model of gender (or gender ideology) clearly reflects the socio-economic inequality that characterises the relationships between men and women.

PEASANT GENDER IDEOLOGY

People hold a model or ideology of gender in which gender differences and the bases and justification for differences between the sexes are explicated. In the final analysis it is clear that this ideology reflects certain realities about men's and women's lives, while at the same time reinforcing and maintaining the status quo in terms of economic and social relations. The peasant gender ideology in the villages studied conceptualises distinctions between men and women. It is articulated in proverbs, jokes and myths, and in formal and informal discussions.

The essence of the local gender ideology is contained in the expression, "Ezenkanankana n'ekisiki, tezaaka" ("Two equal pieces of wood do not start a fire"). Whenever I asked why men and not women were said to be decision-makers, this was the typical response. The people said that men and women are distinct entities with different perceptions, tasks, responsibilities, privileges and attributes. They also argued that the differences were natural and God-given. To be masculine means to provide for and control women. To be feminine is to be pleasing and acceptable to men. The ideology does not emphasise the role of women as producers and reproducers.

According to elderly men and women, such emphases are new. They told me that in the past a woman's worth was measured more in terms of her productive capacities. Hence when a young man was looking for a wife, he would ask of the woman recommended, "Wansi awunyawo"—"Does she smell the ground?" or "Does she know about gardening?" Today the productive values of women are undervalued regardless of the character of their produce.

In specifying differences between men and women, people say that men must have access to cash. A "mere woman" (*omkazi bukazi*), they say, does not need money because she will get married and be cared for. When I pointed out that in their conception men seemed superior, the women would argue that women cannot be compared with men. Women have influence but they are like the small piece of wood which helps in preparing a fire to light the bigger piece of wood. God created men first. Men must control the household.

The beliefs and ideas of the unequal gender ideology have real effects on Ugandan society. Men have greater access to activities in the cash sector of the economy and greater knowledge of the external world. They are also favoured in formal educational opportunities. The destiny of a woman is commonly regarded to be that of a dependent wife. Girls are more likely than boys to drop out of school. Females are consistently under-represented in educational institutions.

Those who dominate in any situation can construct and impose ideologies that serve their interests. We can therefore conclude that the peasant ideology of gender inequality briefly summarised above represents the dynamic relationship between village men and women, and their differential involvement in two unequally valued economic sectors. The ideology expresses female subordination at the same time it expresses the unequal relationship between the subsistence sector and the cash sector. When women talk of themselves as "mere cultivators" who "know nothing" it is because this is the way subsistence activities have been regarded in comparison with the activities of the cash economic sector over the years.

WOMEN'S ORGANISATIONS IN UGANDA

Existing gender inequalities continue to work to the disadvantage of women in Uganda. During recent years women and girls have often been treated brutally, and female trafficking (internally and internationally) and high female morbidity and mortality rates as a result of a lack of health facilities are continuing problems. There has been a need for women to speak out for and act towards positive change in the country. Yet no effective forum for this has emerged. What is the explanation for this?

In examining this issue, a brief historical exploration of the evolution and processes of the National Council of Women will be given. This will give us a clearer picture of the kinds of problems that have made attempts by various women's organisations to further women's interests persistently ineffectual.

The current National Council of Women, which was created by military decree in 1978, has a long history. It owes its existence to the fact that Ugandans have long believed in the effectiveness of mobilised women in development. But it is also this fact which, as we shall see, has been responsible for the ineffectiveness of the Council as a national forum.

As early as 1963, long before the women's decade was declared and years before Boserup's "Economic Roles of Women" was published, Ugandan women were already writing about the importance of women in development. The Hon. Florence Lubega, at the time Deputy Minister of Community Development, had the following to say (1963: 1-2): "It is essential that we work hard for our independent country, with a conscious desire to benefit the nation as a whole, starting right at home, joining the small local activities in our villages until we can understand affairs better and are able to participate in discussions at an international level. Nation building means more than just politics and social welfare. . . . It is essential for women to take part in public life, to understand politics, the way their country is governed, and world affairs. Whenever political, economic and social thinking takes place, women must and will play a vital and important part in the development of the home, the community and the nation."

The mobilisation of women in groups has always been the goal of successive governments in Uganda. As early as 1946 a women's section was established in what was then the Department of Social Welfare. The establishment of the Council of Voluntary Social Services in 1953 was in part a response to the increasing number of women's voluntary societies. In 1957, realising the importance of women's groups, the Uganda Government signed an agreement with UNICEF under which UNICEF was to provide training for more than 3500 women's club leaders who would then work voluntarily in the promotion and extension of the women's club movement in the country. UNICEF at the time also donated teaching equipment for distribution to rural training centres, and vehicles to be used in the supervision of women's work in the districts. In 1966 under the initiative of local as well as expatriate women members of a variety of different organisations, all women's voluntary organisations were formed into the Association of Women's Organisations.

This association served efficiently as a forum until 1973. In that year a number of people were sent to observe various organisations among the people of Guinea. One of their observations upon their return was that the multiplicity of women's organisations in Uganda could not benefit fully from government policies because of overlapping interests and involvements. They thus recommended that there should be only one women's organisation, as was the case in Guinea. Idi Amin, the military president, welcomed this for it promised him the possibility of more effective control and coordination. In turn, however, a three-day conference was organised and a committee to write the constitution was formed. But before the document which was to create the new organisation—and which was the product of the seminar—could be finalised, Elizabeth Bagaya, its principal architect, fell out of favour with the regime, and the entire matter was temporarily closed.

The next landmark in the creation of a woman's machinery came in 1975 when the UN advised that all member states should have only one national machinery. A committee was then set up in 1976 to work out the formation of the National Council of Women, and a national conference was held in Kyambogo in 1977. Again the message that too many organisations which depended on foreign assistance in the support of their activities could sabotage local interests, was passed on by the military president. And this time, though women now as before opposed the formation of a single national machinery, Amin was powerful enough to force the formation of the National Council.

Women's organisations basically maintained their identities and continued to receive funds from friends and sympathisers outside the country after the 1977 decree forming the National Council of Women was passed. But there was now an important and far-reaching difference, for Article 4 of the decree read as follows: "For the avoidance of doubt, it is hereby declared that with effect from the commencement of this decree, no women's or girls' voluntary organisations shall continue to exist or be formed except in accordance with the provision of this decree." All women's voluntary organisations were to be disbanded.

The full effects of the 1977 decree were never fully realised; upon the advice of a woman minister, personnel in the Ministry of Culture and Community Development did not actually implement the orders passed. The decree was received with antagonism by all women's organisations, however, and the Ministry of Culture found that the support it had once enjoyed from women's organisations was totally withdrawn. In order not to be labeled saboteurs, women's organisations continued to send delegates to conferences and other functions whenever so requested: But they tended to send only delegates with whom officials could not really communicate and delegates who had very little influence within the groups they represented.

The ineffectiveness of the National Council during the 1970s cannot be isolated from the apathy under which the general population suffered during this period under military dictatorship. Amin had identified women's organisations as an important tool to be utilised in reaching the grass-roots population through the formation of a national machinery. Women resisted the efforts of the National Council, uninterested as they were in what was being dictated to them.

The continuing failure of the National Council to represent women's interests into the 1980s can be seen, on the one hand, as the result of the divisive interests of the government in power, and on the other as the result of government suspicions of the powers of mobilised women. Perhaps the biggest handicap of the National Council between 1983 and 1985 was the deliberate attempt by government, especially through the women's wing of the Uganda Peoples Congress (UPC), to use the organisation for political purposes. Decisions of the Council could be overruled by the UPC women's wing. Because of political interference, non-UPC members of the Council were often led to understand that the Council was a party organ. Council leaders were often accused of taking anti-government stands.

The credibility the Council was able to establish after 1980 was destroyed by June 1985. With the coup of July 1985 the Council had to demonstrate again that its role was to protect all women's organisations and to serve as the women's "mouthpiece" on issues that concerned them. By agreeing to organise the September 1985 women's peace march in Kampala, the

Council partially proved that it was not a party organ.

The prospects of the National Council of Women under the Museveni Government, which came to power at the end of January 1986, are still not clear. The Council will have to be strengthened, however, if it is to operate effectively as a women's forum. As long as it is attached to a weak ministry (weak in that it is a resource consumer rather than a resource generator), its interests will continue to be ignored in development policies or exploited for political purposes, particularly during periods of governmental instability.

Ultimately the women of Uganda and Uganda as a whole have suffered the consequences of a lack of an effective national forum for women. Attempts to mobilise the women of the country for grass-roots development in the future will have to guarantee the autonomy of women's organisations from party manipulations and recognise the significance of the participation of women in national affairs.

CONCLUSION

The important roles played by women in household and village economies in Uganda are not suitably remunerated either in kind or material. Women in Uganda continue to suffer acts of personal injustices and remain without an effective forum in relation to which to express their concerns and demand action. They are beginning to ask how they can form themselves into an effective forum which will be able to mould the National Council of Women into a stronger national machinery, and a strong new voluntary organisation of women has already been formed. But much remains to be done.

It is commonly asserted by men and women in Uganda that women really have no problems in reference to inequality. Addressing a group of women in a monthly talking point organised by the National Council of Women on 4 April 1984, for example, the Deputy Minister of Labour stated that a woman in Uganda ". . . is a free person, very much emancipated by Dr. Obote. Women are thought of as useful members of society in all professions. Where ladies are, things have not been messed."

The fact is that women will continue to occupy unfortunately subordinate positions in Uganda until men as well as women come to understand that women work and live within systems of thought as well as action that are characterised by gender inequality, and then do something about it. The low percentages of females in formal employment sectors, educational institutions and leadership are directly related to the existing lack of equal opportunities and the unequal distribution of resources. There can be no equitable development if development plans continue to ignore the very real differences that persist.

And this brings us to two final points. The first is that we must recognise that many women in Ugandan communities today live alone and not under male umbrellas. The fact that the phenomenon of female-headed households is new (at least, not more than fifty years old) is not enough for us to continue planning and operating as if all women live with and under the protection of men. We can no longer close our eyes to the reality today that there are communities where up to 40 percent of all households are female headed. The greater positive integration of women into the social and economic life of the nation is essential for equitable development.

Secondly, it must be understood that women in Uganda are not simply a welfare group to be paid attention only during emergencies or when there is an excess of resources. So-called development planning which assumes that there are greater development issues than those which are posed by women's issues, is false development. When women's issues are dealt with, it is not at the expense of development but as a step towards development. People must always be at the centre of developmental concerns, and women are people!

REFERENCES

Bryson, Judy C. 1981. "Women and Agriculture in Sub-Saharan Africa: Implications for Development." In Nelson, N. (ed.), *African Women in the Development Process*. Frank Cass and Company.
Hong, Evelyn. 1984. "Rural Women in Development." *Ideas and Action* (special issue on rural women), No. 158.
Kaal, Marilee. 1984. "Introduction." *Ideas and Action* (special issue on rural women), No. 158.
Leacock, E. 1978. "Women's Status in Equalitarian Society: Implications for Social Evolution." *Current Anthropology*, 19.
Lubega, Florence. 1963. "Women of Uganda." *The Journal of the Ministry of Community Development*. Kampala: Ministry of Community Development.
Okeyo, A. Pala. 1980. "Daughters of the Lake and Rivers: Colonization and the Land Rights of Luo Women." In Etienne, M. and E. Leacock (eds.), *Women and Colonizations*. New York: Praeger.
Ortner, S. and N. Whitehead (eds.). 1981. *Sexual Meanings: The Cultural Construction of Gender and Sexuality*. Cambridge University Press.
Tadria, Hilda M. 1985. "Changing Economic and Gender Patterns Among the Peasants of Ndejje and Sseguku in Uganda." Unpublished Ph.D. thesis, University of Minnesota.

THE UGANDAN FAMILY IN TRANSITION

Josephine Wanja Harmsworth

The institution of the family in Uganda has been under increasing stress in the past ten to fifteen years as a result of war and violence, hyperinflation, the processes of urbanisation and commercialisation, and the long-term erosion of the system of education. As a result traditional practices and values are being abandoned. Clan, lineage and extended family are becoming less and less significant in organising the lives of members. The conjugal family is emerging as a more isolated unit and is no longer inevitably a unit of production and consumption. Within the conjugal family, marriage alliances are becoming more informal and fluid. There are increasing numbers of one-parent families. There is a trend towards greater individualism and less communal activity and sharing.

Such trends should not be overly exaggerated. Kinship is still the most important determinant of identity within Ugandan society, and the network of kinship ties continues to provide a framework of assistance and support. Family relationships remain emotionally and materially more important than those of any other social grouping.

The changes occurring are important, however, and are the subject of this paper. The paper draws for its historical material on documentary sources, and for empirical data on two recently completed studies in which I was involved: one a 1984 study of the "social and institutional profile of Uganda" (an internal publication of USAID, Kampala, of which I was co-author), the other a UNICEF-sponsored survey of the economic status of rural women in Uganda in 1985.[1] Other perspectives and materials have

---

[1] The USAID "profile" study focused on the survival strategies of a sample of more than 1000 rural households drawn from four different ethnic aras of Uganda: Busoga, Kigezi, Buganda and Teso. In each area three villages were purposively selected according to certain criteria including distance from major towns and population. Within each town clustered random samples of households were selected for interview purposes. Data obtained through interviews with household members were supplemented with data obtained in interviews with district and village-level officials. The UNICEF-sponsored survey of the economic status of rural women was carried out in two villages in each of nine districts: Arua, Gulu, Lira, Mbale, Jinja, Kasese, Kabale, Mbarara and Masaka. Fifty women, many of them members of women's clubs or groups, were interviewed in each district. Group meetings were held with women in each village surveyed to probe certain issues more deeply. Meetings were also arranged with women leaders at the district level.

been possible through participation in family, neighbourhood and more general community affairs in Uganda over the past six years. Earlier published studies of the family in Uganda do not focus on or analyse the issues which are currently crucial, and no recent general studies of this institution in the country have been conducted. The only published figures so far available from the 1980 Uganda Census have been the gross numbers of males and females by administrative divisions. In general, this paper explores ideas and possible hypotheses rather than seeking to arrive at definitive conclusions.

The family in Uganda does not refer just to husband, wife and children, nor even an extended group which also comprises other immediate relatives such as grandparents, aunts and uncles. Not only are many conjugal families polygamous, but the extended family includes a much broader range of kin, and everyone is a member of a clan. Uganda is a country of great ethnic diversity although some broad similarities are to be found within roughly defined tribal groupings—the Bantu and Nilotes, for example.[2] From early times there has also been much interchange, conquest and migration, leading to assimilation and integration between disparate groups. It is therefore not surprising that although the traditional kinship systems of these groups differ in detail, they have certain common customs and traditions.

All Ugandans are born into a clan which claims common descent from an original ancestor, and often also clan unity is expressed through symbolic totems and taboos. All kinship systems are patrilineal, although some bilateral elements are to be found among the Lugbara in the extreme northwest of the country. Property, particularly land, is passed through the male line, and in most places land has never been owned by women. In the southwest women also have never owned livestock. Ugandan families are customarily largely patrilocal. Men usually reside near their fathers, and on marriage women join their husbands' homes. All kinship systems in Uganda recognise multiple marriage for men, and men with many wives have traditionally been accorded high esteem. All Ugandan kinship systems provide for the regularisation of marriage through the payment of dowry by the prospective husband and his kin, to the father and male kin of his prospective wife. Thus traditionally the whole extended family and lineage had an interest in maintaining the stability of a marriage. Ugandan families are by tradition strongly patriarchal. Accordingly, men are the decision-makers, the rulers of their families, wives and children, and their villages and nations.

In pre-colonial times the family in its manifestations of lineage and clan formed the basic building block for many of the indigenous political systems and was an integral element in others. It was an important organising unit not only because certain positions in some systems were hereditary, but because the largest polity in others could be limited to a number of families with authority residing in a council of family elders or lineage heads. The assumption of reciprocity and continuity in social relationships within and between families was also important in the transmission and maintenance of mores and norms of behaviour.

The value systems of the peoples of Uganda also had much in common,

---

[2] Sources are too extensive to be listed here. There are ethnographies on nearly all ethnic groups. A useful compendium is contained in the Ethnographic Survey of Africa series.

although it has been suggested that the Bantu groups differed from the Nilotes in the degree to which aggressive behaviour and male physical valour were stressed. The norms and mores of any society at any one time support behaviour which will strengthen the group, further solidarity and encourage harmony within it through an ordered set of relationships which reinforce its authority system. In particular, all Ugandan value systems have underlined respect for elders, men in general, mutual assistance within the family, and prohibitions on the killing of, or theft from, other members of the society. They have also regulated conflict and provided rules in respect to property, marriage and so on.

In more recent times the family has continued to provide a support system both to ensure conformity to accepted behaviour and for economic assistance. It has also to some extent continued to have political dimensions. In the north as well as the south, political leaders have attempted to mobilise support through clan and lineage structures.

The clans, and indeed extended families or lineages, while they may occupy a territorily discrete area, also nearly always have members who are more widely located. Thus while the lineage may be mainly concentrated in one village, it has linkages both in neighbouring villages and, in modern times, much further afield in towns or other rural areas of the country. The recent 1980 Census does not document place of birth, but according to the 1969 Census 19.6 percent of Ugandans of African origin were born outside their districts of residence (enumeration), and nearly 8 percent were born outside of Uganda altogether. Of those born outside their districts of residence, more than half were male.

The dispersal that has occurred affords opportunity to seek aid, both in terms of basic resources and in financial terms. When land becomes scarce in a man's father's home he may seek to obtain a plot in another village where he has lineage or clan mates. Customarily also, mutual assistance has often been given through the sharing of food and help with cultivation. Families can provide lodging and food when it is necessary to visit other villages and towns. Kin may also be used for contacts to those who control the allocation of jobs, houses and other commodities of facilities such as scholarships and passports. Since family members have customarily contributed not only to their own nuclear units but also to the general welfare of the wider family, it has also been common to provide assistance for the education of children other than one's own.

The most immediate factors impinging on such family traditions are inflation and civil strife. The effect on families of the former has been pervasive and insidious. The effect of civil disturbances has been more dramatic and no less fundamental.

Inflation has been a fact of life since 1972 when Asian residents were expelled and many other citizens went into exile. Since 1979 it has assumed even larger proportions, and the rate at which prices have increased has accelerated. To provide one example of a generally used commodity: in 1972 a bar of washing soap cost about Shs. 3. By 1979 it was officially Shs. 17, but on the blackmarket retailed at Shs. 50. In December 1985 the price was Shs. 2000 or more in Jinja, and upcountry prices were 50 percent or more higher than this. Another item in most family budgets is school fees. In 1972 the annual cost of secondary boarding school fees for two boys was equivalent to slightly more than half the monthly salary of a graduate teacher, i.e., Shs.1300. And the fees at the time covered both school uniforms and essential books. For the first term of 1986, in comparison, school fees for *one* child came to nearly double the monthly salary of a teacher, or Shs. 80,000, and no longer covered uniforms or essential books.

As a result of such changes, families are increasingly subject to financial pressures and constraints. Many in town are reduced to seeking to earn money for daily food on a daily basis. Money for larger expenditures in both towns and villages is extremely difficult to obtain. The net effect is a shrinkage in perceptions of family responsibilities. In the villages kin no longer assist freely with farm work or give food to relatives outside their own homestead. Increasingly relatives avoid giving help with school fees, clothes or medical treatment. Today a man is frequently no longer able to help with expenses for his brothers' children. Whereas in the past visitors from a natal village came with stocks of food, they now visit more frequently empty handed, while the hospitality given to them in turn is increasingly limited. For other favours kin are becoming unprepared to extend assistance without payment.

A further effect of inflation is on both the formalisation and stability of marriage. Because many find it difficult to afford the dowries demanded, valued as they are in terms of so and so many head of cattle, alliances are no longer as frequently regularised by social groupings. As a result, it is often the case that few people other than the couples themselves have much interest in or influence over whether or not they work out. Other factors have resulted in increased geographical mobility for men, which has made it easier for some of them to opt out of difficult relationships and form new ones.

Again, whereas in the past many wives and more children meant wealth, today the reverse is often true. Each additional wife or child requires food, clothing, shelter, medical treatment and school supplies. Many men find themselves unable to manage the financial responsibilities of even monogamous unions. Some seek solace and forgetfulness with other women, only to find eventually that their new unions add to their problems, helplessness and sense of frustration.

In many Ugandan societies a man's prestige at one time depended not only on the size of his conjugal family but also on the degree to which he contributed to the welfare of his extended family or lineage relatives. Today such avenues are generally open only to those who enrich themselves through illegitimate activities. Legitimate endeavors seldom provide the means for largesse.

The various practices labeled *magendo*—which involve dishonest or corrupt activities in the pursuit of monetary gain, and in which almost every Ugandan must be involved in order to survive—are often also in conflict with stated norms and values. Children can hardly avoid seeing and hearing what dubious activities their parents must engage in in order to earn enough money to hold their households together, and how community leaders they are encouraged to respect build their fortunes from embezzled funds. In short, there is a dichotomy between what children are taught is good behaviour, and what they see as the real actions of their parents and other elders, which can have far-reaching and damaging effects on family solidarity and parental authority.

An important kinship ritual which appears to have survived and even thrived is that of funerals. Funerals are still occasions for the expression of kinship solidarity and for the redefinition of linkages and relationships. The status of elders at such occasions is still recognised and reinforced through their leadership in decisions as to the distribution of the assets of the deceased. But even here the inroads of change are at work. Binding decisions have been more difficult to enforce, and now more often than in the past there is strong competition between contending interests, between wives and cognates and between wives themselves. As a result of civil disturbances it has sometimes not been possible in the past several years to check on the actual occurrence of death. At the end of 1985, as at other times of great disorder, customary burial in a deceased person's natal place was often made impossible because of the closure of roads. For the poor, inflation has sometimes had the same effect because of the costs involved in the transportation of the body.

In the past, when a man died it was customary for wives and especially children to be cared for if not absorbed into one of the families of the deceased's male kin. This was an important aspect of the support system. It still is in many contexts, of course, but equally clearly this is no longer to be expected. Cognates often seize most of the property left and leave widows to bring up their children unaided. If lucky, the widows may be left in possession of a house or land as long as they do not remarry. In many parts of the country they are totally deprived of shelter and resources, particularly if their children are young.

It is difficult to quantify the kinds of changes just referred to. Base-line figures on the kinds of measures developed in the two surveys in which I was involved are unavailable. Some indications of the degree to which kin continue to or no longer provide certain kinds of support, however, are provided in Tables 1 and 2. Overall the tables show that little monetary or other support is today freely exchanged beyond the limits of the household unit.

Inflation has also affected the degree to which rural families resort to off-farm work in order to earn money.[3] Between 25 and 63 percent of household heads in the "Social and Institutional Profile of Uganda" (SIP) survey were fully engaged in some kind of off-farm work. In the UNICEF-sponsored survey of the economic status of rural women, between 22 and 98 percent of the women interviewed in the nine districts selected were engaged in some kind of non-farm income earning activities. Such activities do not tend to contribute to family unity. Where a husband knows that his wife has made money on her own account he may withdraw support he was previously giving for the purchase of food for the home. Women who are out earning during the day may be too tired or preoccupied in the evening to lend a willing ear to their children. Attention to family matters often suffers. Income from both farm and employment tends to be managed separately rather than jointly.

---

3 A further element in this is the breakdown in extension services which has made cash crops often not readily marketable, at the same time that producer prices have increased more slowly than those for consumer goods. Plant and animal diseases have proliferated when tools and agro-chemicals have been difficult to obtain and very expensive.

Table 1.
Source of Unpaid Assistance to Women Cultivators (percentages)[a]

	Source of Unpaid Assistance				Hired Labour
	Husbands	Children	Other Rel.	Non Rel.	
Acholi	38	4	6	12	62
Buganda	54	23	10	2	40
Busoga	56	28	8	8	52
Ankole	32	2	0	4	48
Kigezi	34	25	2	0	78
Bugisu	42	12	2	0	48
West Nile	60	4	6	12	88

*Source: Compiled from data collected in the UNICEF-sponosred survey of the economy status of rural women in Uganda in 1985.

[a]Some respondents were single, widowed, separated or divorced. All types of assistance were obtained irregularly.

Table 2a.
Source of Assistance to Household Heads in Cultivating (percentages)

Area[a]	Household member	Non-kin	Hired Labour
Busoga	20	7	19
Kigezi	8	15	35
Buganda	9	0	40
Teso	22	31	35

Table 2b.
Percentage of Households Obtaining Financial or Food Aid from Relatives in Time of Famine or Food Shortage

Area	Food Aid	Financial Aid
Busoga	7	1
Kigezi	5	0
Buganda	6	7
Teso	6	2

Table 2c.
Percentage of Respondents Who Borrowed Money from Relatives for Housebuilding or Cultivation in Year prior to Survey

Area	Housebuilding	Cultivation
Busoga	1	2
Kigezi	7	5
Buganda	3	3
Teso	3	7

Table 2d.
Percentage of Respondents Obtaining Remittance from Relatives Including Adult Children as Part of Regular Income

Area	Percentage Receiving Remittances
Busoga	8
Kigezi	6
Buganda	26[b]
Teso	18

*Source: Extracted from data obtained for the "Social and Institutional Profile of Uganda" (USAID, 1984).

[a]The areas referred to in Table 2 correspond to the 1962 districts which were largely coterminous with ethnic divisions.

[b]The Buganda subsample included an unusually large number of women household heads, many of whom were looking after grandchildren.

In fact in many instances it appears that a deliberate policy of secrecy is followed. The men reserve as much as possible for private enjoyment and are suspicious that their womenfolk may be doing the same. Traditional male supremacy is challenged by the increasing economic independence of women. Their roles as providers, protectors and decision-makers are fragmenting.

While inflation has had an unavoidale effect on all families, some have evaded the worst traumas of the civil disturbances which have raged since 1979 in many parts of the country. Nevertheless an increasing number of areas are, or have been, in the "frontline", and the effects of war and violence are not only felt by those immediately in the line of fire. The effects of the various violent episodes on the family have not been researched, but some are visible. Foremost is the existence of many more widows and orphans—that is, children without fathers in the Ugandan sense of the term—and therefore of single-parent homes. Women, because of the pressures already described, do not tend to remarry. Secondly, the dispersal of many families has resulted in their breakup and has made problematic the continued functioning of the extended family. Physical contact among the members of such families has become increasingly difficult. Rituals can no longer as easily be properly performed.

Violence also often reinforces the effects of inflation. Many families whose homes have been looted by disorderly soldiery or other armed groups have been totally unable to recoup their losses or restore themselves and their families to previous modest levels of prosperity or even comfort. Large numbers of people have been more or less permanently uprooted from rural homes and now exist on the peripheries of towns.

Violent incidents also result in major movements of population from one place to another. Apart from the breakdown of both extended and conjugal families under such circumstances, the physical and moral welfare of children are undermined. It is sometimes difficult for children to recover from such conditions and events, particularly where refugee status persists over a longer period of time. Not only have higher rates of infant mortality and malnutrition been recorded, but older children also suffer interruptions to their education due to the breakdown of social services. In this respect all the family units of large areas are deprived of normal existence, sometimes for years at a time. In such cases many families will never be able to fully reintegrate themselves. In the meantime children have become adults, and patterns of life have become completely altered. Abnormality has with the course of time become the daily routine. New relationships have been established.

Other influences on family development are the results of urban influences and commercialisation, and, over the longer-term, education. With the departure of the Asian community in 1972, black Ugandans moved rapidly to fill empty businesses and houses in towns throughout the country. In addition, over the intervening period, many more and larger trading centres have been established. Many Ugandans have moved in less than a generation from farming into trade. Informal trade activities also provide employment to many young people who are jobless as a result of economic stagnation and the lack of access to land as well as knowledge and experience of farming practices. The styles of life associated with business and trade are quite different from the styles associated with wage earning and farming, and this affects family life. In particular, the changes underway have opened up new economic opportunities for women, and it is probable that there are today many more women-headed households in towns and suburbs than in most rural areas. It is also easier today for women to avoid social censure and thus to adopt lifestyles of greater sexual freedom and economic independence. Such activities, however, are not always conducive to the welfare of children nor to their ordered upbringing. Certainly new patterns have often eroded the unit of the conjugal family.

Town dwellers have different concerns and interests than their rural friends and relatives. These can conflict. There are other dimensions to town life. Few women agree to share a town house with a co-wife, and it does not yet appear that urbanisation has in any way acted to limit polygamy. This results in increasing pressure on available housing and a physical distancing of fathers from their children. Men may also not only have wives in different houses in town but others in the village. Few wives will cooperate with each other in managing a business. Thus business development is at times handicapped by domestic conflicts. The alternative is for members of a family to pursue their separate economic interests alone.

In town young people are subject to more influences outside the family. Often the sheer congestion of their homes leads them to play and socialise outside. They often grow up without adequate parental guidance either because their parents are too busy with other concerns, or because they are not living with their parents at all. It is also the case that women are not expected to discipline boys, or the children of other wives. Where the father is absent, as so often happens due to divided residence or the pursuit of pleasure outside the home, boys may be left to bring themselves up. Such situations are frequently made worse by contrasts between ideal parental behaviour and the demands on the parents for economic survival. Respect for parents is undermined by the disparity between what they teach and what they are often forced to do under the circumstances that exist.

There are many needs and temptations, all of which cost money. Thus has grown up a class of *bayaye*—youngsters devoted to shady deals, if not outright theft, as a way of making that money. Some have to finance all their own living expenses as families become less and less able to cope with the needs of all their members. No longer will a good job, the major objective of education, pay for normal needs; thus there is a further trend towards deliberate school drop-out. This and a shortage of jobs due to a shrinkage in employment and the result of economic stagnation, coupled with lack of access to land, leaves many young people footloose and idle.

Education itself is another divisive factor in family life. Pursuit of education often causes prolonged separations of family members. It also effectively removes an increasing number of young people from their rural birthplaces. The content of syllabi are totally unrelated to the actualities of rural living, and do not involve moral training related to marriage and the family. The aim of all education is more education and eventually a good job in town. An objective which is all the more obsolete since no job pays the worker enough to live on, let alone aspire to a high standard of living. Education separates the young from their elders and invites them to consider book learning superior to the wisdom of experience. It can ultimately also provide them with the financial means with which to assert their independence from their elders.

Often children in Uganda start their schooling when they are older than is common in developed countries. Thus many are already physically mature by the time they leave primary school, and more by the time they have completed secondary school (thirteen years of schooling). They often form relationships with the opposite sex which through ignorance, carelessness, or even perverse desire, result in pregnancies. For the girl this is likely to be the end of her studies. For the boy it may be a mere incident, as responsibility is difficult to prove and forced marriages take place less and less frequently.

CONCLUSION

Uganda today is witnessing a process of radical change in the family as an institution both in its extended form and in conjugal units. The traditional forms of extended family corporateness and cooperation are breaking down under economic pressures.

The cooperative and caring relationships between spouses and between parents and children which are essential to stable and secure family life are also being eroded by the exigencies of political and economic instability. Some trends are part of a long-term process, others the result of more traumatic short-term events. This situation needs more examination, precise definition and analysis through studies focusing on particular issues.

The family is still the most important social institution in Uganda. Families are the foundation from which individual strengths, and all other relationships, develop. When the family is no longer strong and united, and loses concern for the welfare of its members, other institutions of Uganda's national life will be corrupted. While most Ugandans are still struggling to fulfill meaningful and responsible roles as parents and as members of both conjugal and extended families, they often do so against the odds, and some fail. When leaders talk of moral and physical rehabilitation their concerns must start with the family.

REHABILITATION OR REDEFINITION OF HEALTH SERVICES

Cole P. Dodge

Summary

Uganda once had one of the best health care delivery systems in Africa. The decade of misrule by Amin saw a collapse of the country and an exodus of doctors and other professionals. The 1979 war and subsequent political instability and insecurity further aggravated the poor health services then available. When political stability was temporarily restored in December 1980 the cash crop export sector took priority over social services and the health budget declined. Emergencies in West Nile, Karamoja, the Luwero Triangle and other areas continued to plague rehabilitation efforts through 1985.

Alternate strategies for improving health are proposed, including female education, increased budget allocations, food and nutrition policy and health information. Uganda's prospect for rebuilding the health services has begun with immunisation, control of diarrhoeal diseases, nutrition surveillance in Karamoja and an essential drugs programme, but the success of these is dependent upon political stability and improvement in overall security.

BACKGROUND

The recovery of the health services in Uganda following the 1979 liberation war proved to be much more difficult than anticipated. The reasons for this are easily understood when the decade of Amin's rule between 1971 and 1979 are considered. Firstly, predictions in the early 1970s had already been that Uganda would not be able to maintain its health services without major changes, especially considering unexpected and increased costs of fuel imports (see Scheyer and Dunlop, 1981). Secondly, Idi Amin's expulsion of the Asians in 1972 deprived the country of many doctors, pharmacists and other health care professionals, as well as of the backbone of the trading community which linked the pharmaceutical industry in the distribution of medical supplies throughout the country.

---

*Editor's note: Reprinted with permission from *Social Science and Medicine*, 22 (7), Cole P. Dodge, "Rehabilitation, or Redefinition of Health Services", Copyright 1986, Pergamon Journals Ltd.

Thirdly, after Amin's atrocities against doctors and professionals in general, many from such cadres fled the country to neighbouring East African or other countries. Between 1967-68 and 1979, for example, the number of doctors dropped from 978 to 574, the number of dentists from forty-two to twenty-four and the number of pharmacists from 116 to fifteen (Scheyer and Dunlop, 1981). Fourthly, the overall plundering of Uganda's economy by Amin's people and army and others over the years eroded the government's tax base, thus depriving the country of its economic viability and ability to sustain investment in health and other social services.

The overall breakdown of services in the country was so dramatic by 1979 that the organised provision of health services ceased in many areas. Monthly salaries for civil servants—including doctors and nurses—was insufficient to sustain a family for more than a week. Inflation was running in three digits, forcing many to take on additional jobs or to rely upon the produce of family gardens to sustain themselves for longer periods. Salary payments were frequently in arrears.

Political stability was not again achieved until 1981. In mid-1985 the Obote Government was overthrown in a military coup. Then the succeeding military council was overthrown in January 1986. Though it is still too early to tell how things will turn out, the Museveni Government formed in early 1986 is committed to the promotion of health and the prevention of disease through the encouragement of community participation in the definition and provision of health services, and the guidance of correct political leadership.

RECOVERY PROGRAMME PRIORITIES

The priorities of the government as established in the Recovery Programme (Uganda, 1982), and presented at the World Bank consultative group meeting, identified agriculture as the first priority with 30 percent of the envisioned expenditures over the 1982-84 period. Industry was earmarked for 28 percent, transport for 21 percent, minerals and energy for 6 percent and social infrastructure (including education, water supplies and health care) for only 15 percent.

The government's subsequent Revised Recovery Programme (Uganda, 1983) identified industry over agriculture as taking precedence with 35 percent, followed by agriculture with 27 percent, the social infrastructure with 20 percent and transportation and communication with 14 percent. The health sector of the original recovery programme was oriented towards the rehabilitation of the health services, while the revised recovery programme reflected donor preferences for immunisation, primary health care and manpower training (see Table 1 for health sector budgets in the recovery programmes). Overall, the proportion of the budget to the Ministry of Health dropped from a consistent 7.5 to 10 percent of budget from 1935 through the mid-1970s, to less than 3.5 percent of the budget in the early 1980s.

The sector priorities of Uganda's recovery programmes were established to reflect basic economic needs. It was argued that unless the cash crop, marketing and processing sectors were revived to generate revenues, and unless the country could feed itself from agricultural production, there was

Table 1.
Recovery Programme Health Sector Budget (in millions of U.S. $).

			April 1982	October 1983
S1	05	Rehab. of Mulago Hospital complex	5	3.07
S1	06	Rehab. up-country hospital	5	5.06
S1	07	Primary health care facilities	15	10.32
S1	08	Blood transfusion services	0.2	0.3
S1	09	Purchase of drugs	5	(Transferred to S1 05, 06 07, 20 and recurrent budget)
S1	28	Strengthening PHC		3.0
S1	29	Health training and planning		4.98
S1	30	Accelerated immunisation		5.22

*Source: Uganda (1982) and Uganda (1983), respectively.

no prospect of reversing the country's problems. Agriculture therefore received the highest priority. While the health services did not receive priority attention, the identification of the need for concentration on the economic situation was clearly reasonable.

In his first term in power between 1962 and 1971, President Milton Obote was identified with socialistic policies. When he came back to power in December 1980, he adopted a more capitalistic, mixed-economy approach, giving priority to private ownership and even allowing the Asians who had been expelled under Amin to return to Uganda and claim, or be compensated for, their properties. Several economic and fiscal policies were introduced in mid-1981 (Uganda, 1981), under advice from the International Monetary Fund (IMF). The accomplishment of these objectives was however frustrated by mid-1984 and into 1985 by increasing pressures from the IMF towards more dramatic adjustment programmes. At a time when the country needed a degree of political stability, the adjustments encouraged had a negative impact on the financing of the social sector (despite two years of real GDP growth and a positive balance of payments in 1983-84). Stringent economic policies must be combined with adequate financial support for essential social services if short-term catastrophe is to be avoided and long-term development is to take place. In short, effects upon the physical quality of life—as measured in consideration of mortality rates, literacy rates, life expectancies and other indicators—must be considered alongside economic factors.

In contrast to recovery programme estimates, actual expenditures for "security" in 1980-81 amounted to 44 percent of the budget. While expenditures for security dropped to 25 percent of the 1981-82 budget, major problems around internal security continued to plague Uganda through 1985. While it is important to recognise that spending for defence and security have taken a substantial share of budget expenditures during the 1980s, more important has been the impact of the "insecurity" of recent years on the health and well-being of the civilian population. In the "Luwero Triangle" to the north and west of Kampala, an area which encompasses a population of an estimated 750,000 people, the International Committee of the Red Cross in 1985 found an infant mortality rate of 305 per 1000 live births among displaced people residing in Red Cross-assisted shelters (Dodge and Henderson, 1985). This Luwero region, West Nile, the Banyarwanda population around Mbarara and Karamoja have experienced varying degrees of insecurity since 1979, placing increased demands on Uganda's budget for "defence" and the immediate relief of displaced peoples. Problems of insecurity in many parts of the country in 1985 again put the provision of normal health services into question.

HEALTH PROGRAMMES

Social services in Uganda during the early 1980s have been supported by voluntary organisations and church and mission groups, as well as bilateral and multilateral donors. After the disastrous decline of all services in the 1970s, some health services were revitalised during this period. Sixty-three percent of all Revised Recovery Programme health sector targets were funded by October 1983. Major donors included Overseas Development Administration (ODA) of the United Kingdom, for Mulago Hospital; Canadian International Development Assistance, through the African Medical and Research Foundation (AMREF), for health manpower training and planning; UNICEF for rehabilitation of 100 health centres, immunisation, transportation, equipment and maintenance, and essential drugs; Save the Children Fund for immunisation and Mulago Hospital; Red Cross for blood transfusion services, and the European Economic Community for primary health care facilities.

A National Expanded Programme of Immunisation (EPI) was launched in 1983 with support from UNICEF, Save the Children Fund and Catholic and Protestant churches. Following plans and programmes established in the late 1960s, immunisation coverage in Uganda had reached an all-time high at over 70 percent of children immunised with BCG in 1973, but had steadily declined thereafter. By 1980 less than 10 percent of age-eligible children were immunised with BCG, and less than 5 percent for DPT, measles and polio. The objectives of Uganda's immunisation programme today are to achieve universal coverage for the six immunisable diseases by 1990, principally through static health units. Despite the coup of July 1985, an urban immunisation campaign planned in June and July was launched on 27 August and involved thirty-one health units (including four military medical facilities) in the greater Kampala area. Save the Children Fund provides a five-man technical assistance team to the Ministry of Health (MOH), while UNICEF support includes the provision of suitable offices and storage facilities, transportation, training and social marketing/health education, and the development of a nationwide solar cold chain to locations where a reliable electric power supply is not yet available. AMREF provides technical assistance and material development support for continuing medical education at the national level throughout Uganda (see Wood, 1985). The Canadian-supported Child Health and Medical Education Programme (CHAMP) provides paediatricians on a rotating basis to the Department of Paediatrics, and Minnesota International Health Volunteers support the Institute of Public Health in rural health training. The United States Agency for International Development provides support to the control of diarrhoeal disease programme, and family planning. The Danish Red Cross, with funding from DANIDA, began a five-year essential drug programme in late 1985, and the World Bank is planning its first assistance to the health sector to commence in 1987.

The rehabilitation of Uganda's medical services to the level that existed in the 1960s has received the most emphasis in the period since Amin was ousted. Uganda enjoyed one of the best health care delivery systems in Africa in the 1960s. Uganda pioneered immunisation programmes through the Preprimary Protection Programme which was established under Makerere University in Ankole District (Cook, 1967). The Makerere Medical School was recognised for excellence during the pre-Amin years, and Mulago Hospital was one of the best of its kind in sub-Saharan Africa.

A dilemma that presents itself in Uganda today has to do with the fact that the thinking and innovations that come out of its university community generally have a lag time of from five to ten years before they are reflected in policy adoptions by the government. Given the decline of Makerere and government services during the Amin period and thereafter, health system definitions and policies were frozen in place when Amin came to power or shortly thereafter. Government policy therefore continues to reflect the academic thinking of the mid-1960s. Little innovation or policy change took place in the 1970s, and the emphasis during the 1980s has been on rehabilitation alone. Ugandan health professionals were not in a position to "internalise" the vigorous dialogue that took place surrounding the Alma Ata conference and the world-wide attention to primary health care in the 1970s. Expatriates, Asians and leaders in the academic field fled or were forced out during the 1970s. Those who were left behind were generally preoccupied with problems of decay and insecurity, and the maintenance of existing programmes and services.

The academics who returned to Makerere in the early 1980s found an extremely difficult and trying situation. Buildings and equipment had been severely looted. Morale was very low. Makerere had been forced to limp along with a much larger enrollment than in 1970 but without the money, equipment, faculty, books and other resources necessary in the provision of good education and training.

While Uganda has the skeleton of a good health infrastructure (Alnwick et al., 1985), this infrastructure must be rebuilt, coordinated and utilised in an effective manner. The 42 percent of the country's hospitals that are owned and operated by Catholic and Protestant churches (Table 2) are not well integrated into the government's basic health strategy, though they have provided on an uninterrupted basis the majority of health care in the country throughout the years of national turmoil. Many government health facilities have not been rehabilitated and do not provide basic services because of low salaries and lack of materials. The immunisation programme of the Ministry of Health has recognised this and offered free immunisation materials to all health facilities. The essential drugs programme assisted by the Danish Red Cross will centralise the procurement and distribution of all essential drugs imported to government as well as church health facilities. Other such short-term stop-gap measures, and longer-term strategies which involve vigorous health planning, must be developed.

Table 3 gives figures for the leading causes of death in selected Ugandan hospitals in 1970 and 1981. Clearly, priorities in health services must be shaped by the epidemiological experience rather than a simple interest in rehabilitating the facilities established in earlier years. Immunisation can be readily established as a priority.

Table 2.
1984 Health Facilities

	Government		Nongovernment		Total
	N	%	N	%	N
Hospitals	46	58	33	42	79
Health centres	101	90	5	10	106
Dispensary/maternity units	70	75	23	25	93
Dispensaries	48	62	29	38	77
Maternity units	30	73	11	27	41
Subdispensaries	351	96	16	4	367
Aid posts	145	90	16	10	161
Totals	791	86	133	14	924

*Source: Uganda (1984).

Table 3.
Leading Causes of Admission and Death in Selected Government Hospitals (Inpatients, 1970-71 and 1981-82).

	Admissions %		Case fatality rate %		Proportion of deaths %	
Disease	1981	1970	1981	1970	1981	1970
Measles	12.4	5.3	9.5	4.3	25.6	5.4
Pneumonia	7.3	5.0	8.3	9.4	13.2	11.3
Malaria	9.8	9.1	2.5	3.0	5.2	6.6
Gastroenteritis	7.1	7.2	5.5	5.5	8.4	9.5
Tetanus	0.4	0.5	48.2	46.6	4.5	5.5
Anaemia	3.6	3.6	5.4	6.1	4.3	5.2
Dysentery	2.9	0.6	3.5	4.3	2.2	0.6
URTI	2.7	3.0	3.3	2.7	1.9	2.0
Pertussis	1.4	1.0	7.4	3.4	2.3	0.9
Total above	47.6	35.3	6.5	5.5	67.6	47.0
All other cases excluding maternity	52.4	64.7	2.8	3.4	32.4	53.0
Totals	100.0	100.0	4.6	4.2	100.0	100.0

*Source: Alnwick et al. (1985b).

ALTERNATIVE MEASURES/OPTIONS

Any attempt to improve the health situation in Uganda must take into consideration several underlying and related issues.

Female literacy

The relationship between maternal and infant mortality and the level of education of the mother are closely related (Grant, 1983). The need for female education/literacy is underlined if the health standards of the population are to be maintained or improved. The question which arises is the following: Which educational strategy should be adopted in order to achieve improved health and other objectives?

Priorities for budget

Another major question is whether to continue to concentrate on the expensive training of medical doctors and specialised medical practitioners at the university level, or to embark upon the general training of primary health care (PHC) workers and traditional birth attendants (TBAs) at the village level. Vested interests at Makerere University and Mulago Hospital vigorously defend their fiscal and resource requirements. Within the budgeting and allocation process at Mulago, allocations are justified in order to stem the outflow of resources for the foreign medical treatment of senior government officials and their families. Within the Ministry of Health there is some reluctance to incorporate TBAs into the official health system because of adherence to a former national health policy which encourages deliveries in maternity units at hospitals, health centres or dispensary-maternity units, even though this encouragement is not practical in consideration of the severe fiscal constraints involved. Some observers feel the incorporation of TBAs will increase competition for scarce Ministry of Health resources. But whatever the nature of the arguments that have arisen and will continue to arise around the allocation of scarce resources, it should be noted that the infant mortality rate in 1985 was still estimated at 120 per 1000 live births. This was the *same level* achieved in 1969 (Dodge and Henderson, 1985).

Food and nutrition policy

Understandings of the relationships between nutrition, health and agricultural patterns are important. Uganda has not yet established a food and nutrition policy. Recovery programmes have placed top priority upon cash crop exports despite the adverse nutritional effects this may have on young children. The cash cropping of tobacco in West Nile was noted in the late 1960s and early 1970s as having an adverse nutritional effect upon children (Dean, 1985). Similar findings have been reported for other settings.

Health indicators

The need for the adequate monitoring and evaluation of health outcomes is evident as Uganda does not have a viable health data collection system. Even estimates of morbidity and mortality are not readily available. The need for such is apparent for the planning of health services and the allocation of very scarce resources to, and within, the health sector. With the breakdown of health services in recent years, many voluntary agencies have been at work and various approaches have been adopted in the thirty-three different districts, often without reasonable coordination. Effective planning will only be possible when demographic, socio-economic and epidemiological data are available.

The changed situation has necessitated changes in church health facilities as well. During the Amin years Kuluva Hospital in West Nile saw the disappearance of many pharmaceuticals. As a result the hospital's treatment potential was constrained. Between 1978 and 1979 many expatriate doctors were forced to leave. The rise of measles admissions records for the mission hospital when immunisation services were discontinued in the 1970s (as illustrated in Figure 1; see Williams, 1985), reflected similar changes in morbidity/mortality patterns in the country as a whole.

Similarly, the delivery of basic services based upon a well maintained network of roads, buses and other communications and transportation facilities was severely disrupted by the early 1980s. This necessitated village-based services as opposed to concentrations of such services in health centres, market towns and district headquarters.

Morbidity and mortality patterns have changed during the past fifteen years. A survey of selected hospitals in 1981-82 (Alnwick, et al., 1985) revealed that measles was the number one cause of death in hospitals, standing at 25.6 percent of all recorded hospital deaths (see Table 3). A study at Mulago Hospital in the same period revealed that 46.6 percent of all paediatric deaths were measles related (Wotton, 1985). Such findings give clear indication of the priority of immunisation in the reduction of both morbidity and mortality in the country.

AN AREA OF SPECIAL NEED

Considerations of health in Uganda must include the special needs of Karamoja. Famine struck Karamoja in 1979 and lasted through mid-1981, claiming the lives of an estimated 50,000 people including 25,000 children (Biellik and Henderson, 1981).

The major problems with health service delivery in Karamoja revolve around the following considerations:
1. The semi-aridity of the region.
2. The dispersal of the population over a very large area.
3. A low literacy rate in comparison with other parts of the country. Less than 5 percent of the women and 18 percent of the men are literate. As a result of low educational levels, health care professionals must be recruited from neighbouring ethnic groups rather than locally.
4. The infrastructure of the region is weak and vulnerable. When automa-

Figure 1.

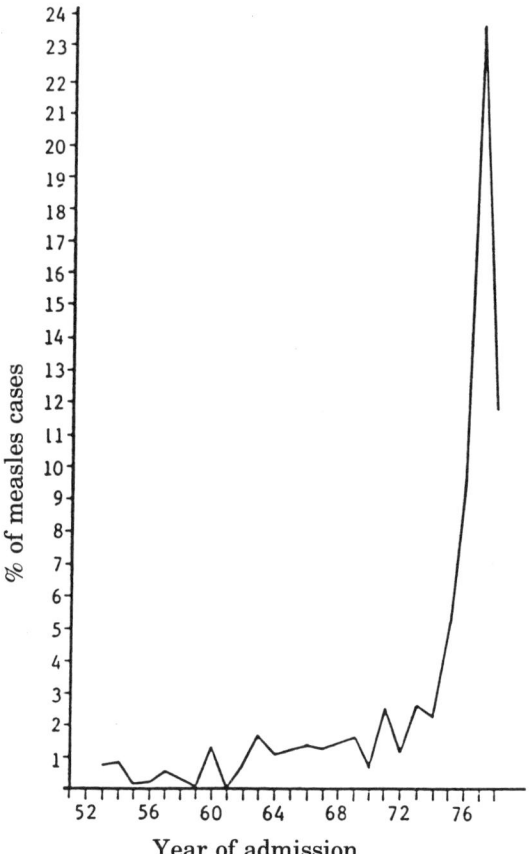

Measles cases represented as percentage of total admissions, Kuluva Hospital

tic weapons were introduced to the traditionally organised cattle-raiding Karamojong in 1979, insecurity increased dramatically, with the result that many civil servants were forced to return to their home areas. This led further to the concentration of cattle, the main supply of food for much of the population, in the hands of one or two of the clan groups and deprived and rendered vulnerable to starvation the balance of the Karamojong people. Trade relations broke down to such an extent that cattle could no longer be traded to neighbouring groups for food supplies. Roads became insecure and security forces frequently closed regional borders.
5. The social service infrastructure of the region broke down almost entirely in 1979 to render hospitals, health centres, water supplies and administrative services unavailable to the Karamojong.

Major questions face the Karamoja region, questions around the restocking and disarming of the Karamojong or their settlement in the more fertile and higher rainfall western rim of Karamoja. When such questions are examined by government, and when a clear policy is established, a more coordinated and coherent approach to the development of the region will be possible. The Ministry of Health has fortunately lowered the educational requirement for health workers in the district, and a school for nurses has been established at the Catholic hospital at Matany. A nutritional surveillance programme—which operates in twenty-five locations and provides a dry ration food package to children weighed fortnightly who are less than 80 percent of their expected weight-for-height—has also been established using Karamojong workers trained by voluntary agencies during the period of famine. The severely malnourished are treated in intensive feeding centres at hospitals and health centres.

A high rate of immunisation coverage together with nutritional surveillance and appropriate food aid helped contain a major catastrophy in 1985. Because of malnutrition (less than 80% of expected weight-for-height), thirty-five percent of pre-school children in Karamoja were enrolled in the nutrition programme during May. A drought had destroyed the 1984 crop in northern Karamoja, while cattle raiding in southern Karamoja had spilled over into neighbouring districts and Kenya. The subsequent joint Uganda/Kenya military operation to quell the violent raiding had displaced an estimated 75 percent of the population in the extreme south in Karamoja and had helped to render the whole of Karamoja famine-prone in early 1985.

PROSPECTS

Despite the serious deterioration of facilities, Uganda has the latent infrastructure for a good health care delivery system. Nearly 60 percent of the population lives within ten kilometres of a health unit and therefore can be theoretically reached by such public health programmes as immunisation, the improvement of TBA practices and the control of diarrhoeal diseases.

A model of social paediatrics introduced at Mulago Hospital with assistance from CHAMP (Ndugwa, et al., 1985) now needs to be encouraged in all hospitals. PHC and community-based health care systems have been introduced of necessity in Catholic and Protestant medical, as well as in other voluntary, programmes. The government must now evaluate these for widespread replication, given that Uganda's population increased by 40 percent between 1969 and 1985 while very few new health facilities were opened, and existing facilities deteriorated. Issues of accountability between service providers and patients as well as motivation in service and the quality of patient care have not been adequately addressed. The deterioration of such dimensions of health care was caused by outright destruction during the 1978-79 liberation war and has been encouraged since by neglect, the lack of maintenance of existing facilities and periodic looting. Finally, given the low budgetary priority given to health in contemporary Uganda, continuing problems with the economy and modest donor support for the social sector, Uganda must confront the issue of user cost or cost recovery.

Whatever the cause of the breakdown of health services, Uganda must decide if the simple but expensive rehabilitation of a 1960s-style system is desirable and possible, or if the more difficult but potentially more appropriate redefinition of health services is needed for the remainder of the 1980s and beyond.

Cost is one of the main issues facing the health sector. In reference to user costs, the government will have to consider two proposals:
1. patients paying for services and medicines, and
2. communities paying for PHC workers.

Patients already pay for some services and medicines in the health facilities operated by the churches, and the 42 percent of all hospitals operated by the church today provide for the vast majority of all health services in the country. Church hospitals and health centres are largely supported by "users" and are owned and operated by the Church of Uganda or the Catholic Church. While foreign church donations are considerable, they do not provide full operating costs. Foreign church personnel continue to assist in many facilities, but overall management is in the hands of Ugandans, and basic running costs are generated locally. Based upon this example, the government is considering the introduction of a fee-for-service element in their health care delivery system. Similarly, the World Bank pre-project technical assistance review identified cost recovery as a priority. Public health programmes such as immunisation, the control of diarrhoeal diseases and health education would be supported by government, and, according to preliminary thinking, the bursary would be utilised to provide services for those who could not afford to pay for services.

Uganda is in a reasonably good position to adopt such an approach. It was never colonised. Land ownership is fairly equally divided and the country's leading cash crop, coffee, is not an estate produced crop but rather a crop produced by smallholders. All crops except sugar and tea are similarly produced by small cultivators. Incomes are relatively evenly distributed. Geographic disparity is problematic, however, and a system of "block" grants from central government to poorer districts could prove necessary if services are to be equally accessible and of the same standard in all districts of the country.

The second question of communities paying for PHC workers has ample precedence in other countries. But the initial PHC proposal for Uganda called for adding PHC workers onto the civil service payroll, and some NGO-supported PHC projects in Uganda have provided salaries for workers. Such introductions are against the principles of PHC and would be too costly for the country to consider at the present time.

Uganda's health services are being rehabilitated following breakdown in the late 1970s and early 1980s. New ideas are circulating with a view to the eventual change of focus required, given population growth and economic constraints. It is too early to predict, however, what the country will decide in reference to the related issues of female education, user costs and budgets for health, cash cropping and a food and nutrition policy, a health information system, the chronic problem of underdevelopment in Karamoja and the overall insecurity and political instability still plaguing the country.

REFERENCES

Alnwick, D. J., M. R. Stirling and G. Kyeyune. 1985. "Population Access to Hospitals, Health Centres and Dispensary/Maternity Units in Uganda, 1980." In Dodge and Wiebe (1985).

Alnwick, D. J., M. R. Stirling and G. Kyeyune. 1985b. "Morbidity and Mortality in Selected Ugandan Hospitals, 1981-82." In Dodge and Wiebe (1985).

Biellik, Robin J. and Peggy L. Henderson. 1981. "Mortality, Nutritional Status and Diet during the Famine in Karamoja, Uganda, 1980." *Lancet, 11* (12 December).

Cook, R. 1967. "The Health of Children in Ankole: The Ankole Pre-School Protection Programme, 1964-67." Makerere University, Department of Paediatrics, mimeographed.

Dean, V. L. B. 1985. "Social Change and Lugbara Subsistence Agriculture in West Nile District." In Dodge and Wiebe (1985).

Dodge, C. P. and Peggy L. Henderson. 1985. "Recent Health Surveys: Towards and Morbidity and Mortality Baseline." In Dodge and Wiebe (1985).

Dodge, Cole P. and Paul D. Wiebe (eds.). 1985. *Crisis in Uganda: The Breakdown of Health Services.* Oxford: Pergamon.

Grant, James P. 1983. *The State of the World's Children.* Oxford University Press.

Ndugwa, C., D. A. Hillman and E. S. Hillman. 1985. "Child Health Crisis at Mulago and Makerere." In Dodge and Wiebe (1985).

Scheyer, S. and D. Dunlop. 1981. "Health Services and Development in Uganda." *Rural Africana,* No. 11 (Fall).

Uganda, Republic of. 1981. *Background to the Budget 1981.* Ministry of Finance.

Uganda, Republic of. 1982. *Recovery Programme.* Ministry of Planning and Economic Development.

Uganda, Republic of. 1983. *Revised Recovery Programme.* Ministry of Planning and Economic Development.

Uganda, Republic of. 1983. *Uganda 1983 Yearbook.* Ministry of Information and Broadcasting.

Uganda, Republic of. 1984. *Health Facilities and Manpower Report.* Planning Unit, Entebbe.

Williams, E. H. 1985. "The Health Crisis in Uganda as it Affected Kuluva Hospital." In Dodge and Wiebe (1985).

Wood, C. H. 1985. "Voluntary Agencies and Health Services: AMREF in Uganda." In Dodge and Wiebe (1985).

Wotton, K. 1985. "Paediatric Mortality in Mulago Hospital, June 1982 to June 1983." In Dodge and Wiebe (1985).

KASANGATI HEALTH CENTRE: PAST, PRESENT AND FUTURE

J. M. Namboze and E. S. Hillman

Kasangati Health Centre was initiated in 1957 to establish a base for teaching community health to Makerere University medical students and to introduce students to the concept of "community diagnosis". The site chosen was nine miles north of Kampala in a subsistence-farming village area.

The development of the Kasangati Health Centre was steady. In 1958 the colonial Development and Welfare Fund provided a grant to build a small health centre, a house for a health educator and a house for a caretaker and interpreter for medical students while they conducted longitudinal family studies in the community. In 1960 the health centre was expanded to accomplish the following objectives: (1) to develop a defined area for teaching public health and carrying out research, (2) to provide a complete range of health services for the benefit of those living in the defined area and (3) to promote wider interest in health centres as ideal units for rural work in East Africa. At the time the Makerere University Medical School was serving Kenya, Uganda, Tanganyika and Zanzibar.

With the help of Rockefeller Foundation support between 1962 and 1966, the Kasangati Centre was expanded in terms of personnel, services, facilities and buildings. By 1967 the centre's staff included twenty-three persons in promotive, preventive and curative work, including a director, medical officer, health visitor, health educator, demographic scout, midwives and laboratory and other assistants (see Namboze, 1968).

An initial requirement of a teaching health centre is to have a defined area with a population of known size and composition. Six nearby villages were surveyed in 1961 by medical students in a house-to-house mapping and census procedure, with the assistance of *muluka* chiefs and village headmen. The small area so identified soon became overexposed to medical students conducting survey research, however, and considerable resistance to further research along such lines was encountered. As a result, the defined area of the health centre was extended in the middle 1960s to include twenty-nine villages with a total population of about 12,000.

The main features of the Kasangati Health Centre were teaching, service and research. Teaching was the first priority and was carried out in all five years of the medical school course with graded responsibility and interdisciplinary teaching which included anthropology and sociology. With the defined area as their community laboratory, students learned how to deal with common rural health problems in visits to houses, seminars and demonstrations. The teaching provided was of the highest quality and in many ways included techniques far ahead of the times.

The services provided at Kasangati in the 1960s were comprehensive when families came to the centre. Excellent antenatal care was provided; many babies were born in the well-equipped and well-staffed maternity centre; follow-up care was provided through home visits. Immunisation and nutritional monitoring and counselling of the highest order were provided in young child clinics to the 25 percent of the families in the designated area who visited the centre. A "morbidity clinic" was available for the treatment of illnesses, and transportation to hospital was available for those who needed hospitalisation. Every effort was made to provide wide coverage and overcome distance problems. Mobile clinics reached out to those families who did not come to the centre (see Namboze, 1966).

Health education courses were organised for teachers from each of the fifteen schools in the centre's defined area, and health centre staff and students frequently visited these schools to teach about health. Every family in the defined area had a "family folder" in which family members and relationships were identified, and a photograph of the family in front of their house was included. Each folder also contained information about the household's environmental situation and water and food supply.

Two of the springs in the defined area were protected in 1960; by 1966 nineteen springs were protected. Some villagers formed self-help committees during the 1960s with interests in housing improvements and the further introduction of pit latrines. "Community-based health care" was encouraged on all fronts. A study conducted in 1967 revealed that 93.4 percent of the mothers who delivered during the year received antenatal care from medical institutions within or without the defined area, and that 79.2 percent of Kasangati mothers delivered in medically staffed institutions. In the rest of the country at the time only about 32 percent of deliveries were taking place in hospitals or clinics (Namboze, 1967).

In reference to the research emphasis at Kasangati, probably no community has been so extensively studied. The studies were well done, very detailed and widely published.

DECLINE AND REHABILITATION

Good and well-established as were the Kasangati Health Centre programmes during the 1960s, they deteriorated badly during the 1970s and early 1980s. A suitable water supply could not be developed, given shortages in funding. Gradually the externally funded vehicles started to break down, and parts and gasoline became too scarce or too expensive to purchase. Drugs were soon in irregular supply at best. Vaccines were wasted as the electricity supply became unpredictable. Buildings deteriorated and could not be reconditioned. Student visiting, teaching and other centre programmes had to be cut back because of lack of funds and, increasingly, especially towards the end of the period under question, continuing problems of insecurity and violence.

Various international visitors came to see the plight of the once famous health centre in the years after the 1978-79 war, some at very odd times and at very short notice. Most of them left, never to be heard from again.

The only people who proved to be serious in their interests in helping the Kasangati Centre back onto its feet were the Minnesota International Health Volunteers (MIHV) of the United States. MIHV sent a feasibility study team to visit the centre in 1983 at the request of the co-directors of the CHAMP (the Canadian Child Health and Medical Education Programme), and shortly thereafter decided to become involved in its work. The first MIHV team—consisting of a paediatrician, an internist, a nurse and a maintenance engineer—arrived in late 1983. Since then, except for during the period of exceptional insecurity towards the end of 1985 and through January 1986, MIHV has supplied volunteers regularly. And during the period it has been in the field, with the help of funding from UNICEF and labour provided from Makerere University, a number of Kasangati's old programmes and many of its buildings have been rehabilitated.

In May 1984 a field survey was conducted in the area of the Kasangati Centre. The results revealed a total population of approximately 15,000 people, with 22.4 percent of them children under the age of five as the target for immunisation. The survey also revealed an infant mortality rate of 93.17 per 1000 live births. Unpublished reports from 1964 showed an IMR at about the same level (90.1). During the intervening years, with health centre involvement in the area, the IMR had dropped dramatically (see Table 1).

DISCUSSION

Immunisation rates in the Kasangati area in 1965, after intensive input, fell far short of the expected goal of 80 percent of the children under five years of age started on their programmes of immunisation. In actual fact 58.8 percent had *not* been given full immunisation in 1965. And thereafter the rates began to fall.

A survey done by A. Kekitinwa in 1984, when the National Immunisation Programme had been re-instituted, showed a rise from 1.16 percent to 34.6 percent of children under five fully immunised after a year of intensive work: a remarkable rise, to be sure, but still a long way from the 80 percent

Table 1.
Trend of Infant Mortality Rate at Kasangati Health Centre

Year	IMR/1000 live births
1964	90.1
1967	42.2
1968	30.4
1969	24.9
1970	27.2
1971	33.5
1984	97.17

coverage to be achieved by the year 2000 according to country plans.

Why did the efforts of the 1960s fall short? Why do efforts continue to fall short? How can health programmes less likely to be undermined in the withdrawal of professionals, experts and outsiders be established? Surely we must recognise by now that superimposed "top-down" programmes will not work and that "health education" is not "health learning". The pioneers of the 1960s—Josephine Namboze, John Bennett and others—accomplished much. But it did not last. Will the year 2000 see another decline from the efforts of the 1980s?

A programme of preventive care must be community based, seen as a priority by the community and organised by community members themselves if it is to be maintained. Until each takes responsibility for the health of its own members, all efforts will fall short and bursts of enthusiasm will generate little upward trends but no long-term achievement. Perhaps now, under President Yoweri Museveni, we will see this develop, as local committees will be the basis of his decentralised administration.

Consciousness for development can be modest in dimension, slow in pace, moderate in success and without any significant external flow of funds, yet heroic in relation to the odds being faced. Such a programme is planned at Kasangati where the aim is to move people by the cumulative momentum of their social conscientiousness, pooled energy and village-organised activity through constructive, educational and cultural channels relevant to resolving the issues that come up daily as recognised priority issues—security, water, school fees and, somewhere down the line, health.

In the Kasangati area, in the reasons given for parents not attending the clinics in the 1960s and again in the 1980s, the same themes are repeated—"too far to walk", "child ill", "mother ill or pregnant", "card lost", "did not know about need for immunisation" and, sometimes, "don't approve of immunisation". Important though such reasons may be, they are not the most important reasons. Why then do we hear them round the world? We have not convinced mothers or community leaders of the importance of attending clinics; we have not selected the right incentives; our advertising techniques are wrong; we have rushed too quickly over traditional beliefs. In the 1960s there was considerable community participation: now there must be deeper and meaningful community involvement as well.

The time has come to take new and more positive approaches to programme designs which contain methods of measuring outcomes in behaviour. We found (Namboze, et al., 1984) that 50 percent more children were immunised in 1984 than in 1983. But we have continued to neglect the assessment of community knowledge and attitudes about the prevention of disease and the need for sanitation and clean water. We have not studied actual community practices in reference to immunisation, nutrition, growth monitoring and personal hygiene. The imposition of an outsider's standards and practices will not work. Going to the market on a certain day will remain more important than going to the clinic, unless we change our approach.

The future beyond the present crisis in Uganda will be bright if the urge to accomplish goals determined and achieved by the community is present. There is enough food and there is now water. And there is less dependency on vehicles, drugs, buildings and outsiders than there once was. The changes necessary will take a generation or two of advocacy for women and children, and other vulnerable groups. They will take intersectoral cooperation in health, agriculture, education and local planning. They will require curriculum changes in primary and secondary schools, in training centres and in Makerere, and they will require practical, goal-directed education for those not in school, particularly women, in the new child survival strategies that have been shown to be effective.

Hakon Torjeson, president of the MIHV group, in a report to his Board of Directors in July 1985, emphasised the progress made in child survival in the Kasangati area in 1984. The most obvious change was in measles mortality and morbidity with the number of cases of measles at the centre declining from 50 per month in early 1984 to 5 per month in 1985. Of concern to him was the overwhelming impression shared by all of us that the percentage of families making meaningful use of the centre was only about 20-25 percent. Bennett in the 1960s stated that less than 50 percent of homes were reached even then. Even though there was an improvement attributed to the extensive home visiting programme of 1985 over 1984, the concept of active intervention in the health of one's own children does not yet seem to be a realistic option for most families, especially among the poorest who are, of course, the least well educated. We are encouraged that the intensive home visiting programme of 1985, focusing on the need for immunisation, encouraged five of ten village health committees to express a serious interest in establishing community-based programmes in their villages. If this degree of decentralisation can be accomplished in the next few years (it won't occur overnight) the crisis in Uganda of recent years will turn into a success story.

Given the long agony and chaos of Uganda and the worsened security situation after the military coup at the end of July 1985, the dedication, morale and team spirit at Kasangati has remained remarkably good. Looting was a problem. Shooting, as elsewhere in Uganda, was a daily terrifying experience. The Kasangati staff spent more than one evening in the dark, hands linked, praying for peace. When the overseas volunteers were advised to withdraw, work continued at Kasangati as it did at Makerere University. Now, under the new regime, the American volunteers have returned, and under the new government of the National Resistance Movement there will be new skills and enthusiasm in motivation of the community-based committees and the empowerment of the people themselves towards health.

One of the early objectives in the Kasangati project was to help Makerere University develop a reproducible model teaching clinic in primary health care for undergraduate and postgraduate students at Makerere University, and for other cadres concerned with primary health needs in Uganda. Another objective was to help the university develop faculty, curricula and a research base in the field of primary health, particularly in community-based health-care strategies.

In the Kasangati success story of the 1984-85 period, incidental benefits have included deep and lasting friendships between the North American volunteers and their Ugandan counterparts, shared skills in creative leadership, role modeling in the hard work and "let's get our hands dirty together" necessary to restore and repair a functioning health facility, a meaningful learning experience for Ugandans and for Americans and the strength that can come from the shared agony and fear of war and violence. "We cannot let this happen again," has become a strong and motivating understanding. New linkages have developed between postgraduate and undergraduate training programmes at Makerere.

The proposal for Kasangati in the second half of the 1980s is to develop the centre as a *community health unit* whose achievements are recognised and utilised by the Ministry of Health. It will be supported by both the Institute of Public Health and the Social Paediatric Unit of the Department of Paediatrics and Child Health at Makerere. Although service will come before teaching and research, one objective of this unit will be to conduct epidemiological studies and health services "operational" research in infectious diseases in order to train students in the skills necessary to carry out such studies and provide the Ministry of Health with health and management information required for evaluation and monitoring. Staff for this unit will be trained in the unit and in the communities served by the health centre through both classroom and practical field exercises for all cadres of trainees, just as in the "old days". But with our newer knowledge this will not be the prime purpose in Kasangati. Health by the people will be more important, and health education—or health learning—will be improved to better motivate village populations around Kasangati to participate in primary health care activities and to accept the responsibility for improving their own health situations. Community development aims at freeing people through educating them to an awareness of their own potential. This cannot be done by others. It can only come about when people have the possibility of organising themselves to ensure their voluntary participation in making, adjusting and controlling decisions at the local level.

Emphasis in the Kasangati area as elsewhere in Uganda now should be on the *training* of traditional birth attendants, village health workers, mid-level managers and health workers in a position to teach others, by the Ministry of Health in collaboration with the African Medical Research Foundation (AMREF), UNICEF and other donors.

A health learning unit based at Kasangati can be developed to strengthen the educational support of primary health care activities in the area through the following:

— Short-term training for health education technicians in mid-level management and supervision of maternal and child health and development activities.

— Short-term training for health visitors and health inspectors in basic audio-visual methodology including the training of a video film technician to develop locally produced video films on immunisation, nutrition, female education, control of diarrhoeal disease, etc.

— Provision of equipment and supplies to support this unit—for example, a duplicating machine, overhead projector, video camera and film, primary health care manuals (such as those published by AMREF and UNICEF Uganda for the Ministry of Health, as well as *Where There is no Doctor* and *Teaching Health Workers to Teach*). The services of a graphic artist should be made available to the centre. A vehicle for the exclusive use of the health education part of centre programmes should also be made available.

The existing laboratory can be updated to establish laboratory tests to support immunisation, control of diarrhoeal disease, family planning and other primary health care activities. A microcomputer and solar calculators for the centre's staff and training in the use of these as well as in information collection and analysis will be required.

We need to find support for a monthly newsletter aimed at and developed by the members of the community-based primary health care system themselves, with help from UNICEF and Kasangati staff.

What explains the persistent lack of motivation and the sometimes intransigent attitudes of village people? Andreas Fuglesang, in "The Myth of People's Ignorance" (1984), says the answer is the ineffectiveness of the educational programme itself, the irrelevance of its professional message, the falsity of its staff and the incompetence of its management. Cynics cry that health and nutrition education do not work. The fact is that such education has never actually been tried. At Kasangati we are given a highly motivated staff and a "model" and accessible community as a clean slate on which to write a plan for the future.

Many still say the poverty of the developing world is due to ignorance. This twisted truth allows the new middle-class in the third world to direct social energies into charitable activities. The conclusion is that poverty can be solved by education, and suddenly a plethora of educational projects are developed such as adult literacy, nutrition or sewing classes which, from a government point of view, are conveniently visible, even conspicuous and harmless. But such projects obscure the deeper causes of poverty. Really needed are an equitable distribution of resources and structural changes which allow more widespread participation in all activities that concern the people. Only in this way will health by and for the people, and other such developments, be achieved.

Ensuring good social relations is as important as producing food. Too often the long time needed to ensure smooth community action is misconstrued by outsiders as laziness on the part of community members. We should have learned our lessons by now. Perhaps we have.

We need to recognise that fundamental failures in communication are the consequences of a lack of trust. It takes social intelligence to realise that knowledge is the result of a process in which all sectors of society have a stake. This understanding offers us a specific opportunity to develop a community base for development which is valid: knowledge must be communicated through trust. People who trust each other communicate well and develop a sense of mutual well-being. It is difficult and time consuming to build trust, but it is possible. Social transformations do not work well when one group or another thinks it knows best.

We can utilise such principles of community development at Kasangati. The efforts at Kasangati have not failed. They were prematurely tried with considerable success in the 1960s and the opportunity is there now to carry the newer knowledge of community-based primary health care through to outstanding and reproducible success in Uganda and other African countries.

Even though the community health worker and other provisions for primary health care at the village level—such as mobile clinics, mass immunisation, home visiting, antenatal and young child clinics—can all contribute greatly to health, they are not enough by themselves. Such resources bring new concepts into a peasant society and may influence some families to change behaviour, but their impact on traditional practices and attitudes is minimal. The important lesson to be emphasised is that all interventions need to be *with* the people, and *by* the people, to succeed. There is no other way.

Proposed strategies to develop and sustain community participation in the Kasangati area currently include:

— The provision of mass media recognition of community efforts;

— Rewards for community members who remain committed to improving their community, even if only through media recognition or letter;

— Encouragements to staff to *stay* with the communities they serve in order to ensure better results in community participation;

— The arrangement of visits by community members to other communities to share experiences;

— The matching of resources raised by a community (and hence the encouragement of local fund-raising);

— The further development of Kasangati's reputation for community celebrations with noted guests and dancers, good food and recreation;

— The acquisition of the resources required for community participation. When people get together, money is often needed for the support of group activities or because money is not earned while members work for the community. The reluctance of community members to participate may be due to their anticipation of what their participation will cost them, while they are still unsure of benefits. In a marginal economy this is a difficult problem and innovative solutions must be sought by community leaders.

In the future Kasangati will serve again as a visible functioning Ugandan model of community-based health care involving a community, various non-governmental organisations, a university and the government.

REFERENCES

Bennett, F. J., G. A. Saxton, J. S. W. Lutwama and J. M. Namboze. 1964. "The Use of a Rural Community in the Curriculum of a Medical School in a Developing Region (East Africa)." Unpublished manuscript.

Fuglesang, Andreas. 1984. "The Myth of People's Ignorance: Development and Dialogue." Uppsala: Dag Hammarskjold Foundation.

Namboze, J. M. 1966. "Mobile Clinics at Kasangati Health Centre Defined Area." *Journal of Pediatrics and African Child Health Monthly*, 12, No. 2.

Namboze, J. M. 1967. "A Study of Births and Deaths in the Defined Area of Kasangati Health Centre in the Year 1967." *Journal of Tropical Pediatrics*, 15, No. 3.

Namboze, J. M. 1968. "Maternal and Child Health Services at Kasangati Health Centre, 1965-67." *Preventive Medicine*, publication No. 5.

Namboze, J. M. 1974. "The Trend of Births and Deaths in the Defined Area of Kasangati Health Centre." Included in the proceedings of the Scientific Conference of the East African Medical Research Council, "The Child in the African Environment: Growth, Development and Survival." Nairobi: East African Literature Bureau.

Namboze, J. M., B. K. Asaba, R. B. Biritwum, J. F. Mafagiri, N. Nickerson and F. S. Ngabirano. 1984. "Community Health Survey of Kasangati Health Centre." Mimeographed.

UGANDAN ECONOMIC CRISIS: DIMENSIONS AND CURE

Vali Jamal

INTRODUCTION

Although crisis has by now become a commonplace term to describe the economic condition of most sub-Saharan African countries, it would be true to say that perhaps no other African country has experienced as wide a range of misfortunes as Uganda. As in other African countries there were the negative impacts of the recession in the West, two oil-price shocks and the ravages of inclement weather. But unique to itself, Uganda had to adjust to the break-up of the East African Community, to a war with Tanzania—and to General Idi Amin Dada as the supreme economic planner and political overlord. During a regime of singular economic mismanagement and repression he reduced a once prosperous and promising country to one of the poorest in the world.

Amin's singlemost important foray into the economic field and one which set off the decline was his self-proclaimed War of Economic Independence against the Asian community in 1972. The consequent and almost predictable collapse of the modern sector that the Asians controlled, spread, through the collapse of the infrastructure, to the export sector, bringing ruin to all other sectors. Although in general the chain of events leading to the collapse has been known, nothing specific has been documented about its extent or its impact on living standards and economic relationships in Uganda. The objective of this paper is to fill these lacunae. We shall also examine the policies adopted by the government in the first half of the 1980s to revive the economy. Although at many places gaps in the statistics have to be filled with our own estimates, it is considered that these are of the right order of magnitude and afford us a rare glimpse into the workings of a troubled economy.

THE "LOST DECADE"

Figures of GDP give us a preliminary picture of the major trends in the economy in the last decade compared to the 1960s. These figures are shown

*Editors' note: This paper is based on data collected in Uganda in February 1985 during an FAO/WCARRD mission. The use of the present tense should be seen in that light. The author wishes to thank Dharam Ghai, Samir Radwan, Ajit Ghose and Hamid Tabatabai for helpful comments on an earlier draft.

in Table 1. Between 1970 and 1980 aggregate monetary GDP fell by 25 percent, implying a decline of around 42 percent in per capita terms. Practically all the economic sectors registered declines, except for "government" whose aggregate output more than doubled. Per capita monetary agricultural GDP fell by 45 percent,[1] whereas "others" GDP fell by 55 percent. The latter group comprises the sectors generally subsumed under the rubric "modern sector". Thus we get a clear indication of the great decline in that sector. Moreover, in deriving the per capita figures, we have for simplicity divided aggregate figures by total population; had we divided by the number of operatives in the modern sector as we strictly should, we should find even a bigger fall in the average income because of the massive "informalisation" of the modern sector following the Asian exodus. For the moment the relevant fact to note is that modern sector output fell by 42 percent, and that this was shared by a greatly expanded class of operators.

The debacle in the 1970s was in sharp contrast to the performance in the 1960s and to some extent since 1980. Between 1963 and 1970, with high

Table 1.
GDP Performance, Aggregate and Per Capita, 1966-83, Selected Years (aggregate in million shillings at 1966 prices; per capita with 1970 = 100)

	1966	1970	1980	1983
Aggregate (Shs. m., 1966 prices)				
Monetary GDP	4,248	5,077	3,822	4,440
Agriculture related[a]	1,628	1,957	1,377	1,710
Government	371	413	882	909
Others[b]	2,249	2,707	1,563	1,821
Subsistence GDP[c]	1,871	2,149	2,293	2,935
Per capita (1970 = 100)				
Monetary GDP	95.1	100	58.3	62.5
Agriculture related	94.6	100	54.5	62.4
Government	102.2	100	165.6	157.1
Others	94.5	100	44.8	48.1
Subsistence GDP	99.0	100	83.0	97.5

*Source: Uganda, *Background to the Budget, 1984-85* and earlier years.

[a] Agriculture (in most years 85-90 percent of total); crop processing; and forestry, fishing and hunting.

[b] Mining and quarrying; manufacturing; electricity; construction; commerce; transport and communications; and miscellaneous services.

[c] Agriculture (in most years 75-80 percent of total); forestry, fishing and hunting; construction; and owner-occupied dwellings.

---

1 This is quite likely an underestimate. In aggregate terms monetary agricultural GDP is shown to have fallen by 30 percent. In the meantime exports declined by 62 percent. Since exports formed the major part of agricultural monetary GDP (and in any case the quantum of food sales did not increase much), it is difficult to see how only a 30 percent decline in agricultural GDP is obtained.

savings and investment rates (13% of GDP), a yearly growth rate of 4.8 percent was achieved in GDP, with the monetary economy leading with 5.2 percent. Inflation was kept to a minimum, government revenue exceeded expenditure, and a positive current account balance was achieved in most years.

All these growth rates turned negative in the 1970s. Monetary GDP declined at 3 percent per annum; subsistence GDP—meaning mostly food produced and consumed by farm families—held up somewhat and helped to moderate the fall in total GDP. Investment and savings ratios fell to 50-60 percent of their previous levels. Exports and imports declined to two-fifths of their peak values. Cotton exports were particularly hard hit, falling in 1980 to only 15 percent of their 1970 value; coffee exports suffered less, but still ended up at only 36 percent of their 1969 peak value. Industrial production fell by a staggering 90 percent. "Economic collapse" would certainly be an apt term for the catastrophe that hit Uganda in the 1970s.

FOOD PRODUCTION AND CONSUMPTION

In contrast to the gloomy trends in the modern sector and in export crops, it is comforting to report that food production did not decline during the "lost decade". This assessment is based on national statistics of food production, combined with various other pieces of evidence, not least of them the author's own perception of the current situation in Uganda compared to pre-1972. The picture that emerges contradicts the picture from FAO statistics, and thus the argument about the statistics needs to be spelt out in detail.

According to the FAO, per capita food supplies fell by 17 percent between 1972-74 and 1980-82, from 2141 calories per capita per day to 1781 calories. The alleged fall was all the more serious as it came from a level of less than self-sufficiency—from 92 percent of requirement (said to be 2330 calories per capita)—to 76 percent.

FAO's estimates are supposedly based on production figures provided by national authorities. These are converted through a technique known as a "food balance sheet" (FBS) to food available in terms of kg. per capita and then calories per capita. To arrive at the former, coefficients are applied to production statistics for amount used for seed and feed, and amount wasted. Adjustments are made for stock changes and net imports. The quantity figures are then converted to calories, based on the usually available tables of calorie values. There are disputes about all the conversion coefficients, and of course there are grounds for doubting even the "raw" figures on which such estimates are based—i.e., the national production data. Thus one would be amply justified to treat most FBS estimates with a fair degree of skepticism. However, the thrust of our criticism of FAO's Uganda FBS is not that the coefficients used are wrong, but rather that FAO's initial figures of output are at variance with the national figures. The differences are particularly marked for cassava, sweet potatoes and plantains—i.e., for the group of starchy foods known collectively as "roots and tubers"—and somewhat less markedly for maize. The roots and tubers group together provides 40-50 percent of total calories in Uganda, so that any discrepancy in its accounting has a perceptible effect on total calorie figures. The following tabulation shows the differences between FAO's production figures and the national figures (in '000 Mt).[2] Both sets of figures relate to 1980-82. For all three crops FAO's estimates are below 60 percent of the national estimates.

	FAO	National
Cassava	1,583	2,733
Sweet potatoes	730	1,333
Plantains	3,347	5,900

There is one further problem with the FAO estimates. FAO takes Uganda's population in the reference period (1980-82) to be 13.626 million. The 1980 Uganda census showed population to be 12.636 million, which at the inter-censal (1969-80) rate of growth of 2.8 percent per annum would give a population of 12.99 million in 1982.[3] Thus FAO's population estimate was 4.9 percent above the national estimate.

Applying the corrections for the three roots and tubers crops, and for maize, as well as for population, gives 2382 as the figure for calorie availability in 1980-82 (see Table 2). This would make Uganda self-sufficient in food compared to the requirement of 2330 calories.[4] For 1983 a rough food balance sheet using national production figures and FAO coefficients indicates calorie availability at 2754—i.e., 18 percent above FAO norms or 33 percent above Uganda norms.

While it would be wrong to overload the data in view of the known weaknesses of Uganda's statistical base in recent years (a concomittant outcome of the general breakdown of the infrastructure), we do go along with these figures rather than the FAO figures for several reasons. Firstly, FAO has no independent basis for arriving at production figures. It generally uses national figures and only an oversight accounts for the lapse in this case. Secondly, the figures for food imports do not confirm a large and growing deficit. In 1982 Uganda imported 5 kg. of cereals per capita compared to 3.4 kg. in 1974.[5] Thirdly, the FAO figures are inconsistent with known diet patterns in Uganda. If true, they would imply either a very calorie-deficient diet for the plaintain-eating tribes or a very cereal-oriented diet, neither of which is borne out by informed opinion. Indeed the final reason for rejecting FAO's figures is that they just do not conform to one's perception of the

---

2 Source: FAO from food balance sheet computer print-outs; national from Uganda (1984, Table 20: 66).
3 A curiosity should be pointed out. In the Uganda document, *Background to the Budget, 1984-85* (1984, Table 34: 80-81), the projected figure for the 1981 population is given as 13.144 million from the 1980 census figure of 12.636 million. This implies a rate of growth of 4 percent, whereas the inter- censal rate was 2.8 percent. For the subsequent years the 2.8 percent rate is applied (on the *incorrect* 1981 figure). The reason for the different procedure in 1981 is unknown but is quite evidently an error.
4 This last figure, it is worth pointing out, is itself disputed. It is generally based on various factors such as age and sex distributions of the population, activity levels and weights, and climate. John H. Cleave (1968), working with national demographic statistics and estimated activity levels, arrived at 2056 as his estimate of calorie requirements for Uganda. This would make Uganda quite comfortably self-sufficient in 1980-82.
5 Source: IBRD: *World Development Report, 1984*, Table 6: total cereal imports divided by total population. In Kenya and Tanzania the figures in 1982 were 10.7 and 18.2 kg. per capita, respectively.

present day food situation in Uganda or trends in the last decade.[6] By and large most farm families remained as self-sufficient in food as before and might even have intensified their food cultivation, devoting some of the labour freed from export crops to food crops.

The optimistic scenario we obtain is meant to be optimistic in contrast to FAO figures, as well as to any simplistic inference from accounts of "economic collapse". The collapse was confined to the monetary sector; the subsistence sector remained immune from economic and political upheavals, which of course explains its basic strength in most African countries. However, in documenting this contrast we should not go overboard and lose sight of the facts that the surplus is only of the order of 20-33 percent, which could easily be wiped out under adverse weather conditions; that there are regions where food is in chronic short supply and famine is never far away; and finally that even within the food-surplus regions, unequal access to productive assets means that a significant proportion of farmers still fail to meet their food needs.

Table 2.
Food Supplies based on National Production Figures, 1980-82 and 1983: Calories Per Capita Per Day from Selected Foods[a]

	1980-82	1983
Cereals	**615**	**750**
Maize	221	260
Millet	217	250
Sorghum	156	210
Roots and Tubers	**1,139**	**1,376**
Cassava	390	531
Sweet potatoes	175	213
Plantains	550	612
Others (based on FAO)	**628**	**628**
Pulses	201	201
Meat, fish, eggs, milk	132	132
Total	**2,382**	**2,754**

*Source: Cereals and roots and tubers based on national production figures as reported in Uganda, *Background to the Budget, 1984-85*, Table 20: 66. FAO's coefficients for seed, feed and waste and calories are applied to convert to net food available. Figures for "others" in 1980-82 are from FAO, computer print-out, corrected for population error; the same figures are assumed to apply in 1983. Population 1980-82 (1981), 12.99 million; 1983, 13.73 million.

[a] Individual figures may not add to subtotals as only selected foods are shown.

---

[6] Fortunately there is support for this viewpoint in recent missions to Uganda which have specifically looked at the food situation. See, for example, Royal Tropical Institute (1984: 8) and Uganda et al. (1984: 20).

INCOME AND INCOME DISTRIBUTION

In this section we take up in detail the consequences of the collapse of the modern sector for living standards in urban areas. The collapse signifies nothing less than a complete dismantling of economic relationships that existed in Uganda before 1972.

The historical evolution of the Ugandan economy after the introduction of British rule and cotton cultivation resulted in huge inequalities along racial, occupational and geographical lines.[7] The racial element was represented by the Asians, people of Indian descent, who had originally been brought in by the British to build the railway to the coast, but who through sustained immigration came to dominate the economic life of the Protectorate.[8] From this followed the basic division of labour in the country, with the Europeans as rulers, the Asians (and Europeans) as entrepreneurs, and Africans as labourers—farmers and wage earners. After independence there were the first beginnings of a crack in this structure, with the emergence of an African trading class, but still by and large, by the time of the Asian expulsion, Africans were conspicuously absent in large-scale activities in the modern sector.

At this period—the late 1960s—one spoke of wage earners as the "labour aristocracy" in Uganda—of course not in relation to non-African entrepreneurs, but African farmers.[9] Minimum wage had been raised fivefold since 1957, whereas coffee prices even in *current* terms had declined by half and cotton prices by 27 percent. In real terms this amounted to a fourfold increase in wages compared to declines of 40-60 percent for the export crops. Such huge wage increases completely changed the nature of wage employment and the structure of incomes in Uganda. In 1957 the minimum wage would have bought only three-fifths of the food requirements of an average size family in towns, using as the unit of measurement the most basic staple, *matoke* (green bananas) (see Table 3); by 1967 one-half of the minimum wage would have sufficed. In 1957 the average farm income (including subsistence income) was *three times* the minimum wage; ten years later the minimum wage *exceeded* the average farm income by nearly one-fifth.

The turnaround resulted from deliberate government policy, which at the time was geared towards curbing the phenomenon of circulatory migration between rural and urban areas. The belief was that this could only be done by enabling the worker to earn a sufficient wage to support his family in town. The family-based wage remained the norm in wage-fixing from the late 1950s through the first decade of independence. Under its influence the minimum wage was increased sixfold in thirteen years between 1957 and 1970, representing an almost fourfold increase in real terms. The "labour aristocracy" was well ensconsed by the mid-1960s.

Both the "aristocracies" we have been describing were destroyed in the 1970s—the Asian one by one stroke of Amin's pen in 1972 and the labour

---

[7] For the early economic history of Uganda see Cyril Ehrlich (1965), Christopher Wrigley (1957) and Vali Jamal (1976).

[8] A history of the East African Asians may be found in J. Mangat (1969). For their socio-economic profile in the 1960s, see Dharam P. Ghai (1965).

[9] J. B. Knight (1967: 233-64) contains an analysis of wages policy in relation to farm incomes.

somewhat gradually in the few years following. The ultimate outcome for income distribution of the disappearance of the Asian class remains ambiguous; the outcome of the fall of the wage-earning class was devastating.

In expelling the Asians, Amin was of course not motivated by any notions of equality, simply by a dislike of what he considered to be foreign domination of the economy. During the various rounds of distribution that followed, most Asian assets fell into the hands of Amin's army favourites. The bigger industries were handed over to parastatals. Gradually the assets lost their productivity, because of lack of spare parts, foreign exchange and maintenance. Simultaneously the axis of economic power shifted to the *magendo* (or parallel) economy, where also Amin's favourites reigned. The essence of *magendo* was a preferential freeing of the markets, for while price control was generally disregarded, it was enforced where it suited the power brokers: at the ex-factory level but not the retail level, at the farm-gate but not at the market or the borders. Those who had access to factory or farm supplies made fortunes, and these were of course those who had the protection of the government. Thus although all-round incomes fell in Uganda, it would be difficult to say that urban income distribution improved after the expulsion of the rich Asian class.

The outcome for the wage earners was decisive. With the decline in modern sector productivity, a wage structure which supported an independent class could no longer be sustained. Either the labour force had to shrink or wages had to fall. The labour force actually *increased*, from 329,800 in 1972 to 367,600 in 1977 (1977 is the last year for which wage data are available), so that adjustment had to come through a fall in real wage and the mechanism for this was inflation. Table 3 shows the rise and fall of the wage earning class. The figures are so fantastic—minimum wage down to 10-15 percent of its 1972 value in the 1980s—that one is bound to wonder whether there is not an error here somewhere—perhaps all those zeros in the inflation?[10] Well, inflation was a hard fact of life in Uganda after the mid-1970s and the arithmetic of deflation does indeed yield the figures in column 3. To clinch the issue, in column 4 we have shown the purchasing power of the minimum wage in terms of the basic staple, *matoke*. In 1972 the minimum wage would have bought 1.67 times an average family's food requirement (reciprocal of column 4); towards the end of 1984 only 22 percent could have been bought. This signifies a fall of the same sort of magnitude (87%) as given by the price index (91%).

The question these figures prompt is how does the urban population cope—or is there massive starvation? Our answer is that the people do cope, although at a much reduced level of living. The first thing that has happened is that people have changed their diets to conform to their incomes. All tribes have had to reduce their consumption of the preferred foods (meat, milk, fruits, etc.) which in the 1960s was absorbing a sizeable and growing propor-

---

10 A note is in order here about the impact of inflation on *our tables*. It may be noticed that in many tables we have dropped the decimal point after the 1970s. This is not only because it would be spurious to retain it in most cases, but for a more down-to-earth reason: where figures are in shillings the decimal implies shillings and cents. With inflation, the cent can buy nothing and has completely gone out of circulation. Even shilling coins are no longer in circulation. In Table 3 we have reproduced an official table; the decimal point is an arithmetic operation.

tion of their income. Even within the category of staple foods there have been switches, particularly to maize-meal, which in relative terms is now a cheaper source of calories than *matoke*. For the non-Baganda tribes this signifies a continuation of past trends; for the Baganda it signifies a major departure in their diet patterns. The important factors behind this switch have been income declines and changes in relative prices. The *matoke*:maizemeal calorie-price ratio reached 3.2 in 1982, after hovering at 1.5 during most of the previous two decades. This was enough to induce a major switch to maizemeal by the Baganda, which was in any case imperative as *matoke* supplies were dwindling.

Table 3.
Minimum Wage in Nominal and Real Terms, 1957-1984, Selected Years

	Minimum wage (Shs./mo.)	Price index (1972 = 100)	Real wage (1972 = 100)	% of min. wage to purchase 9000 calories
1957	33	61.4	29	164
1959	75	62.4	65	
1962	138	67.0	111	
1964	150	70.9	114	
1967	150	75.2	108	49
1970	185	90.2	111	
1972	185	100.0	100	60
1976	240	368.0	35	
1980	400	3,348.0	6	
1981	950	6,068.0	8	
1984 (av)	6,000	22,000.0	15	
1984 (Nov)	6,000	35,000.0	9	450

*Source: Minimum wages up to 1972 from reports of minimum wages advisory boards and Knight (1967: 233-64); after 1972 from information provided by the Ministry of Labour. Price index from Uganda, *Statistical Abstract*, and idem, *Background to the Budget*, various years. Figures in the last column derived from *matoke* price data.

These substitutions would still leave a big gap between family needs and income. How then do such families survive? The answer is found in two major changes which occurred in the urban sector. One of these relates to the process of "stabilisation" that had occurred in the 1960s and the other to a break-up of the wage-earning class. "Stabilisation"—i.e., the sedentarisation of the labour force—was not only halted but put into reverse after the mid-1970s. Trips back to the family farm (*shamba*) became common and some members of the family were actually permanently sent back to tend such farms. More significantly, urban families began to grow their own food, something that had always happened, but was on the decline because of increasing "specialisation" and influx of migrants who did not own land near Kampala. With the departure of these migrants Kampala became more a Baganda city than it ever was—and with the cultivation of food crops, a more rural city.

Before 1972 most urban budget surveys showed that Kampala was 20 percent self-sufficient in calories; in the 1980s that figure quite likely doubled.

The second structural change that took place concerns the break-up of the wage-earning class. With the wage down to 10-15 percent of its value, a person also effectively worked that much less. Some of his free time he devoted to organising side activities and this meant "business", the buying and selling of small items of consumer goods. More significantly, the wage earners' family members took to this kind of trading, the opportunities for which increased because of the gap left by the Asians. Compared to pre-1972 one is struck by the visible increase in street-trading. Of course something like that has happened in most African cities, but in Uganda the reasons were different, for the fact is that unlike other African countries migration actually slowed down or even changed direction,[11] and yet the informal sector grew. What happened was that a great part of the trade previously in the hands of the Asians was shared by an increasing number of petty traders. Thus we have the phenomenon of the expansion of the informal sector without migration.

The culmination of these two changes was that after the mid-1970s the distinct classes that had existed in urban Uganda in the 1960s coalesced into a grand trader-cum-wage earner-cum *shamba* growing class. How did its real income compare to the 1960s? The following table sets out the orders of magnitude involved (Table 4). The first part shows the known income position of urban families in terms of wages and an estimate of own *shamba* food. This is compared to the cost of a typical food budget and to the 1967 average wage income valued at 1985 prices. These are the "targets". The shortfall has to be made good from trade income. The shortfall to attain the food budget is Shs. 20,070—effectively equivalent to profits from the sale of just eight bottles of soda per day. This should be well within the reach of most urban groups.

The attainment of the 1967 average wage levels presumes a great deal more income from trade. We had shown in Table 1 that modern sector GDP fell by around one-half in per capita terms in the 1970s. Taking this as a rough proxy for the drop in urban trade income would yield a figure of Shs. 95,000 as the income from trade in 1985. Thus the total income for the urban household may be estimated at Shs. 113,000. This would imply a decline of 30 percent in average urban incomes. Calorie intake would be maintained quite comfortably, albeit with a reduction in preferred-foods calories, but nonfood consumption would be down by three-fifths. This sort of decline, although smaller than indicated by wage figures, is not to be scoffed at. Moreover, from the point of view of the economy the estimate actually *understates* the decline in total urban incomes because we have been dealing with African incomes only. A large chunk of urban income earned by the Asians— not to mention the physical structures that went with it—was lost forever.

---

11 The growth rates (percentage per annum) of the four largest towns between 1969 and 1980 were as follows: Kampala, 3.2; Jinja, -0.7; Mbale 1.7; Tororo, 0.5. Compared to this, the overall population growth rate was 2.8 percent. Now up to 1972 the towns were growing at 5-6 percent per annum. Thus between 1973 and 1980, all towns (including Kampala) registered lower growth rates than the natural population increase, implying reverse migration. Source: Uganda: *Background to the Budget, 1982-83*, Table 1.26: 50.

Table 4.
Illustrative Figures on Urban Living Standards, c. 1985 (shillings per month)

Income		
Wage	8,000	(1.33 wage earners per family)
Own food	10,000	(40% cals. from own *shamba*)
	Target	**Shortfall**
Food budget	38,070	20,070
1967 average wage earner household	150,000	132,000

*Source: Illustrative figures. Figure against food budget shows the cost of an assumed food basket in which 60 percent of calories come from *matoke* and 10 percent each from maizemeal, groundnuts, sugar and "others". 1967 average wage is converted to 1985 terms.

PRICING POLICY

Given the massive structural shifts in the economy, pricing policy for agricultural export crops is at the heart of macro-economic management in Uganda. Table 5 shows in a succinct form the trends in crop prices between 1972 and 1980. By 1980 the structure of prices was in complete disarray. Food crop prices had increased 20-25 times, whereas export crop prices had increased less than sixfold. In real terms, food crops prices were at 64 (*matoke*) to 150 (maize) percent of their 1972 values whereas export prices were at 20 percent.

Table 5.
Crop Prices in Nominal and Real Terms, 1972 and 1980

	1972	1980	1980:1972	1980 in 1972 terms	1980:1972 real terms
	—Shs/kg—				
Prices					
Coffee	1.19	7.00	5.9	0.21	0.18
Cotton	1.25	6.00	4.8	0.18	0.14
Matoke	0.17	3.00	21.4	0.09	0.53
Maize	0.60	20.00	33.3	0.60	1.00
Returns ratios					
Matoke: coffee	0.9	3.8			
Maize: cotton	0.6	5.7			

*Source: Uganda, *Background to the Budget,* various years, for coffee and cotton prices; *matoke* and maize prices based on data provided by Ministry of Agriculture.

The deterioration in farm prices may be brought out even more dramatically by comparing the movement in farmers' terms of trade with external terms of trade. Concretising in terms of soap, in 1972 the farmer could purchase around 7 kg. of soap with 100 kg. of his produce (a rough average for both cotton and coffee since prices were similar); in 1980 he could purchase only 1 kg.—a fall of 86 percent. On the external market the country could buy 18 kg. of soap in 1972, and in 1980, with an improvement in external terms of trade, 20 percent more. Thus if we take 1972 as the base year, we can visualise the exchange accounts as follows in terms of kg. of soap consumption per 100 kg. of exports:

	Farmer buys	Country buys	Basis
1972	7	18	Farmer gets 39 percent of export proceeds.
1980	1	21.6	Country's terms of trade up 20 percent; farmer's terms down 86 percent.

In 1972 the farmer was being taxed at 40 percent of his potential income. This was through the "normal" mechanism of the export tax and contributions to a price stabilisation fund, which had operated in the colonial as well as post-independence periods, and the rate was also about "normal". Up to this time inflation was also proceeding at a "normal" pace (5.9% per annum between 1967 and 1972). So we may take 1972 as a base year in terms of neutral "exchange-rate taxation". By the time we come to 1980, internal inflation was rampant (*33.5-fold* increase in prices between 1972 and 1980) and the farmer was able to buy only 1 unit of soap at a time when the country was buying 21.6 units. Clearly the farmer was being taxed heavily—at a rate one shudders to calculate (at least 75%, allowing for processing and marketing costs). The mechanism was an "overvalued exchange rate", which we have translated into the difference between what the farmer received for his produce and what the country did.

When the Obote government finally secured some semblance of control over the country, it turned its attention to the economy and quite rightly perceived the problem facing it to be the revival of the export sector. The chosen instrument for this was higher producer prices and the chosen vehicle for articulating this, devaluation. Given the nature of the economy, the huge distortions that had crept into the price structure and the implicit taxation of export income that was going on, these were correct measures at that time. However, we suspend further judgement till we see how things developed.

The story of the devaluation—or rather devaluation*s*—may be quickly told by means of Table 6. Through the various opening, closing and merging of various "windows" (Window I was the managed float, Window II the auction-determined rate), the shilling went from 8 per dollar to 77 to 326 in the course of three years. More was yet to come, for with the merging of the two windows, the dollar was systematically bid up in the weekly auction (by around Shs. 50).[12] By February 1985 — i.e., within eight months of the merging—the dollar had reached Shs. 570 (an increase of 74%), and was still climbing.

Table 6.
Official Exchange Rate, May 1981-February 1985 (Shs. per U.S. $)

	Window I	Window II	
May 1981	8		
June 1981	77		First devaluation
August 1982	100	300	Window II opened
May 1984	292	326	Windows unified in June. Thereafter exchange rate determined through auction.
February 1985	570		

*Source: Bank of Uganda, May 1981 to May 1984, as quoted in Uganda, *Background to the Budget, 1984-85,* Table 8: 55; February 1985 personal information collected by the author.

One of the reasons sometimes advanced for a devaluation is to capture the parallel market in foreign exchange. The Uganda devaluations did not succeed in this. Before the first devaluation the parallel market rate for the dollar was Shs. 80 compared to the official rate of Shs. 8. With the devaluation (to Shs. 77), the parallel rate jumped to Shs. 200 (differential of 159%). When Window II opened (at Shs. 300) it had risen to Shs. 350 (differential of 17%) and by November 1983, with Window II at Shs. 330 it was Shs. 400 (differential of 21%)(see IBRD, 1983, Table 2.1: 29). So the opening of Window II did bring about a narrowing of the differential between the parallel market and the official market, an outcome the proponents of devaluation seized upon to demonstrate the success of devaluation. Well, in February 1985 the Window III rate was twice the auction rate and diverging daily.

The initial devaluation enabled huge price increases for export crops, which was of course its main justification. Prices were increased fivefold, practically restoring the parity between coffee and *matoke* and extensively repairing that between cotton and maize (see Table 7). In real terms prices increased by 2.7-fold, bringing them to around 40 percent of their 1972 levels. The problem of course was that inflation continued and even increased. In the face of this, prices had to be adjusted every year and with the establishment of an Agricultural Secretariat, in 1982, prices were raised to more than compensate for the inflation. In four years producer prices were increased 30 times over, signifying a tripling in real terms. All this happened in the face of declining external terms of trade so that farmers were effectively being given a bigger share of a shrinking fund.

---

[12] At the beginning of 1985 some US$ 3 million were being auctioned each week, equivalent to the bridging loan of the IMF.

Table 7.
Export Crops/Food Crops Parity: Coffee vs *Matoke,* Cotton vs Maize, 1972, 1980, 1981 and 1984 (prices in Shs/kg and ratios)

	Coffee/*matoke*			Cotton/maize			Memo item:
	Coffee (Shs/kg)	*Matoke* (Shs/kg)	Ratio	Cotton (Shs/kg)	Maize (Shs/kg)	Ratio	Min. wage (Shs/mo)
1972	1.19	0.17	7.0	1.25	0.60	2.1	185
1980	7.00	5.50	1.3	6.00	20.00	0.3	400
1981	35	7	5.0	30	25	1.2	950
1984	210	30	7.0	180	65	2.8	6,000
Ratios							
1980:1972	5.9	32.3	-	4.8	33.3	-	2.2
1984:1972	176.5	176.5	-	144.0	108.3	-	32.4
1984:1980	30.0	5.5	-	30.0	3.3	-	15.0

*Source: Uganda, *Background to the Budget,* various years, for coffee and cotton prices; *matoke* and maize prices from data provided by the Ministry of Agriculture.

Obviously what is going on in Uganda is a massive redistribution of income in favour of the farmers. This might be justified by quoting real-price trends and showing that recent price increases merely reversed the redistribution that occurred in the 1960s. That certainly is a perspective worth having, but we also have to have the perspectives of farm incomes in their totality and in relation to incomes of other groups. From these viewpoints the two facts that need to be emphasised are that farm incomes did not fall as drastically as urban incomes, and that farm incomes in real terms are now much higher than most urban incomes. Both of these facts depend on giving a proper valuation to subsistence consumption. When this is done, farm incomes in total fell by less than 30 percent or so,[13] compared to the 30-50 percent fall in urban incomes in their totality, not to mention the 90 percent fall in urban wages. And as for absolute incomes, in 1984, we would have to give the farmers Shs. 456,000 as the imputed value of their subsistence consumption.[14] On top of that, coffee farmers made around Shs. 60,000 from coffee and Shs. 17,000 from food crop sales. Thus their total income would come to Shs. 553,000—over five times the average urban wage and *nearly one-half* of *average* urban incomes—for all intents and purposes average *trading* income. Cotton farmers did not fare as well because of stagnant output,

---

[13] A notional figure based on the fact that cash incomes formed around 30 percent of total farm income (including subsistence production/consumption) in the 1960s. Even if we assume that all of the cash income disappeared, the drop in total income would be only 30 percent.
[14] Food budget A. Quite likely their diets might even be better than that. We have to resort to this method to estimate farm subsistence incomes as GDP accounts do not give current-value figures of subsistence production (as of other components). In any case we might have done this, the underlying argument being that equal baskets of food should carry equal price tags. Thus the operative assumption here is that farmers produce and consume a food basket of the budget A type—i.e., a basic starchy-staple basket. This assumption may not stray too far from reality.

but even their "income" would easily come to 40 percent of urban incomes in real terms.

These figures are obviously not offered as the last word on the subject but merely to show that in a subsistence context price trends of export crops do not tell the whole story about levels of living, or income distribution. Given these perspectives then, the advocacy for higher farm prices loses some of its force. For the fact is that the real-term price increases that have occurred since 1980, despite adverse external trends, imply a redistribution of income in favour of export crops, and such a redistribution is not now self-evidently justified, since at least some of this is occurring at the expense of fixed-income urban groups, such as wage earners and civil servants.

The final reason for questioning the government's pricing policy is that its basic premise—that higher prices are needed to bring forth greater output—is not vindicated by experience. Thus the poor output performance of the 1970s cannot altogether be blamed on low prices, and the experience with high prices in the 1980s has not altogether been satisfactory. Between 1973 and 1975 cotton output fell by 57 percent while prices fell by (only) 28 percent. Even the most ardent proponent of prices would not argue that elasticity was as high as 2. Clearly other factors were at work bringing down the output. At the other end of the period, while cotton and coffee real prices doubled between 1980 and 1982, coffee production increased by a mere 16 percent and cotton by 59 percent, quite a large part of the latter because of a change of stocks as ginning capacity was increased to take care of the backlog of unginned cotton.

Thus it is obvious that factors other than prices have been responsible for the supply response in Uganda. What these are should not be difficult to imagine, given the total breakdown of the economic and political orders in Uganda. From a vast potential list we should single out at least five as of significant importance. Firstly, there is a continuing lack of security in the rural areas, and farmers still live under the threat that their crops might be commandeered by troops or guerrillas. Although this is not a factor in food production because of the subsistence orientation of the farmers, it certainly applies in the case of export crops because of their high value. Secondly, there is a total lack of transport and processing facilities. These in particular explain the poor response in the case of cotton, which is a weight-losing commodity. Thirdly, the most basic farming implement—the *jembe* (hand-hoe)—is not available in the rural areas. Farmers have to make do with hoes that should have been discarded years ago. Fourthly, consumer goods are scarce in rural areas, another reflection of the breakdown of the infrastructure. Finally, farmers are not paid on time for their produce. The last two factors ensure that the price increases do not translate into anything tangible. Lack of consumer goods has kept the farmers in the "subsistence mode", while late payment has broken their remaining confidence in the marketing authorities. Farmers would rather take their *debe* (tin) of maize to the roadside and sell it to the passers-by for instant cash than grow cotton, to be paid in chits.

While high farm prices have failed to elicit a significant supply response, inflation has become an integral part of the economy, an outcome of the exchange-rate regime in operation. Each week the price of foreign exchange is bid up by the traders to secure a very lucrative resource, in anticipation of continuing inflation. With the economy now more than ever dependent on imports, the higher foreign-exchange price translates directly into higher prices for consumer goods: the 5-10 percent *per week* inflation in the exchange rate that Uganda has been experiencing recently is thus a major cause of the 80-100 percent *per annum* general inflation that is its lot.

The country is thus caught in a spiral of devaluation-inflation-high prices-devaluation. While the original devaluation was justified to pay higher prices to farmers, the latter devaluations have become simply part of a vicious circle in which the real sufferers are the fixed-income earners. The prospect of them again becoming full time wage earners or university professors or government officials is continually receding and this cannot but be at the expense of productivity in the economy.

CONCLUSION

The Ugandan economy has undergone massive structural shifts in the last decade. In the rural areas exports declined catastrophically, while in the modern sector wages were continually eroded and wage earners ceased to be a viable and independent economic class. Real incomes fell in all sectors.

Despite such huge upheavals, the country's food situation remained healthy. The reason for this was the basic strength of the subsistence sector. In the urban areas too the food situation remained healthy, despite the massive fall in urban wages and the disruption of supplies. This paradoxical situation has been explained in terms of the informalisation of the modern sector, whereby a greater part of the trade originally in the hands of Asians passed into the hands of Africans. Many of the previous wage earners or their family members were absorbed into this trade sector, which after the mid-1970s provided the dominant part of urban incomes. At the same time the urban groups also turned to subsistence farming, producing some of their food requirement on their own garden plots. Thus, while urban incomes fell quite sharply, the total income available to urban groups from trade and wages and own-farming was sufficient to keep the urban population well above basic food poverty.

Given the dominance of export crops in the economy, its revival now requires an increase in export crop production, and this puts agricultural pricing policy at the core of macro-economic management in Uganda. In the 1970s with the increase in inflation, the basic parities between food crops and export crops were completely disrupted. Government had to intervene in the price field and with Uganda's inflation having gone way out of line with imported inflation, the basic remedy was devaluation—and a massive one. This came in 1981 and prices were raised in real terms. After this the currency was kept on a float and underwent almost continuous devaluation. Farm prices were adjusted periodically to keep pace with the inflation. These subsequent actions are open to question. They place preponderant weight on higher prices as the cure for exports, whereas the poor output response has vindicated the importance of non-price factors in export production. The floating of the shilling has by itself become a source of inflation in Uganda because of the country's new reliance on imported consumer goods. The continuing erosion of urban fixed incomes that this implies is detrimental to the revival of a diversified modern sector.

Thus when we change the perspective from the food situation to the economy as a whole, we cannot but be dismayed by the immensity of the task that remains to be accomplished. Nothing less than the reintroduction of export crops is involved, with its concomitant investments in marketing, processing and transport facilities. And it involves recreating the whole modern sector. No doubt, even without this the Ugandan farmer will continue to grow his own food and the towns may become even more self-sufficient, but the economy will remain two steps backwards.

REFERENCES

Cleave, John H. 1968. "Food Consumption in Uganda." *East African Journal of Rural Development*.

Ehrlich, Cyril. 1965. "The Ugandan Economy, 1903-1945." In Harlow, V. and E. M. Chilvers (eds.), *History of East Africa (Volume II)*. London: Oxford University Press.

Ghai, Dharam P. (ed.). 1965. *Portrait of a Minority: Asians in East Africa*. Nairobi: Oxford University Press.

IBRD. 1983. *Uganda Country Economic Memorandum*. Report No. 4733-UG. December.

Jamal, Vali. 1976. "The Role of Cotton and Coffee in Uganda's Economic Development." Unpublished Ph.D. thesis, Stanford University.

Knight, J. B. 1967. "The Determination of Wages and Salaries in Uganda." *Bulletin of Oxford University Institute of Economics and Statistics*, 29 (No. 3, August).

Mangat, J. S. 1969. *A History of the Asians in East Africa, c. 1886-1945*. London: Oxford University Press.

Royal Tropical Institute. 1984. *Towards a National Food Strategy (Volume I): Main Strategy Report*. Amsterdam.

Uganda, Government of, with FAO/WHO/OAU. 1984. *National Food and Nurtrition Policies and Programmes*. Accra: FAO.

Uganda, Government of. 1984. *Background to the Budget, 1984-85*. Entebbe: Government Printer.

Uganda, Government of. 1982. *Background to the Budget, 1982-83*. Entebbe: Government Printer.

Wrigley, Christopher C. 1957. *Crops and Wealth in Uganda: A Short Agrarian History*. Kampala: East African Institute of Social Research.

THE IMPACT OF THE ECONOMIC CRISIS ON FIXED-INCOME EARNERS

Firimooni R. Banugire

INTRODUCTION: THE ECONOMIC CRISIS

The present economic crisis in Uganda may be characterised as that of increasing absolute poverty and persistent economic stagnation arising out of extended structural economic decline. It is useful here to distinguish between three successive stages of economic decline in an agrarian neo-colonial economy like Uganda's. The *recessionary stage* consists of a general decline in the rate of growth of incomes and expenditures and can usually be associated with one or a combination of the following: a fall in export prices, a fall in demand for agricultural and mineral products, severe supply bottlenecks, crop failures due to droughts, and abnormal dislocations such as political disturbances and wars. The second is the *structural decline stage* wherein persistent recessionary decline and structural dislocations generate substantial changes in the roles of the various production, consumption and trade components of the economy. In particular the leading dynamic sectors and sub-sectors decline in relation to the traditional and informal sectors in both rural and urban areas. Persistent structural deterioration eventually leads to the third stage, that of the *regressive* or *magendo* economy.[1]

The Ugandan economy in recent years has been a *magendo* economy. Practically no Ugandan wage earners have been able to meet more than 10 percent of their "basic needs basket" out of their formal wage incomes. Most Ugandans have been involved in a continuous struggle for survival.

Overall economic decline in Uganda is revealed by the following indicators of long-term economic trends. First, GNP per capita declined by 1.1 percent per annum during the 1970s and early 1980s because of a decline of 1.5 percent per annum in national output (GDP) in the face of a population growth rate of 2.7 percent. Secondly, while the agricultural sector accounted for 40 and 59 percent of monetary and total GDP respectively in 1970, per capita agricultural and food production fell by 2.1 and 1.0 percent per annum respectively between 1970 and 1982. Thirdly, export performance, which con-

---

[1] See Banugire (1985a) where the *magendo* economy is defined as an economy in which the basic needs basket for the majority of the population is several times greater than their formal wage incomes.

stituted the primary engine of economic development over this period, deteriorated in volume terms because of dislocations in production processes and shifts away from non-food cash crops to food crops. Poor export performance in value terms, plus a drastic fall in net capital inflow, generated a steady decline in import values and rising import prices. Rates of inflation averaged 47.4 percent per annum between 1970-82. Inflation and declines in income over this period were aggravated by an absolute decline in industrial output due to the lack of investments and low levels of capacity utilisation (10-20% by 1981).

The structural deterioration that has occurred in Uganda in recent years is amply illustrated by the following shifts in socio-economic structures:

1. The share of non-monetary output in the GDP is estimated to have increased from 32 percent in 1970 to about 40 percent in 1982.[2]
2. The overall share of agriculture in the GDP increased from 52 percent in 1960 to 82 percent in 1982, and the corresponding share of the labour force in agriculture fell only marginally from 98 to 83 percent.
3. While industry and manufacturing accounted for 12 and 9 percent of the GDP respectively in 1960, they accounted for 4 and 4 percent respectively in 1982. The share of the industrial labour force increased only marginally over this period, from 4 to 6 percent, having actually fallen during the 1970s.
4. The share of services in the GDP declined from 36 to 14 percent although the share of the labour force represented here increased slightly from 7 to 11 percent.
5. The rate of growth of the urban population fell from an average of 7.1 percent during the 1960s to an average of 3.4 percent during 1970-82, resulting in a very small rise in the percentage of people living in urban areas (which stood at 9 percent in 1982).
6. Public sector expenditures accounted for 3.2 percent of GNP in 1981, as opposed to 21.8 percent in 1972, and the share of government current revenue in GNP fell from 13.7 percent in 1972 to 0.7 percent in 1981.
7. The shares of gross investment, gross savings and exports in the GDP fell from 11, 16 and 26 percent respectively, to 8, 5 and 5 percent. The traditional positive balance of trade was reversed to persistent deficits standing at -3 percent of GNP in 1982. Indeed, in absolute terms, real consumption, investment and volume of exports declined by 4, 8 and 9.2 percent per annum respectively during the 1970-82 period.

The *magendo* economy stage in Uganda was created by persistent structural changes in the above directions. Declines in the performances of leading sectors of production and export have generated chronic foreign exchange shortages. In Uganda's case these shortages have been further made problematic by a drastic decline in per capita net foreign resource flow, to US$ 12.2 in 1982, as compared with US$ 33.6 for Sub-Saharan Africa, US$ 39.2 for Tanzania and US$ 31.2 for Kenya. Chronic foreign exchange shortages have led to inflation through the continual devaluation and/or depreciation of the dollar value of the Uganda shilling, as well as shortages of imported

---

[2] Official estimates tend to exaggerate the share of subsistence. Grass-roots evidence indicates increasing dependence on market purchases for foodstuffs.

and domestic goods. Chronic shortages and inflation have led to a continuous erosion of the real incomes of the majority of the population, especially fixed-income earners, as illustrated in Table 1.

The following tendencies emerge clearly from the Table 1 estimates of expenditures in the ten low-income and ten middle-income households represented. A "basic needs basket" refers to a wage sufficient to ensure a tolerable standard of living in consideration of the standard enjoyed previously.

1. The basic needs gap for the Low Income Group (LIG) was rising within the 1:20-1:30 range during 1983-84, then accelerated to 1:40 in 1985, and 1:80 in early 1986, in response to accelerated price rises.
2. The basic needs gap for the Middle Income Group (MIG) was significantly less than it was for the LIG in 1983 and 1984, though it showed an upward trend within the range 1:15-1:20. It was slightly reduced in 1985 by the salary increase of 1984, then adjusted back to 1:24 during 1986.
3. There is an increasing tendency towards both poverty and inequality among low and middle income earners, as basic needs gaps widen.
4. The formal income gap between the MIG and the LIG is wider than the corresponding basic needs requirement gap, and the difference has tended to increase with inflation (i.e., from 5.9 to 11.0, as compared to 4.5 to 3.0, in 1983 and 1985 respectively).
5. The dramatic wage increases of 1984 temporarily closed the needs gap, but more so for the MIG than the LIG. However, inflationary adjustments later reversed this improvement, especially for the LIG.
6. Escalation in the cost of living harms the LIG more than the higher income groups.
7. The upward shift in inflation during 1985-86 has significantly reduced the proportion of income to be spent on food by the LIG from about 61 percent (1983-84) to 38 percent (1985-86), given the same basic needs basket. This implies a greater rise in prices of non-food expenditures including essential transport, education and medical expenses. The inability to purchase the basic needs basket affects such expenditures most, thereby creating misery and frustration.

The *magendo* economy in Uganda is sustained through spiral inflation promoted by the stagnation and decline of agricultural production and an ever worsening foreign exchange position. This foreign exchange trap has been aggravated by complete reliance on the IMF exchange rate policy package as the key cure for the *magendo* economy disease. In fact, the strategy of trying to approach the black market exchange rate through the guided depreciation of the "official" or "auction" exchange rate has only served to accelerate capital flight, inflation and disinvestment. It has not promoted foreign exchange earnings through increased agricultural exports. Substantial rises in wages and producer prices have failed to maintain the share of fixed-income earners in national incomes and production, thereby increasing the absolute and relative surpluses of the groups who control the production and marketing of major products.

In conclusion, the economy has continued to regress towards the absolute limits of utter misery and degradation for the majority of Uganda's wage

Table 1.
Estimates of Monthly Household Expenditure and Basic Needs Income Gaps, 1983-86 (Shs. "000")[a]

	Low Income Group				Middle Income Group			
	1983	1984	1985	1986	1983	1984	1985	1986
Food (value)	25.94	39.78	100.50	242.20	63.63	85.30	219.80	582.00
	59%	63%	36%	40%	39%	44%	32%	34%
Non-food (v)	17.71	23.46	177.80	368.74	101.00	110.50	474.41	1,127.40
	41%	37%	64%	60%	61%	56%	68%	66%
Total expenses (v)	43.65	63.24	278.30	610.94	164.63	195.80	694.21	1,709.40
Savings (v)	-	-	-	-	32.93	39.16	138.85	351.85
Total BN income	43.65	63.24	278.30	610.94	197.66	234.96	833.06	2,060.25
Formal income[b]	2.10	2.30	6.90	7.60	12.40	12.70	76.80	84.50
BN gap	1:21	1:28	1:40	1:80	1:16	1:18	1:11	1:24
LIG/MIG I-gap	1	1	1	1	5.9	5.6	11.0	11.0
LIG/MIG BN-gap	1	1	1	1	4.5	3.7	3.0	3.4

*Source: Banugire (1985a, Table 1) and calculations. Estimates for 1986 refer to January prices; estimates for the other years are based on second quarter prices. V = value, BN = basic needs.
[a] The data presented refer to estimates based on interviews with twenty workers.
[b] Gross formal income includes benefits such as housing, medical allowances and transport allowances.

earners, and only a small minority among them have been able to maintain or improve their standards of living. Furthermore, the mechanisms of a *magendo* economy are now so deeply embedded in the country's political, administrative and economic institutions that major institutional surgery will be necessary in order to spur the economy towards recovery and reconstruction. The current crisis is the product of a vicious triangle of poverty, economic exploitation and political repression.

TRENDS IN THE LABOUR MARKETS
Employment Trends

Overall wage employment trends are shown in Table 2 (which is not up to date because statistics are unavailable after 1978). Employment grew rather steadily during the period 1967-73, from 256,799 to 368,635, but thereafter stagnated, being estimated at 371,000 in 1978. Yet the labour force was growing at about 2.12 percent during the 1970s, all of which implies there was a diminishing ratio of wage employment in the labour force over this period.

Before 1973 private sector employment exceeded public sector employment; thereafter, the latter exceeded the former, being estimated at 56.6 percent of total wage employment in 1978. The shift away from the private sector is partly explained by an institutional shift to the public sector. It is largely explained by the decline of the private sector and the tendency towards over-employment in the public sector.

Uganda's working population may be broken down into a number of subgroups. The High Level Manpower Survey of 1967 classified wage employees into eight groups, of which seven were defined as high level manpower (HLM).[3] These included (a) top managers (1200), (b) junior managers (3840), (c) professionals (3610), (d) technicians (7840), (e) craftsmen (9420), (f) clerical workers and office executives (10,100) and (g) others including primary teachers (14,900). Given that wage employment was estimated at 257,000 at the time, HLM represented 20 percent of total wage employment, while semi-skilled and unskilled workers represented 80 percent.

HLM requires substantial periods of human capital formation (education, training and experience). Table 3 shows Uganda's HLM in 1967 categorised by the level of education "desired" for relevant posts in the private and public sectors. It shows that most HLM (69%) was in the public sector plus the teaching service. With the rise of the regressive economy, the ratio of HLM to total wage employment in the public sector is likely to have fallen rather than risen, as previously expected. This would be indicated by the tendency towards overstaffing, especially at the level of semi-skilled and unskilled manpower, and by the withdrawal of HLM into exile or self-employment. The same ratio in the private sector, on the other hand, is likely to have risen, given the institutional shift towards the parastatal sector, the decline of the economy and the fact that skilled workers in this sector have been more

---

3 The coverage was estimated at 90 percent overall, being highest for categories (a), (c) and (d) at 95 percent, and lowest for (e) at 80 percent and (f) at 85 percent.

Table 2.
Employment and the Wage Bill

Employment	1967		1970		1978	
(thousands)	No.	%	No.	%	No.	%
Private sector	162	63	184	59	161	43
Public sector	95	37	128	41	210	57
Totals	**257**	**100**	**312**	**100**	**371**	**100**
Wage bill (million Shs)						
Private sector	590	60	780	59	960	40
Public sector	384	40	550	41	1,420	60
Totals	**974**	**100**	**1,330**	**100**	**2,380**	**100**

*Source: Uganda (1984) and statistical abstracts.

Table 3.
Manpower by "Desired" Education Level, 1967[a]

	Manpower by Sector				
Level of education	Private	Public[b]	Education	Total	%[c]
9	40	140	810	990	1.9
8	1,340	1,390	940	3,670	7.2
7	450	110	560	1,120	2.1
6	50	2,060	-	2,110	4.1
5	870	1,750	470	3,090	6.1
4	1,600	2,740	1,660	6,000	11.8
3	4,120	6,200	200	10,520	20.7
2	5,650	4,670	9,590	19,910	39.1
1	1,410	2,000	90	3,500	6.9
Total manpower (HLM)	15,530	21,060	14,320	50,910	99.9
Total employment (N)	140,000	84,000	33,000	257,000	
HLM/N (%)	11	25	43	20	
Distribution of manpower (%)	31	41	28	100	
Distribution of employment (%)	54	33	13	100	

*Source: Uganda (1968: 11, Table II and IV).

[a] Employers were required to state the level appropriate for each post.

[b] Public refers to non-self-financing government sector (i.e., excludes public sector enterprise).

[c] Refers to people holding the post at time of survey.

likely to retain their jobs than semi-skilled and unskilled workers. In general, unemployed unskilled workers have spilled over into informal *magendo* markets in both urban and rural areas.

Wage Rates and Wage Bills

Changes in consumer prices, agricultural producer prices and wage rates have been characterised by structural imbalances. As a general rule, consumer prices have moved much faster than agricultural producer prices, thereby ensuring deteriorating terms of trade and real incomes for peasants, who predominate in the processes associated with national income formation and export performance. Secondly, in that wage rates have risen only marginally in comparison with producer prices, the attractiveness of wage employment vis-a-vis income-generating agricultural enterprises has declined. No wonder then that the rate of growth of the urban population during the 1970s was generally less than half of the expected rate of 7 percent. The rate of migration from rural to urban areas was accordingly reduced. The share of the government wage bill in recurrent expenditures declined from an average of 41 percent in 1970-73, to 16.6 percent in 1982-83.

Except for expected annual wage increases (10%), and the wage award of 1976-77 (which came to about 10-15%), wages stagnated during the 1970s. On the other hand, export and food crop producer prices increased severalfold. Again, between 1980 and May 1984 producer prices increased 12-15 times, whereas wages increased by about 2-2½ times. With respect to the public sector, the salary raises of July 1980 were designed to counteract the worsening trend in the context of the dislocations of the "liberation war", and the raises of July 1981 to counteract the effects of floating the shilling from US$ 1 = Shs. 7/80 to US$ 1 = Shs 78/00. The raises of July 1980 and 1981 were followed by (1) the June 1982 exemption of civil servants from salary income taxation (PAYE), the effect of which was estimated at about a 20 percent salary increase, (2) the April 1983 award of a 20 percent salary increase and (3) the July 1983 award of a 50 percent salary increase for all employees.

The three awards of 1982 and 1983 increased civil servant salaries by approximately 216 percent, and it may be assumed that salaries in the private sector were adjusted accordingly. Makerere University personnel were given an additional 15 percent raise in January 1983, and a 40 percent raise (rather than a 20 percent raise) in April 1984, multiplying their total wages by about 2.7 times over their 1982 wages.

The dramatic June 1984 awards were also designed to redress the imbalances between the earnings of fixed-income earners and peasant agricultural producers—whose prices had risen periodically—as well as business owners, who were reaping increasing surpluses due to persistent inflation. Yet the overall result was again to fuel inflation and raise the cost of living for everybody, particularly fixed-income earners. Dramatic as they were, the wage increases were effectively counteracted by rising consumer prices, and fixed-income earners continued to suffer in the erosion of their standards of living.

The 1984-86 period of hyper-inflation exacerbated the problems of the fixed-income earners.

Trade Unionism

The social, economic and political forces that undermined other organisations also generated institutional disintegration *within* the trade union movement, and *between* the movement and the government and employers. The relative financial positions of members and unions declined towards negligible proportions, thus negating their ability to finance organised political pressure in the negotiating process. The tendency towards the pursuit of selfish interests on the part of union leaders intensified. Given the prevailing political repression and the continuous struggle to make ends meet, members tended to lose interest in collective bargaining mechanisms. In short, the trade union movement during the period lost credibility both among workers and employers.

Between 1981 and 1984 the UPC Government tried to establish UPC Workers Councils in places of work, especially large establishments and parastatals. The Councils were designed to weaken the actual and potential roles of the trade unions in a strategy of depoliticising the workers and denying them independent defences against worsening social and economic conditions, and were successful in their objectives. With the tendency towards factionalism within the ruling party further aggravating the position of the workers vis-a-vis their employers and the government, it is no wonder that the position of workers continued to deteriorate, and that 1983-84 became a period of intensified industrial unrest (see Akkiki, 1984).

MODES OF EMPLOYMENT: WORKER RESPONSES
Modes of Employment and Lifestyle

The best way to grasp the dynamics of structural decline is to focus on the labour process as the core of the production process. This helps to ascertain the impact of economic decline on manpower utilisation, productivity and basic needs satisfaction. Indeed the social crisis in Uganda is primarily a crisis of the working population: a crisis of employment, income and poverty. The *magendo* economy exploits workers by paying them less than is necessary to ensure a decent standard of living, and less than is necessary for them to meet their social obligations. This leads to their dissatisfaction with their place in the "social relations of production" and feelings of alienation and exploitation.

Socio-economic progress is propelled by the expansion and improvement of the production process in society. A mode of employment refers to how a specific group within the working population participates. Given the coexistence of the peasant and capitalist modes of production in Uganda, there are three broad classes, namely the peasants, workers (or proletarians) and capitalists. Uganda's class structure is also characterised by cross-breeds between classes, however, especially between the workers and the peasants. Almost all agricultural workers—and to a lesser extent industrial workers—have one leg in the peasantry in the sense that members of their families remain peasant producers; they are therefore peasant workers rather than proletarians. Some have one leg in self-employment within the "informal" sector and depend significantly on "petty bourgeois" incomes. Overall, very few workers do not own some kind of productive property—especially land, but also buildings and other capital assets, though their proportion has been falling with the increase in poverty

A major impact of the regressive economy in Uganda has been an increased mobility of workers among different modes of employment and lifestyle. The principal alternative modes of employment available to the fixed-income earner in recent years have been:

1. Alternative formal wage employment;
2. A shift to "informal" wage employment in the "informal" or *magendo* sector;
3. Withdrawal wholly or partially into rural peasant activity;
4. Entry into commercial (agrarian capitalist) farming;
5. Entry into small or medium-scale (petty bourgeois) businesses;
6. Opting out of the *magendo* economy into economic exile.

In general, the lower the level of income and the lower the level of skill, the more affected has been the mode of employment of the income group. Members of higher income groups can afford to buy in bulk at cheaper prices, and often have more access to scarce commodities. Skilled workers tend to have more options, including self-employment, the chance to perform several jobs within the same time-table, and outmigration to greener pastures.

Worker Responses

The deterioration in standard of living among workers has been closely associated with their depoliticisation and their alienation vis-a-vis their employers. These tendencies lead us to two vital questions:

1. What are the possible responses in the struggle to alleviate or avoid immiserisation among workers?
2. What are the consequences of these responses in terms of individual and institutional efficiency as well as social justice and equity?

Worker responses may be classified under the following categories. The first involves efforts to increase "formal benefits" within the same mode of employment, including bargaining for higher incomes, more and better social welfare benefits, or housing. Whereas workers often have limited room for manoeuvering in such directions, the opportunities for those in productive enterprises critically depend on enterprise performance and worker bargaining strength, both of which have deteriorated. The only major alleviations in this context have been periodic salary increases which have been woefully inadequate and which, in any case, have generally been more than offset by the inflationary effects of the same increases.

The second set of responses involves the resort to "informal" income-generating activities even while continuing within the same mode of employment. Such responses have given rise and impetus to *magendo sharing mechanisms* within governmental and state enterprises, and within the private sector. Thus workers within organisations, right from unskilled messengers up to top decision-makers, have devised ways and means of living on their jobs through the collection of *tributes* from users of the services they are in a position to dispense. And thus to every role has been attached the "right to survive" (or "eating") from service users, which increases the costs of using such services to everybody. Fees are collected in order to pay the fees necessary elsewhere in the system, and collections are generally considered to be sharing mechanisms among fixed-income earners as they seek to meet their basic needs.

At the same time the "fees" have no doubt become sources of capital accumulation for persons at lucrative choke points. Those who have been able to control public resources have been able to use their positions with impunity in the transfer of public assets and revenues to their private use. As a result public services have been further undermined.

Thirdly, there is the possibility of a shift from one type of formal employment to another, whether or not the old job is retained. Thus the most seriously affected institutions (especially non-self-financing services) have lost workers to more lucrative jobs in other institutions. The teaching profession has been notorious for this kind of response in recent years as teachers have taken several jobs in several institutions, and non-teachers (especially civil servants) have taken teaching jobs. The "poaching" has led inevitably to less and less efficient teaching, and to declining standards. Another example of this kind of response has been the medical profession, as most doctors have been doubly employed in both the public and private sectors. In that many second jobs are informally rather than formally organised, they serve as entry points into *magendo* activities.

Fourthly, there is the alternative of opting out of fixed-income modes of employment into other modes of employment where incomes are less restricted. Some of the workers who have taken this option are workers who have all along had access to other modes of employment—for example, unskilled workers, whose families subsist as peasants in the rural sector, and bureaucrats who own commercial farms or business enterprises on the side. But, in general, complete switches from fixed-income earning are infrequent, for the tendency among workers is to keep one's eggs in several baskets. Some of the people who have taken up this option are the very few persons who have found it profitable to leave fixed-income employment for business activity, or even farming, despite the increased insecurity possible in such a move. Most of the workers who leave fixed-income positions must find work in the informal sector.

The informal sector embraces both legal and illegal activities. It has swallowed up most of the urban and rural unemployed, adults and children alike. It has also attracted women who would otherwise have remained unemployed, and has thus led to the greater participation of women in income-generating activities. The share of retail trade and other services handled by the informal sector has risen dramatically over the past decade and a half, and represents a drive to share dwindling economic surpluses more evenly.

Lastly, there is the option of escaping the difficulties of finding employment in Uganda through escape to another country (the "brain-drain" alternative). This option has been taken mostly by professionals (especially doctors, teachers and accountants), with the main reason being the income motive, although this is often disguised as the fear of insecurity. Other reasons for migration include the search for personal security and the problem of political insecurity. In general, the younger the job seeker, the more attractive the search for greener pastures elsewhere. Similarly, the greater the degree of know-how and technical skill, the greater the opportunity and tendency to migrate abroad.

Consequences

The main consequences of the immiserisation of workers in Uganda may be considered as follows:
1. The extent to which *magendo* incomes fill the basic needs of workers in various categories of employment;
2. Impact on the "productive" efficiency of enterprises and service delivery systems;
3. Impact on distributive justice or equity in society;
4. Impact on cultural and value systems.

In the first place, informal incomes, whether or not originating from the same institution, have assumed predominance over formal wages in both public and private sectors. The Salaries Review Commission concluded in 1982 that the failure to ensure living wages to civil servants had created a "retainer fee syndrome", the tendency to regard salaries as a means of retaining positions in government.[4] The Commission estimated that the civil servant worked effectively on an average for only one to two days per week (about two to three hours per day), and spent more time chasing other lines of income. Although reliable estimates are difficult to obtain, it is entirely clear that informal incomes are several times formal incomes, and that the margin tends to be greater the higher the status of the worker.[5]

Secondly, social and economic institutions have systematically deteriorated in organisational efficiency, largely through what we may call the *privatisation syndrome*, especially in the public sector. *Magendo* responses have opened the way for the predominance of self-interests over the interests of the public among managers, thereby promoting personal "chiefdoms" in the public sector. Individual efforts tend to be valued in terms of access to informal income, *not* in terms of knowledge or institutional objectives. Activities leading to the acquisition of knowledge and technical, research and planning skills are devalued in favour of informal income-generating activities. Thus, because of spare parts problems requiring as little as US$ 5000 to remedy, a factory can be grounded.

The persistent downward push on personal efficiency and cost-effectiveness in contemporary Uganda can be remedied with time. The reversal necessary, however, will be impossible without a reorganisation from above, which will require a reorganisation of the political process as the key coordinating mechanism. Contrary to what the Salaries Review Commission as-

---

[4] A living wage is defined as "a wage that does not grossly compromise the standards of living of the employee in keeping with his social status" (Uganda, 1982: 293, section 441).

[5] Those whose jobs are literally mines generally have no interest in leaving them even for profitable private enterprise. A side effect is that the easier the money, the less the tendency to invest the surplus in productive agricultural or industrial enterprises, and the greater the tendency for luxurious consumption, capital flight and speculative real estate.

sumes,[6] an improvement in real formal incomes will not be enough to generate and promote efficiency.

Thirdly, there are two approaches to the issue of equity effects. One is that *magendo* earnings within the network of bureaucratic roles represent a mechanism for sharing the community cake more evenly among workers than would otherwise be possible, even though the persons who man key check points generally end up exploiting the poor in their capacity to do so (see Banugire, 1985a: 14). The second treats *magendo* earnings simply as "corruption margins" possible because of a decline in standards of morality.

Both perspectives are instructive. The first, however, is more analytically useful and generates more appropriate policy prescriptions than the second, for the degradation of poor workers through poverty and exploitation is not directly attributable to any social group per se, but is inherent in the dynamics of overall economic decline and social disintegration. Accordingly, society as a whole is *collectively* responsible for the disease and must therefore bear collective responsibility for the redress of inequalities and exploitation, which inevitably implies the need for political transformation as a precondition for long-term social justice.

The last issue concerns the cultural values implied by the *magendo* economy. The evils of this typically regressive system are integrated with the evils of political repression in the form of human rights violations and the lack of political freedom, and create an intoxicating brew from which both the exploited and the exploiters drink. The political factor in all of this, however, constitutes the primary base in which the dynamics of socio-economic change are grounded, whereas the economic element (the regressive economy) constitutes the superstructure corresponding to it. This is a central characteristic of the lopsidedness of an economy which has reached the *magendo* stage of economic retrogression. The evidence of this is clear in the systematic depoliticisation of the worker, the destruction of collective bargaining mechanisms, the distribution of positive rewards for the inefficiency which is associated with *magendo* incomes, and negative rewards for the pursuit of organisational efficiency, and by the use of "mafia" tactics in business, administration and politics. The workers' choice to survive is nothing but a recognition of the pervasiveness of the evil and criminal methods of management that are currently common in the economic and political life of Uganda.

Practically all public services show signs of the above responses and their consequences. The civil service, for example, swallows up any funds poured into it without generating a corresponding increase in services or effectiveness. Indeed, the Salaries Review Commission (Uganda, 1982: 110) concluded that the level of productivity obtaining at the time of reporting could be easily achieved by ". . . half the size of the current manpower employed in the public service if such manpower worked full time and put its

---

6 The Salaries Review Commission found the following: ". . . the civil servant had either to survive by lowering his standard of ethics, performance and dutifulness or remain upright and perish. He chose to survive. We have evidence that the choice was a painful one in general, not one taken without a pang of conscience. However, we likewise have suggestive evidence that the average Ugandan is still morally sound and not only capable, but also proud of good work if only there was an improvement in his real income" (Uganda, 1982: 109, section 163).

back into the job." A World Bank mission in 1984 recommended a 50 percent reduction in public service personnel and the privatisation of certain publicly provided services. But neither such reductions, nor subsequent wage increases, would lead predictably to increased services or cost-effectiveness because of the in-built *magendo* incentives operating and the great magnitude of the problem.

SUMMARY AND CONCLUSION

The Ugandan economy has deteriorated through the recessionary stage into the structural retrogression stage and into the state of a regressive or *magendo* economy. The core of the current economic crisis is a basic needs or poverty problem whereby the capability of the majority of the working population to afford a living wage has been continuously eroded through commodity shortages and a rising cost of living.

Employment may be broken down into four categories: (a) formal wage employment, (b) informal sector self-employment, (c) formal business self-employment and (d) peasant employment. Fixed-income earners generally have one leg in the first category, the other in the second, usually through their spouses. While formal wage employment has stagnated, informal sector employment has absorbed most of the job seekers and has enabled them to share in the dwindling national cake.

Formal wage earners often also participate in *magendo* activities either within their places of employment or outside in the informal sector. Because such activities generally provide more income to the worker than do formal activities, they often receive more time and attention, at the expense of efficiency in employing institutions.

The immiserisation of the working population through increasing levels of absolute and relative poverty has continued unabated since the early 1970s, and reached explosive proportions by the end of 1985. It has been indicated by the following:

1. Widening gaps between living wages and formal wage earnings in excess of 40:1 for the LIG, and 20:1 for the MIG, with the former gap widening faster than the latter;
2. Generally unsuccessful attempts to fill such gaps through informal earnings, with the result that yawning gaps revealing poverty and degradation have persisted;
3. Drastic reductions in the availability of consumer goods and services, with serious consequences in terms of poor nutrition and health, increasing alcoholism, the inability to afford transport services, failures to meet extended-family obligations and family disintegration;
4 Great strains in providing for the education of children.[7]

Women's roles as income earners and family supporters have been increased to the extent of equal partnership. Under current circumstances women often bear the brunt of frustration in the struggle to make ends meet.

---

7 This is regarded as a fundamental obligation not to be defaulted. Many are unable to provide education for their children at serious psychological costs.

They are often simultaneously forced to struggle with the escapism and alcoholism of their husbands.

Labour and institutional productivity have fallen not only because of the misery of the workers but also because of the mismanagement of decision-makers who reap excessive *magendo* incomes. Given the heavy weight of the institutional and psychological factors involved here, plus the problems associated with excessive poverty, no wage raises will solve the existing problems without institutional reorganisation being effected.

Other aspects of the misery of the workers include the distortion of lifestyles imposed through inadequate and poor housing conditions, severe shortages and high costs of public transportation, the looting of consumer durables (like cars, bicycles and music systems), distorted food and beverage consumption habits, and poor factory working conditions.

Several alternative policy strategies are possible in the alleviation of the problems of fixed-income earners. The following summary statements can be made:

1. There has been a lack of clear objective and planning in giving priority to market mechanisms and government interventions in the hiring and firing of workers in both public and private enterprises.

2. A wage policy has been relied upon to solve the workers' plight, though this approach has proven ineffective and inappropriate. While the policy reforms dictated by inflationary pressures have advocated the extreme liberalisation of the economy through the liberalisation of exchange rates and exchange controls, they have at the same time been biased against wage rises. The drastic wage increase of 1984, presumably against IMF advice, tended to worsen rather than solve the problem given prevailing economic and political constraints.

3. The development of an informal incomes policy seems a better strategy than the development of a direct wage policy in meeting the problems of fixed-income earners, whether or not it involves reforms in the labour contract and payment system. Yet such an approach has hardly been considered by government, and the very few experiments undertaken along such lines have been resisted and sabotaged by employers, often with the connivance of bureaucrats and politicians.

4. In an economy such as Uganda's, the labour contract and payment system should be reformed in favour of workers. There has been a strong tendency towards labour contracting rather than normal wage employment, whereby, for example, a worker earning Shs. 2000 per month refuses to clean one's compound for Shs. 500 per day because this is below the market contracting rate. New emphases would be helpful.

5. The trade union movement needs to be reorganised as a vigorous, independent, democratic movement capable of articulating the real interests of workers.

6. There is a strong need to introduce lifestyle policies as part of the basic-needs policy package to ensure adequate housing and other facilities to the urban population.

REFERENCES

Akkiki, Luke. 1984. "Industrial Unrest in Uganda." *Forward*, 6 (No. 2).
Banugire, F. R. 1985a. "The Political Economy of 'Magendo' Society: The Case of Uganda." MISR Academic Forum, Makerere University, Kampala
Banugire, F. R. 1985b. "Class Struggle, Clan Politics and the 'Magendo' Economy." Fourth Mawazo Workshop, Makerere University, 26-28 April.
Banugire, F. R. 1979. "Uganda's Development Patterns: An Historical and Prospective Analysis." ILO-JASPA Working Paper, Addis Ababa.
Chango Macho, W'Obanda. 1985. "The World Bank, IMF and Deepening Misery in Uganda: The Mbale Experience." Fourth Mawazo Workshop, Makerere University, 26-28 April.
Dodge, Cole P. and Paul D. Wiebe (eds.). 1985. *Crisis in Uganda: The Breakdown of Health Services*. Oxford: Pergamon.
Doi, Z. A. 1979. "Smuggling Activities Across the Uganda Borders During the Military Regime, 1971-79: Case Studies in Tororo District." Research Paper, DPA, 1979-80, IPA, Kampala.
Green, Reginald H. 1981. "Magendo in the Political Economy of Uganda: Pathology, Parallel System or Dominant Mode of Production?" IDS Discussion Paper, DP 164, Sussex.
Mahmood Akhta. 1985. "Dual Exchange Rate: The Experience of Uganda." Fourth Mawazo Workshop, Makerere University, 26-28 April.
Uganda, Government of. 1968. "High Level Manpower Survey, 1967, and Analysis of Requirements, 1968-81." Entebbe: Government Printer.
Uganda, Government of. 1982. "Report of the Public Service Salaries Review Commission, 1980-82." Kampala: Ministry of Public Service and Cabinet Affairs.
Uganda, Government of. 1984. *The Revised Recovery Programme*. Entebbe: Government Printer.
World Bank. 1984. "Uganda Agricultural Sector Memorandum: The Challenge Beyond Rehabilitation." Report No. 5044-UG. Nairobi: Eastern Africa Regional Office.

APPENDIX A:
SEMINAR PARTICIPANTS

Firimooni R. Banugire - Associate Professor of Economics, Makerere University.

Cole P. Dodge - UNICEF Representative, Uganda.

Josephine Wanja Harmsworth - private consultant on rural development in Uganda.

D. A. Hillman - Professor of Paediatrics, Memorial University of Newfoundland, Canada, and UNICEF Professor of Social Paediatrics, Makerere University.

Elizabeth Hillman - Professor of Paediatrics, Memorial University of Newfoundland, Canada, and Makerere University.

Tarsis B. Kabwegyere - Associate Professor and Head, Department of Sociology, Makerere University.

John Tuhe Kakitahi - Associate Professor, Makerere University, and Director, Mwanamugimu Nutrition Services.

Erisa Kironde - Chairman of the Uganda Red Cross Society, the Uganda National Theatre and the Nommo Gallery.

B. George Kirya - Vice-Chancellor, Makerere University.

Dan Mudoola - Associate Professor in Political Science, and Director, Makerere Institute of Social Research.

Grace Nakintu-Kyeyune - UNICEF Assistant Project Officer, monitoring and evaluation.

Josephine M. Namboze - Professor and Head, Institute of Public Health, Makerere University.

Christopher M. Ndugwa - Head, Department of Paediatrics and Child Health, Faculty of Medicine, Makerere University.

J. M. A. Opio-Odongo - Associate Professor in Rural Sociology, Department of Agricultural Economics, Makerere University.

Raphael Owor - Dean, Faculty of Medicine, Makerere University.

Dennis R. Pain - Oxfam Field Director for Uganda.

Magne Raundalen - Associate Professor of Clinical Psychology, Bergen University, Norway.

Ruhakana Rugunda - Minister of Health, Government of Uganda.

Eustace Rutiba - Associate Professor of Philosophy and Religious Studies, Makerere University.

W. Senteza-Kajubi - Head, Department of Adult and Higher Education, Makerere University.

Hilda Mary Kabushenga Tadria - consultant on women in development, Eastern and Southern Africa Management Institute.

Paul D. Wiebe - Professor of Sociology and Anthropology, Bethel College, St. Paul, Minnesota.

Observers

John Kyabaggu - Assistant Director of Medical Services (PHC), Ministry of Health, Government of Uganda.

Emmanuel Mutabaazi-Kaijuka - Assistant Director of Medical Services (MCH), Ministry of Health, Government of Uganda.

INDEX

African Local Government Ordinance of 1949 57
African Medical and Research Foundation (AMREF) 104, 118
Akena Adoko 19
Algeria 57
Alma Ata Conference 105
Amin, Idi 1, 2, 6, 12-15, 17-19, 22-23, 31, 34, 38, 47, 53, 55, 57, 60, 87-88, 101-3, 105, 108, 121, 126-7
Anyanya guerrilla movement 54
Army organisation 16-19
Asians/Asian population 16-17, 22, 37, 51, 66-67, 102-3, 105, 121, 126-7, 129, 135
 exodus of 122
 Indian troops 17, 24
 trading network 46
Association of Women's Organisations 87

Baganda Growers Association 67
Bagaya, Elizabeth 87
Baker, Samuel 41-42, 49
Bamba/Bakonjo/Batoro conflict 57, 60
Basic needs basket 137
 gaps 139
Bataka Movement of 1922   66
Bennett, John 116-17
"Bifurcated" cash economy 83
Binaisa, Godfrey 1
Boundary issues 12-14, 57
 See also "Lost Counties" controversy
"Brain drain" 146
British 6, 17, 27-30, 32-34, 45, 49, 52-53, 61, 126
 Britain 21, 24, 38
British East Africa Company 27
Buganda Agreement of 1900   27-28, 57, 66
 weaknesses of 28-30
Bugisu Cooperative Union Ltd. 69

Canadian International Development Assistance (CIDA) 104
Cash crops 36, 48-50, 52, 102, 107, 111, 130, 133, 135-36
 export agriculture 66-77, 134

women in cash crop production 81-85
Child Health and Medical Assistance Program (CHAMP) 104, 110
Church of Uganda 30, 111
Churches 26-27, 30-32, 104-105
 medical programmes 110-11
Churchill, Winston 5
Civil service organisation 14-16
Class structure 11, 79, 129, 135, 139, 144-45
Coffee Marketing Board 16, 46, 71
 Bugisu Coffee Marketing Association (BCMA) 70
Colonial rule 8, 11-12, 14-18, 21, 27-30, 36-37, 41, 47, 63, 66-69
 legacies 57-62
Commonwealth team 18
Community-based health care 114-120
Consociational model in development 39
Constitution, Uganda's 20-21, 23
Cooperative movement in Uganda, emasculation of 69-76
 effects of vested interests 70-74
 effects of inflexible adherence to the Rochdalean cooperative model 74-75
 effects of inadequate organisational methods and techniques 75-76
Cooperative movement, revitalisation 76-77
Cooperative movement, vitality 67-68
Cooperative News 75
Cooperative Societies Acts and Rules of 1963 74
Cooperative Societies Ordinance of 1946   67-68
Council of Voluntary Social Service 87

DANIDA 105
Danish Red Cross 195
Democratic Party (DP) 19, 38, 61, 70
Department of Cooperatives 67-69, 75-76
Department of Paediatrics and Child Health 118
Devaluations, currency 131-32
Divide and rule policy 29-30

East African states 17, 121

INDEX

Economy, organisation of Uganda's 21-22, 36-38
  "chiefdoms" in the private sector 147
  immiserisation 145, 149
  "informalisation" 122, 145-46
  magendo (regressive economy) stage 137-51
  pricing policies 130-35
  privatisation syndrome 147
  recessionary stage 137
  specialisation 128
  "stabilisation" 128
  structural decline stage 137
Education and educational facilities and services 7, 30-31, 35, 37
  Acholi interest in 49-52
  in consideration of family life 99
  King's College 31
  Namiryango College 31
  St. Mary's College 31
  Traditional system 33
Elite fragmentation in Uganda 56-58, 62
Emin Pasha 41-43, 45, 49
Employment modes and lifestyles 144-45
Employment trends 141
"Ethno-functionalism", doctrine of 61-62
European Economic Community (EEC) 104

Family organisation 91-100
  decline of extended family 93
  effects of civil strife 94-98
  effects of inflation 93-97
  traditional organisation 91-93
  urban and commercial influence 98-99
Farmers/peasants 36-37, 65ff, 126ff, 131, 134
  farm incomes 133
  farm prices 131, 134-35
  gender organisation among 79ff
  trips to the farm 128
Federation of Uganda African Farmers 68, 75
Female literacy as a health option 107
Fixed-income earners and wage earners 127,137-51
  level of living 127
  lifestyle policies 150
  women's wage-earner roles 149
Food and Agriculture Organisation (FAO) 123-25
Food balance sheet 123-24
Food crops 37, 49, 80ff, 123ff, 130, 135
Food production and consumption 123-26
Foreigners, the early coming of to Uganda 25, 37
Female-headed households 89, 149

General Service Unit 23
Gordon, Charles George 25, 42
Guinea 87

Hannington, Bishop James 26
Health care and medical facilities and services 7, 9, 24, 102-12
  alternative options 107-8
  cost of 111-12
  health indicators 108
High Level Manpower Survey 141
Huntington model of political stability and instability 55

Identity crisis in Uganda 35-36

Ilemangoma 13
Immunisation 104, 108, 110, 114ff
  Pre-primary Protection Programme 105
Income and income distribution 126-30, 138
Indirect rule policy 29, 37
Industries 37, 138
Inflation 93-94, 135
  effects on family organisation 93-97
Informal sector 129
Institute of Public Health 118
Institutionalisation of religion 30-32
International Committee of the Red Cross (ICRC) 104
International Monetary Fund (IMF) 4, 22, 103, 139

Judiciary, inroads into the 19-20

Kabaka of Buganda 27-28, 31-33, 45
  Kalema 27
  Kiwewa 26
  Mutesa I   25-26
  Mutesa II, Edward 21, 38, 57
  Mwanga 26-27
Kabaka Yekka (KY) Party 38
Kabarega 16, 29, 42-44
Kagera salient 12-13
Karamoja, an area of special need 33-34, 108-10
Kasangati Health Centre 113-120
  decline and rehabilitation 114-15
  main features 113-14
  proposed strategies 120
Kenya 6, 12, 24, 28, 35, 37, 45, 57, 67, 71, 113, 138
Kenyatta, Jomo 35
King's African Rifles 17, 41, 45, 49, 52
Kiwanuka, Benedicto 38
Koreans 18
Kuluva Hospital 108
Kyesimira case 19

"Labour aristocracy" 126
Land ownership 28, 111
Lenin 11
Language/tribal regions 4, 32-33, 36, 47-48, 92-93
  allocation imbalances 58-62
  diversity 29
  tribalism 4, 31, 34
  See also tribal peoples
Lint Marketing Board 16, 70-71
  Cotton Export Group 70
"Lost Counties" controversy 13, 28, 56-57, 60
  See also boundary issues
Lubega, Florence 87
Lugard, F. 16, 27, 43, 60
Lule, Yusufu 1, 13
Luwero Triangle 2, 6-7, 16, 19, 103-4

Makerere Institute of Social Research 5
Makerere University 5, 105, 107, 113, 115, 117-18
  Medical School 105, 113
  Faculty of Medicine 5
Male/female role differences in the peasant economy 79-90
Matany Catholic Hospital 110
Mbarara 7

INDEX

Migration 129
Military Commission Government of 1979-80 18, 23, 55
Military recruitment and economic development 53-54
Minnesota International Health Volunteers (MIHV) 105, 115, 117
Ministry of Health 104-5, 107, 110, 118
Missionaries 26-27, 30, 37, 111
 Church Missionary Society 27
 Mill Hill Mission 27
 Protestant 27
 White Fathers 27
Mobilisation approach in development 39
Mountains of the Moon guerrilla struggle 13
"Move to the Left" documents 56
Mozambique 57
Mulago Hospital 104-5, 107-8, 110
Museveni, Yoweri 4, 14, 36, 54-55, 89, 116
 Government 102
Muwanga, Paulo 19
Mweya Lodge 5
 seminar 5

Nairobi peace talks 14, 23
Namboze, Josephine 116
National Commission on the Conditions of Rural Life 77
National Council of Women 86-90
National Expanded Programme of Immunisation (EPI) 104, 115
National integration as a process 39
National Resistance Army (NRA) 1, 4, 14, 55
National Resistance Movement (NRM) 1, 4-5, 14, 18, 23-24, 54-55, 62
 Government 6-8, 36
National Security Agency (NASA) 23
Niger 76
Northern Ireland 32
Nutrition and malnutrition 110
 food and nutrition policy 107-8
 monitoring 114
 standards 7
Nyerere, Julius 35

Obote, Milton 1, 14, 17, 21, 29, 34-35, 38, 55-56, 60, 89, 103, 131
 Bushenyi annual event 22
 Constitution 21
 Government 5, 13, 19, 35, 102
 overthrow 16, 18
 second term 4, 15, 23
 showdown with Mutesa II 56
Okello, Basilio 1, 14, 17, 35
Okello, Tito 1, 14, 35, 55
 army 6
 Government 1, 4, 14, 34-35
 overthrow 18
Opon-Acak, Smith 17
Overseas Development Administration (ODA) 104
Oyite-Ojok, David 16, 17

Pan-Africanism 32
Peasant gender ideology 85-86
Political parties, the position of in Uganda 38-39
Politico-religious conflicts in Uganda 26-27, 30-31, 43, 60-61

Primary health care (PHC) 110-11
 See also community-based health care
Recovery Programme 102, 107
Republican Constitution of 1967   55-56
Resource allocation imbalances 58-62
Revised Recovery Programme 102, 104
Rhodesia 57
Rockefeller Foundation 113
Rwotcamo, Chief of the Payeera 42

Salaries Review Commission 147-8
Save the Children Fund (SCF) 104
Selim Bey 43
South Africa 32
Ssebugwaho, the Honorable 20
Ssemogerere, Paul 19
Sudan 6, 29
 Sudanese 41, 53-54

Tanganyika 113
Tanzania 6-7, 12-13, 18-19, 55, 71, 121, 138
 Ujamaa 35
Teaching Health Workers to Teach 118
Torjeson, Hakon 117
Trade unions 16, 144, 150
 collective bargaining mechanisms 148
Trades 37, 150
Traditional birth attendants (TBAs) 107, 110, 118
Traditional socio-political systems 32-33, 34, 74
Tribal peoples
 Acholi 6, 34-35, 41-46
  clan organization 48
  economic history 48
  Military participation 47-54
 Alur 33
 Baganda 27-28, 30-31, 34-35, 37, 41, 44-45, 128
 Bagisu 69
 Bahima 44
 Bakiga 33
 Banyarwanda 6, 60,104
 Banyoro 41, 43-44
 Bari 44
 Kakwa 34
 Karamojong 6, 7, 33-34, 48, 109-110
 Langi 6, 33-35, 44, 49
 Lugbara 33, 35
 Madi 35, 44
 Nubians 34, 47, 51, 60
  "clans" 41-42
  military participation 41-47, 53-54
  "potential Nubians" 47
 See also language/tribal regions
 Teso 49

Urban incomes and wages 129, 133, 136
Uganda National Liberation Front (UNLF) 13, 23, 54
Uganda National Movement (UMN) 37
Uganda Peoples Congress (UPC) 23, 29, 38, 63, 70, 88, 146
 Workers Councils 144
Uganda Peoples Congress/Kabaka Yekka Alliance 23, 38, 56
United Nations (UN) 87
United Nations Children's Fund (UNICEF) 5,

87, 91, 104, 115, 118-19
United States Agency for International Development (USAID) 75, 91, 105

Value integration, the problem of 34-35
  lack of unity and 39
Village health workers 118
Volunteers, North American 117

Wage rates, wage bills and wage policies 143, 150
Wallis Report 57
West Nile emergency 6-7, 104
Westminister model 14
Where there is no Doctor 118

"Window" currency auction rates 131-2
Women and development 86ff
Women's roles 79-80
  devaluation of 85
  in the cash sector 81-85
  in the peri-urban household economy 80-81
World Bank 4, 22, 102, 105, 111
World Food Programme 7

Zaire 6
Zambia, "humanism" 35
Zanzibar 113
Zimbabawe 35